BeingGazza

Also by Paul Gascoigne

Gazza: My Story (with Hunter Davies)

BeingGazza

My Journey to Hell
and Back

Paul Gascoigne
with John McKeown and Hunter Davies

headline

First published in 2006
by HEADLINE BOOK PUBLISHING

1

A CIP catalogue record for this title is available from the British Library

Hardback ISBN 0 7553 1542 1
Trade paperback ISBN 0 7553 1561 8

Text design: Ben Cracknell Studios
Typeset by Avon DataSet Ltd, Bidford on Avon, Warwickshire
Printed and bound in Great Britain by Clays Ltd St Ives plc

Headline's policy is to use papers that are natural, renewable and
recyclable products and made from wood grown in sustainable forests.
The logging and manufacturing processes are expected to conform to
the environmental regulations of the country of origin.

HEADLINE BOOK PUBLISHING
A division of Hodder Headline
338 Euston Road
London NW1 3BH

www.headline.co.uk
www.hodderheadline.com

www.paulgascoigne.biz

For George Best
1946–2005

Contents

Preface

I was signing copies of my life story in Manchester when I got
the idea to write this book. Someone came up to us at the book signing, and
just quietly told us how much that book helped them. They thanked us for
doing it. I was surprised, and really pleased.

It happened at book signings up and down the UK – people telling me
it was a relief reading the story of my problems, because they thought, 'I
can't believe it – Gazza's got the same problem as me!' I was playing pool
the other day with my sister, and the manager of the pool house came up
and said he wanted to thank me because, after reading my story, his wife's
panic attacks had got less. I was amazed that that book could mean so
much to people.

I wanted to do *this* book even though I knew doing the sessions for it,
and going back through everything, would be hard. I hadn't seen my
therapist – Johnny Mac as I call him – for about a year and I knew I'd have
to go back over all that stuff again – my childhood and all the way up to

today. I knew I'd be digging things up, going over and over things in my head. But I needed help – I'd got into bad times again – and I knew I needed to face places in the past I'd rather not face. So I've faced it, and it has been hard – really hard. I've had an unbelievably difficult year but, with the help of my therapist, I've kept fighting. And the fight's not over yet. I'll always have these illnesses, but I'm learning all the time how to do the right things to stay on top of them and to have a good life.

In that first book I didn't go into the details of these different illnesses I've got. It was later the idea came to write this book to show what it's really been like, and to talk about all the therapy I've done, so that maybe it would help people with the same problems. I hope it does.

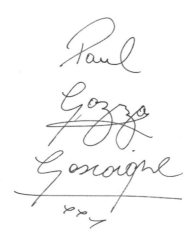

March 2006

Acknowledgements

My thanks go to Mum and Dad, Anna, Carl and Lindsay, Jimmy Five Bellies Gardner, Bill Kenwright, Dr Neil Brener and Dr Fran Moore for all their support. Also, for their help in writing this book, I'd like to thank Johnny McKeown, Hunter Davies and Emma Littlewood for all their hard work, and Jochen Encke, Tim Leighton and Mark Dunn for their feedback and advice. Thanks also to Jane and Kat at JMM Management, to David Wilson at Headline, and to Calum Best. And, finally, thanks to all the other crazy people 'in the rooms' for listening.

Paul John (Gazza) Gascoigne

Chronology of his life, including some dramatis personae who will appear in this book ...

Personal
Born: 27 May 1967, Gateshead, County Durham

Father: John, hodcarrier

Mother: Carol

Siblings: two sisters, Anna and Lindsay; brother, Carl

Education: left school at sixteen, two CSE passes

Marriage: to Sheryl (Shel) 1996, divorced 1998

Children: one son, Regan, born 1996, plus two stepchildren, Bianca
    born 1986, Mason born 1989

Meets Jimmy ('Five Bellies') Gardner, best friend, 1983

Meets John McKeown (Johnny Mac), his therapist, at the Priory
    Hospital, London, 1998

Awards
Young Player of the Year, 1988

BBC Sports Personality of the Year, 1990

Scottish Football Writers' Association and Scottish Professional
    Football Players' Player of the Year, 1996

Gazza: My Story published by Headline 2004, winner of Sports Book of
    the Year, 2004

Football career

1983	apprentice at Newcastle United (schoolboy from 1980)
1985	turns professional at Newcastle United
1988	transferred to Tottenham Hotspur for £2.3 million
1992	transferred to Lazio, Italy, for £5.5 million
1995	transferred to Glasgow Rangers for £4.3 million
1998	transferred to Middlesbrough for £3.45 million
2000	free transfer to Everton
2002	free transfer to Burnley
2003	player-coach, Gansu Tianma, China
2003	Wolverhampton Wanderers reserves
2004	player-coach, Boston United
2005	player-coach, Algarve United
2005	manager, Kettering Town

England appearances

57 caps, 10 goals, between 1988 and 1998, including
World Cup semi-final, 1990, and European Championship semi-final, 1996

ChapterOne

Paul goes to see his therapist

Paul

It's late summer 2005 and today I'm on my way to see Johnny Mac. His office is in a posh street, posh address, in London, but Johnny's far from posh. In fact, in some ways I think his background is similar to mine. I've picked up bits, just when it comes out, in relation to me, and what's happened to me, but he doesn't talk about himself much. They're not supposed to, are they? Bloody hell, I hope not. I'm doing the paying, so he can listen to me – I mean, help me. That's the idea.

He's a real Scouser, which I suppose is why I get on with him so well. He's an Evertonian, though I hadn't yet played for Everton when I first met him. I was still with Middlesbrough. It was in, let me see, must have been 1998 when I first met Johnny. It was at a stage in my life when I was still in denial so, afterwards, I sort of pretended it had never happened, that I hadn't seen him, that there was nothing wrong with me. Well, nothing that a few drinks couldn't cure. That's what I imagined then.

I'm not far from Harley Street. I saw the sign. That's the famous street for doctors and medical help. I've always wondered if there was a Doctor Harley. S'pose there must have been. Was he related to John Harley, that little kid who played for Chelsea a few years ago? I did play against him. I think he went to Fulham. I wonder where he is now? Not heard of him recently. That happens with lots of players. Once they retire, or move down the divisions, they sort of seem to sink out of sight, slip away. I wish I could.

Or it could have been the bloke who invented Harley Davidsons. Funnily enough, I used to come and visit Johnny on my Harley Davidson. This was when I was staying at Shel's (my ex-wife), at a time when I had shitloads of Harley Davidson bikes. About nine at one time. Only one now. I've just bought it. A Hot Rod. Built from scratch.

This area of London is pretty handy for me actually. Although I wish it wasn't. It's very near the Princess Grace Hospital, just round the corner. I have a season ticket for that, ha ha. I've taken all my best injuries there, over the years. I first went in 1991, playing for Spurs, after the Cup final when I did my leg in, my own stupid fault. It looked as if my career was over. I went in an ambulance, while the game was still on. I managed to catch the last bit of the game from my hospital bed. I saw poor old Des Walker head the ball into his own net from a corner. We'd won the Cup, the biggest achievement in my football life so far. I ended up with a winner's medal – but I felt I didn't deserve it. I'd acted like a mad bastard. Typical.

I've just come down to London from Newcastle for the day to catch up on a few things. I've got a rented flat in the Jesmond area of Newcastle. It's a smart new block, but I don't really like it. I hate living on my own. If I get a new job, then I might buy somewhere to live nearby, to be handy for it. I haven't owned a house for, must be the last seven years. I've either been in hotels, flats or hospitals. Don't remind me.

I'm seeing Johnny to go over stuff. It's been a while since I saw him. I was abroad for a fair whack of the summer, in Portugal. I do need to talk about what's recently happened but, in other ways, I feel I don't need him.

I've managed to conquer quite a few things in the last couple of years.

I don't have as many compulsive obsessions as I used to, such as having to have things neat and tidy, all in a certain order. That used to drive me mad – and everyone else.

I remember when I was at Glasgow Rangers I bought this house not far from Ally McCoist's. He was in a panic, thinking I was actually moving next door. I was in fact exactly 1.8 miles from his house. Coisty measured it out.

There was a pub near his house that I used to go to and, one night, I was there till about two in the morning, pretty pissed. I suddenly felt really hungry. I couldn't get a taxi so I thought, 'I know what, I'll break into Coisty's.' I'd been to his house many times so I knew which window was left open.

I get in, as quietly as possible, and make myself a huge sandwich, opening all the tins I can find and taking stuff from his fridge. Coisty is upstairs in bed and he suddenly hears this noise in his kitchen. He gets out this baseball bat that he keeps under the bed to arm himself against burglars – not to practise his swing with (I don't think, anyway). He comes down the stairs, rattling it along the banister, making as much noise as possible to frighten away the intruder.

In the kitchen, he doesn't see it's me at first because I'm on a chair. I've cleaned up all the mess I'd made and I'm now arranging all the tins on his shelf. I was upset that he didn't keep them very tidily.

'It's you, Gazza!' shouts Coisty. 'What a fucking relief!'

I told him I was just tidying his kitchen for him, which of course he couldn't understand. He went back to bed. I was a bit more sober by then so, when I'd tidied everything, I managed to walk home.

Today that story makes me smile, as do all the other times in my life I became obsessed by having things tidy. But I've other things to worry about now, God knows. Probably always will.

I've been through lots of therapists, and therapies, in my life – all sorts, all over the place. I often think some of them have just been watching the clock, not really bothered. Others talk a lot of shite and I've no idea what they're on about. Johnny's been good for me. The best I've ever had. In bad times, I have gone to see him every week for months at a time. At other times I might miss a few months, but we usually still talk on the phone.

I have known Johnny since I was admitted into the Priory Hospital. As I've already said, I don't know too much about him but what I do know suggests that he has had his own personal battles in the past. That comes across when we speak, at times, say, when I am struggling with an issue and he shares one or two examples from his own life. I think he is about four or five years older than me – looks more, ha ha – only kidding, Johnny. He's from a working-class background and grew up in Birkenhead, Merseyside, and is a true Evertonian. He has worked in the counselling field for a long time, I think at other football clubs, and I know he worked in prisons for a good few years. All that stuff helps me to get on with him. I can relate to him easily. He doesn't judge. That's one of the reasons I keep going back to him.

I'm going to start seeing him again, after a gap of about a year, and I know what will happen – I'll have to go over all the same old stuff, to revisit the past, the recent past as well as my childhood. I don't know if I can face that. And since I've decided to do this book, I'll have to think about it and talk about it afterwards – about what it's like, before and after therapy, and about what else is happening in my life, all the other things that are going wrong. I'll be doing my own head in. I'll be awake all night and every night, going over things. So I thought, 'Bugger it, nice idea, but I'm not up to it.'

Then I thought, 'Now that I do need help again, and am going to re-start therapy, that's what you have to do anyway – to open up, you need to go back, visit places you might not want to visit, and contemplate possibilities and causes you've been too scared to think about or admit . . .'

Johnny's place is in this big, seven-storey house. It looks like a house where people live, not like offices or a medical building. In fact, it's two big houses knocked together. It still has two entrances. When I first went to see him there, I didn't know which fucking door to go into.

Inside, it's like a sort of old-fashioned posh hotel. It's got two reception rooms with antiques and classy magazines. They also have stuff like notices and leaflets offering to help you: 'STOP SMOKING IN ONE HOUR – 95% Success Rate.' I never read them as they're all bollocks. Yeah, of course, I still smoke, though I lie about how many, but I'm not bothered. If smoking was my biggest problem in life, I'd be laughing, ha ha ha.

In this building, where Johnny has his rooms, there are about twenty different therapists, specialists, doctors and consultants. I could probably keep them all occupied, if I put my mind to it. Spread my custom around. Give them all a bit of work.

Johnny's room has a white sofa, two white chairs and off-white carpet and walls. The only bit of colour comes from some framed theatre posters on a wall. I find myself looking at them if I get bored. Sometimes I just go for a walk about the room.

I always start my sessions the same way. I throw myself on his couch and say to Johnny, 'Can I smoke?' He then says, 'No you can't.' I say, 'Fucking hell!' Then we get on with it . . .

———————

Dear Paul

I'm taking the honor of writing in your book first. You're such an amazing guy. You light up the room with humor and laughter. Stay true to yourself. I hope we keep in touch.

Love

Patty

Chapter Two

Paul's first session: Getting back on track

John

I hope this book will benefit Paul and benefit his readers and fans. I've known him since 1998, and we've worked together on and off since then. He's wanted to make some of his counselling and therapy into a book for a couple of years, to get across to the readers a realistic picture of what it's like managing and struggling with his illnesses, and hopefully to help anyone with similar problems. It's difficult to put something as private as therapy into the public domain, so he's selected excerpts from some of his sessions that he felt comfortable sharing with the public. Of course there were other sessions and conversations that weren't included, but I think what's here will be revealing in an interesting and helpful way.

It's been some months since Paul and I have had a properly structured one-to-one session. He's keen to get back on track, telling me he's fully committed to doing some more work on himself. Paul had a good stretch of time – over two years – of managing his illnesses very effectively and feeling healthy and balanced. Then things started to go wrong again. So, before we start, I remind him that as we haven't met for a while he should begin by talking about the time from when he feels that everything started to go wrong, and to take his time doing so. He's visibly shaky but keen to get going straight away.

When a client comes to therapy for the first time, or returns after a long break, the therapist usually spends the first one or two sessions gathering as much information as possible. As the therapist, I don't interrupt the client's flow unless it's necessary. It's crucial that the client shares where they are at, what got them there and how it feels to be there. Paul needs to talk.

Paul

Can I smoke? Fucking hell!

I had a really good two-plus years when I wasn't drinking, I was sober, and the other parts of my illness were under control. I was on top of things and my recovery was going great. I was the same person I'd always been, I still had fun, but I was clean. People said to me, 'Why did you ever drink — you're such a great person when you're sober?' I always thought I was just as nice when I was drinking, I couldn't tell the difference myself, but people tell me I'm a pain when I'm drinking.

Anyway, things had been going pretty well for me, the best since I'd given up playing football four years ago. Then I signed up for the TV show *Strictly Ice Dancing* and got injured; it was a terrible injury and it wasn't even through football. I'm used to that at least. At the time, I'd been training really hard. My OCD (obsessive compulsive disorder) had just started to kick in a bit, I'd be training all day every day – and I wasn't eating properly, I was eating just a sandwich and wine gums. The dance programme was a one-off to go out on Boxing Day 2004, but I never actually took part in it in the end. During the rehearsals I fell on my back and injured myself. I was in terrible pain, but still danced one more time.

I then headed to the airport with my dad – I was on the way to Madrid for a charity match – but I never got on the plane. I went to pick up my bag and something went in my neck. The pain was so bad my dad took me straight back into London, to the Princess Grace Hospital where I was given an epidural. That's how excruciating the pain in my back and neck was. I couldn't move my arm. Dave Seaman took my place on *Strictly Ice Dancing* in the end, and won it! I was in the hospital for eight days, and while I was there I was given morphine-based painkillers. That's where the trouble started.

I came out of the hospital and went home to my family for Christmas, but I couldn't really join in with it all or enjoy it. I felt fluey, had a pain in my chest, and was absolutely freezing – I was shivering all the time. I rang Dave Seaman and the physio Gary Lewin at Arsenal who told me to go for an X-ray. After that, I was rushed into hospital – I had pneumonia, and was given injections for the pain.

I just couldn't believe what was going on. It was hard to accept – that I'd got injured through doing something that wasn't playing football, and had then caught pneumonia in the hospital. It's something that happens – people catch infections in hospitals and it's difficult to prevent it from happening. I also got a blood clot while I was in there. Because of all this, I was on *so* many different pills. I had warfarin for the blood clot, strong antibiotics for the pneumonia and morphine-based painkillers for all the pain. I remember thinking I was going to die from that pneumonia, feeling like I couldn't breathe. Now I understand how people can die from that illness.

When I came out of hospital I said I couldn't stay on morphine-based painkillers, because of my addictive personality, but it was difficult because the medical staff didn't really know my background and also I was in terrible pain, and those, of course, are the tablets that help. So they had to give them to me. So I started taking one tablet four times a day, and then it went up to two tablets four times a day, and so on. The OCD came back then. I was constantly checking and re-checking doors and windows, and cleaning and tidying up. All the obsessions came flooding back after I'd been more or less in control for such a good long period of time. The old voice was back in charge again.

At Christmas, when I'd been so ill, I'd taken some of that flu medicine . . . you know . . . Benylin. What I hadn't realised was that there are two types of Benylin – one containing alcohol and one without. Anyway, when I realised I'd been taking the one with alcohol in it I thought, 'That's it, I've just thrown away two years of sobriety. I've had a drink!' So when I was recovering from the injury, I decided I may as well have a drink seeing as I wasn't clean any more anyway. But it was crazy because I started training again, while still taking the painkillers, so I couldn't really tell whether or not I was damaging my body with the training. And then for three weeks, every night after training I'd have just one drink in the evening. Then I began to think, 'I've had one drink, I may as well have another.'

Soon after that I really tried to get it all back under control, knock the drinking on the head, but the old voices were back and it wasn't long before I started drinking Red Bull again – one of my addictive problems I'd managed to get to grips with over that past year. To some people Red Bull sounds like a really harmless soft drink, but it's actually banned in some countries. It contains a lot of caffeine, and I was drinking fifteen cans a day, which is like at least fifteen cups of coffee a day. Way too much, I know. I was on a high all the time, with the shakes. Sometimes I couldn't stop shaking, and I couldn't sleep. I was in my flat in Jesmond at the time. I'd sleep for around two hours, and go for a run at two o'clock in the morning, then go to the gym at 6 a.m. I'd train until about 10 a.m., then go back on the Red Bull. My OCD went off the scale then. I was constantly checking the door, the bed, the light switches, tidying everything away, shutting all the cupboard doors, turning the TV off, turning the stereo off. I have to have everything perfect, and if it's not perfect I can't concentrate. I was absolutely exhausted, I can't tell you how exhausting it was. I'd leave the lights off in the house and I'd be going around in the dark so as not to have to worry about turning the lights off and checking them. Then I'd want a drink or a painkiller to calm me down. People don't understand why you can't stop, but there's always this voice in my head saying, 'Have another, have another.' And I think, 'Fuck it, I've had one, I may as well have another.'

As I've said, I'd had trouble with Red Bull before then. Overdoing it. In fact, when I was in Cottonwood (the clinic in America) in 2004, just for a couple of weeks, to get me straight before all the promotional work for my autobiography started off, the American psychiatrist reckoned the Red Bull that I'd been drinking at that time could have been one of the triggers that helped set off one of my bipolar episodes. What she said was that, as long as I was taking the right medication and not messing around with any other mood-altering substances, the bipolar would be under control, but hitting the Red Bull might have helped trigger another episode. It was she who first diagnosed me as bipolar, back in 2003.

I was in a bit of a state round about then. When I was on the Red Bull for the first time, I got myself into some dangerous situations. One time, before that visit to Cottonwood in spring 2004, when I was out in the car, I suddenly swerved to avoid a big lorry coming at me that I hadn't seen. The car skidded and I went into the back of an Asda van, and the air bag blew up in my face. I was breathalysed at the scene but of course it came up clear as I hadn't been drinking. The paramedics wanted me to go to the hospital with them. I said I was okay but I wasn't, I was in a state so me dad took me to the hospital where they gave me some Valium to calm me down. I wasn't actually injured, and I hadn't thought much about it all, but the next morning when I looked out and saw the car I thought, 'My God, I could have died.' It hadn't hit me at the time, but it hit me really hard the next morning.

Not long after that accident I found a mole on my head and panicked. I phoned Bryan Robson, the Boro manager, about it, who got me to see a doctor in Manchester. I had to go to a lunch, and I came away feeling really full up and like I couldn't breathe, worrying about this mole. When I saw the doctor he laughed, and said that I'd got myself so stressed out I'd burst a blood vessel. It wasn't a mole at all.

Then, later that spring, I tried to come off the Red Bull. But I needed something, I had to have something, so I went gambling. I've never really been a proper gambler, it's not really me, although I did have a phase of gambling years before when I was seventeen. But this time I won on the very first race, and I thought, 'I'm going to keep on winning.' It got to the point with the gambling where I once took £5,000 out in the casino at one time. I was in tears, knowing I was going to lose the whole £5,000. But that time I won £11,000. I got in my car to drive home, drove around the car park and came back. I thought, 'I've won all this money, I may as well have another go at it.' I bet £3,000, lost it, then another £3,000, lost it. All in all I lost £9,000 in two hours.

At that stage I didn't want to go into a clinic because I thought the press would say I was going in for drink. I didn't want to carry on with the gambling because I knew it would get worse – and I knew I'd hit the bottle. I wrote a note at the bookies and signed it, saying I wasn't allowed to go in and place bets there. I did it at the casino as well, banned myself from gambling – but it didn't work because there was another casino I could go to and there are bookies everywhere.

I went to London and went to AA and talked about the Red Bull. Then I did go to the clinic in America, Cottonwood, for two weeks, and told them about the gambling. They got me to go to GA (Gamblers Anonymous). I went to one meeting and knew straight away that it was exactly the same as with the booze: I have an addictive personality. The painkillers, the drink, the Red Bull, the gambling, the food. It's all the same thing.

I've got a battle on my hands every day of my life. My friend Paul Davis, who used to play for Arsenal, asked me, 'What would it be like to have a normal life?' I actually don't know. I don't have a normal life. Every day I get up and I have to deal with booze, food, my OCD, medication for panic attacks, the whole lot. No matter how well I face the battle, I still have to start again from scratch the next day. It's exhausting. I can't take it or leave it like other people. While I was getting drunk it was great, but once I *was* drunk it was a nightmare.

From that time in Cottonwood in 2004 until the *Strictly Ice Dancing* injury I was sober – I had been for a while anyway, since I got back from Cottonwood in 2003, after China where things had been going wrong for me – and on top of things generally. Now here we are in 2005 and since the painkillers, the Red Bull again and then drinking in Portugal over the summer, it's started going wrong again. I've got a little bit of knowledge about how to get back on the right track. Early in the morning, as soon as I wake up, I write my problems down to get them out of the way, and then I shut the door behind me. I can't conquer my fears until I face them. I know I have a chemical imbalance and I have to take medication to address the imbalance, and for two to three years while I was getting clean I'd have massive panic attacks. They think that was originally triggered by cocaine, which I took a couple of months after leaving Everton, in summer 2002. People think it's fun to take cocaine but it's dangerous. I found that out the hard way.

I sometimes wake up at night and lie there worrying about dying. I worry about what I've achieved and what I haven't achieved, and whether or not I've got time to get it all done. The thought of dying will make me jump out of bed. I watched *The Running Man*, a film with Arnold Schwarzenegger, set in the future. It's about a deadly reality TV show for criminals, and I hated it; I couldn't stand watching it, but I still watched it. He has to battle to survive. I've got this battle on my hands for the rest of my life. But I know, if I keep on fighting it and fighting it, I'll win in the end.

John

Paul had a lot to get off his chest, and I noticed how much calmer he became as he shared. For the first ten minutes of the session he talked as if he were being interviewed on Radio Five Live, which shows how out of practice he is with the counselling. It *is* a peculiar process after all.

I'm pleased that Paul's as aware as he is of what's currently going on in his life. In the session, he was able to track back to where he felt everything had started going wrong, and how he eventually relapsed back to drink. He knew exactly why he did this and, despite all the awful things that he had to deal with, he was still able to be conscious of picking up that first drink. However, drink he did, and that relapse was the start of a pattern that has lasted for the past nine months. Several issues came out of the session that concern me and they will need to be addressed urgently over the next few weeks. Firstly, Paul is now in a regular pattern of drinking that will only progress and get worse. Secondly, since damaging his neck in the skating accident he has been abusing his prescribed morphine-based medication. Thirdly, as a result of the drinking and pills, Paul has been unable to eat properly and this has triggered his food disorder. Meanwhile, the medication that he normally takes for his bipolar disorder, which also helps with anxiety management, has stopped working because of the alcohol and codeine intake, so he has been suffering from panic attacks, and this has also meant the return of his obsessive compulsive disorder.

With alcoholism, once the balance goes and a pattern of drinking is set up, other conditions that co-exist, such as anxiety and mood disorders, are triggered. Also, for an alcoholic, or any kind of addict, swapping one substance for another doesn't work because it keeps the addiction alive, or re-starts it, as in the case of Paul and the painkillers he took for his neck. This is why many treatment models for addiction are founded on abstinence from all mood-altering chemicals and behaviours – once you get into altering your mood the whole cycle of addiction is jump-started into action.

At the end of the session I advised Paul that, over the next week, he should really try to prioritise his time, put his recovery first and practise better self-care. He should knock out his alcohol intake with the help of a home detox regime, which he could get from his psychiatrist, and return to AA meetings to get some extra support with staying sober. This would also help with his anxiety and, in turn, with the OCD. It would give his normal medication a chance to work. We would have to do some specific work on his eating, but for now he should try and have three regular meals a day. He agreed to try this plan.

The primary focus of our sessions together has to be Paul's alcoholism. Until he stops drinking he won't be able to tackle his other underlying problems. So the focus of our next session will be specifically alcohol, looking at whether Paul has been able to achieve the aim of stopping, and focusing on his drinking history: looking at where and when he started drinking and when it became problematic.

Cheers Paul!

It's been so great having you in our group. You always have such smart and sensitive things to say and I know you won't relapse which you are worried about.

You are always so kind and funny. I hope we can keep in touch. I'm excited to read the book you told us about. It's got to be more interesting than the crap books they give you in here.

Kiss,

Stacey 'the lovely lass'

Chapter Three

Paul's road to therapy

Paul

I had my first therapy session when I was ten. Lots of shit had started to happen. The worst was about a little kid I was supposed to be looking after, Steven. We were in this shop, mucking around, when Steven ran out into the road. An oncoming car went right into him. I ran out and stood over his crumpled little body screaming, 'Please move, please move!' It was the first dead body I had seen – and I blamed myself for it.

Then my dad, who had been away a lot, for months on end, in Germany and elsewhere, came home at last – and started having seizures. I was with him once, on my own. I tried to pull his tongue out to stop him swallowing it, thinking he was going to die.

It was around this time I started having twitches, and making lots of stupid noises. I also developed obsessions. I became fixated on the number five, everything had to be touched five times. I'd put the light on and off five times, or close the door five times.

My mam got worried about all these twitches and took me to a doctor. He said I had to see a psychiatrist at Queen Elizabeth Hospital in Gateshead. My mam was working that day, so my dad took me. This psychiatrist made me play with a load of sand which I thought was fucking stupid. I refused to go again. My dad thought it was silly as well. So all the twitches and stuff just carried on.

Looking back, I don't regret stopping going, but I'm not saying I still think it was all rubbish. The thing about therapy is that the timing has to be right, and you have to be right. It can be right for you at seventeen or thirty-seven or fifty-seven, or never.

At seventeen, the signs of various obsessions were getting worse, but I don't think therapy would have helped me. Not at that time. I wasn't ready for it. I would not have accepted it. It wasn't for me.

Yet I've never been one of those who were cynical about therapy, who said it was all stupid or just for rich, daft people to indulge themselves. I remember going to see *One Flew Over the Cuckoo's Nest* – and it terrified me. I thought, 'That could be me, I could end up in an institution like that.'

When I was playing for Rangers, I was in a terrible depressed state at one time, feeling suicidal. I asked the Rangers doctor if I could have a word with him. 'These people,' I said to him, 'who want to top themselves, why do they want to do it? What makes them flip?'

'People who flip,' he said, 'don't know they've flipped.' In a way, that reassured me. The fact that I knew I was feeling crazy suggested I might get through it. It's people who don't know who end it. I don't know whether this is true or not, but it helped at the time. I'll have to ask Johnny.

When I was with Sheryl, and everything was going wrong with me and the marriage, Shel insisted we went to see a marriage-guidance counsellor. I agreed to go once – but never again. I thought it was useless. I didn't listen to a word he said and denied everything. But Shel went a few times and seemed to think it helped her, for a bit anyway.

It was landing up in the Priory, in 1998, that's what started me off on the therapy road. I was playing for Middlesbrough at the time and had been on the piss for days. In Dublin, on a break, I had drunk thirty-two whiskies.

Didn't know where I was or what I was doing. One of my best mates, Davey, had just died suddenly, and I was blaming myself, again.

Late in the evening, having flown back to Newcastle, I somehow got myself on a train to visit Shel in Hertfordshire and got off at Stevenage. I was in such an emotional state that I wanted to throw myself in front of a train – but the last train had gone. So I just sat there, on an empty station, crying.

Finally, I somehow managed to ring Shel – but she refused to let me come to her place, not in the state I was in. She'd been through all that before. But she did ring Bryan Robson and he drove down overnight and picked me up. By that time, I was out of it, had no idea where I was or what had happened.

When I woke up, there appeared to be metal bars keeping me in so I said, 'Where am I?' They said it was the Priory. I said, 'Why am I here?' – and they said, 'For alcoholism.' I said, 'I'm not a fucking alcoholic, get me out of here!' But they wouldn't let me go. I had a guy coming into my room, staring at me all the time for the first twenty-four hours, in case I did anything stupid.

One day I heard this bloke banging on my door, asking to be let in. I said, 'Fuck off, go away, I don't want to see or talk to anyone.' He kept on banging and eventually I let him in – and it was Eric Clapton. He said he had been through all this, and it had helped him, so I should make an effort just to try it. So I agreed, but not really. I was touched by him bothering to come and see me, but I still thought it was all rubbish, that I wasn't an alcoholic and didn't need treatment. I'd be okay once I sobered up.

I agreed to answer fifty questions, about my life and drinking and that – but decided just to tell lies, say the first stupid thing that came into my head. 'Do you drink in the mornings?' was one question. I said 'No' to that, which was a lie. They asked if I liked the taste of drink and I said 'Yes, love it', which was another lie. I've never actually liked the taste of drink. When I used to go out boozing with people like Chris Evans, I'd often be pouring away my drink in plant pots. I just like the effect, not the taste. Anyway, I scored thirty-five points on this survey, despite telling lies. I thought that, after all, it might prove I needed help. Don't ask me how.

I got put into a psycho-drama session which, at the time, I thought was really daft. I don't think that any more. I've since seen the benefits. But I did think it daft then. We all had to pretend to be trains, and go 'choo choo choo'. 'I'm Paul Gascoigne and I'm a fucking choo choo train.' I refused to take it seriously. I didn't understand the point. In another group session I had to join everyone was having a go at each other. Most of the people there knew who I was, which made it harder.

In one session, I wanted to throw a chair through the window. I threatened I was going to, so they all laughed and clapped and said, 'Go on, Gazza, you can pay for it.' I stormed out shouting at them, 'You're all mental!' Not very nice, I know; but remember, I was pretty messed up. That's my only excuse.

This was when Johnny appeared. I thought at first, 'Who the fuck are you to tell me things? You don't know fuck all about my life, or about football.' Football had got me into this, so I thought. I would not have been in the Priory, but for football. But when Johnny started one-to-one sessions, it got a bit better and I began to realise more. The point is that we are all trying to help each other, to expose the anger and pain.

As I started to settle down in sessions with Johnny, they began to allow me a few concessions, letting me out, for example, on country runs to keep fit. I went on one long run, not knowing where I was going – and found I had run into Fulham's training ground. That was funny. They all shouted at me, 'You can do it Gazza, keep going Gazza!' I think by then most people had heard what had happened to me, and where I was.

After seventeen days, I pleaded with them to let me out. I promised and promised that I would never have another drink, which of course is what all drunks say.

I'd found Johnny not so bad, not a bad bloke, but I still hated being there.

You are meant to have a full twenty-eight days, that's the minimum first treatment if, like me, you have been brought in paralytic. The average number of times someone needs to go for treatment, before it really hits home, is three.

After twenty days, I was ready to run away. And I was serious. So they agreed I could leave, on condition I came back two days a week for the next four weeks, to get me up to the twenty-eight days.

But when I came out, I was still angry. So I didn't give that first visit to the Priory a proper chance. I was still too busy denying I was an alcoholic.

John

When I first met Paul in the flesh he was just as I'd expected: down-to-earth, funny, one of the lads. On hearing my accent he immediately asked where I was from. When I told him I was a fellow northerner he seemed to relax in my presence. I was to be his counsellor in treatment for the next four weeks, so this was a good start. On the surface, Paul was like most people who have ended up in rehab. He had been drinking far too much over a fairly short period and it had all come to a head after one particular bender, resulting in his being brought in to treatment. He, like most, had hit 'rock bottom'.

When you enter a place like the Priory Hospital as a patient, all sorts of things happen to you. First, when you wake up on the day after being admitted you usually don't know where you are. Paul thought he was in the Southampton Priory because that's what was reported on the news. He was actually in London. The Priory is a chain of psychiatric hospitals with addiction clinics attached.

During the first few days most patients are on medical detoxification which increases the sense of disorientation. At some point you are then taken to the unit that specialises in addiction treatment and introduced to your primary group. This is the bunch of people, usually around eight men and women, who will get to know you inside and out over the following weeks. And of course you will get to know them just as thoroughly. So it's a lot to take in.

As Paul began to settle in, he slowly started to take risks both with his group and in our one-to-one sessions. After some initial resistance he settled in to the idea that he could not control his drinking, and began to talk openly about his alcoholism. This was an important breakthrough as it is a convention that all patients begin group therapy by introducing themselves with their first name and identifying themselves as an alcoholic or addict, or sometimes both: 'I'm Jimmy and I'm an alcoholic.' It's important to remind yourself that you are in hospital because of *your* addiction.

During Paul's early treatment I was surprised to observe how supportive he was towards others in group-therapy sessions. He would be the first to give feedback when a fellow patient had shared a painful life story. He would get angry on their behalf and even offer to confront relatives on 'family day'. His insights were important and genuinely helpful.

As time went on it became clear why Paul had so much insight into others' painful lives. This was because of his own painful life, which included early traumas such as the death of a childhood friend and the illness of his father.

Paul had witnessed a lot as he grew up. It's important to add that Paul's family's social life, like that of all their friends and extended family, revolved around alcohol and the pub. It was where people would meet, have a good time, get drunk and sometimes fight. So it wouldn't be unusual for Paul to witness physical violence every now and then.

Early in life Paul began to develop some tics and stammers due partly to the traumatic events experienced at such a young age. He did the best he could to deal with his lot but developed anxiety disorders. For him this developed into various obsessive compulsive disorders, such as counting in certain ways, checking doors, and obsessively cleaning. Paul began to see the world in a certain way, and to be programmed to think and feel in a certain pattern. Once programmed, it's extremely difficult to change a person's mental and emotional blueprint. Every one of us has a programme, but whereas some of us have a way that gets us through life well enough, for others nothing seems to work. It's as if the world is against us – everything we touch turns to dust. Relationships, jobs, friends – whatever it is, something seems to go wrong. We feel victimised, and sure enough we become victims. This is a lifelong pattern for many people. The really unfair thing about this pattern is that it's unconscious. In other words we cannot see it ourselves;

we are not programmed to review our own behaviour. The only time we get to see ourselves is when someone at home or at work points something out to us and by then it's out of hand and we take the comments as criticism or a put-down. So we react defensively, give them a piece of our minds and, guess what, we become victims all over again, crying: 'It's not fair!'

I was going to hear that statement from Paul time and again throughout his treatment at the Priory. The main focus in any addiction treatment centre is on the illness of addiction. I call it an illness because that's precisely what it is. Not everyone who drinks heavily has it; however, some individuals who only drink moderately *do* have it. You either have it or you don't. Paul was admitted to hospital because he could no longer control his drinking. Everyone around him would tell him this, especially those who were close to him. Friends and family would be on edge every time they were in a social situation with him because they wouldn't know how he would behave. He is a classic 'Dr Jekyll and Mr Hyde': when sober, he's a lovely man, kind and considerate and very generous; however, when drinking alcohol he is unpredictable.

He would sometimes be fine. He'd have a few drinks, tell a few jokes and be the popular figure we all love. Other times he would have one too many, get loud, start to say inappropriate things to friends and become aggressive. Everyone around him would be on eggshells – wondering what they should do next, how they would get him home in one piece, avoiding the press and trying to prevent him getting into a fight. Family and friends would cover for him and even tell lies on his behalf. Why do such people, who usually behave honestly and professionally in their lives, suddenly start to cover things up? It's because they don't know what to do; they feel over-responsible for their loved one and this leads to personal compromise. Suddenly the alcoholic is more important than oneself. This issue is very common in families in which alcoholism is present, and it's got its own name: codependency. Codependency is about relationships, and its main feature is that we say or do what we think will control or fix the other person, rather than what is true or good for ourselves.

Paul began to recover physically and mentally and, by the second week, when his detox was completed, he began to focus on what we describe in the treatment field as 'outside issues'. He was, after all, still playing football in the Premiership and was keen to get back on the pitch. His relationship with his ex-wife was stable, and after three weeks he couldn't understand why he shouldn't return to Middlesbrough. His psychiatrist, the treatment team and I all disagreed with his thinking, as it was too early for him to leave.

The suggested minimum stay is twenty-eight days. We called a meeting and invited in his then current manager, Bryan Robson, to thrash out the issue. The result was that Paul would be discharged that weekend but that he would return for two days a week for the next month to complete treatment. The only person happy with this was Paul. But true to his word he came back the following Monday and stuck to the agreed regime.

Alcoholism is described as a three-fold illness that affects the physical, mental and spiritual parts of our being. Physically, people become addicted and start to suffer withdrawal and other harmful symptoms. Alcohol is a depressant. It impedes the functioning of the brain's physiology, which in turn messes up the whole body's rhythm. Mentally, there is an immediate effect on the thinking during drinking and a long-term corrosive effect on decision-making and other cognitive processes. Spiritually, there is a 'loss of the self'. In other words, our natural personality, the person we have been all of our lives, our 'real nature', starts to disappear.

During the last few days of Paul's stay at the Priory, we began to put together an aftercare plan. This was to remind him that the job he'd started was by no means complete. He would need to abstain from alcohol and other mood-altering drugs and, for a short time, stay out of social situations that involve drinking. He should ideally attend one of the many self-help support groups each day for the first ninety days. I would aim to meet with him every fortnight for one-to-one sessions.

The other issue to be dealt with was his depression. Would he need to be on medication for this? Was he actually clinically depressed or was the depression caused by his drinking pattern and subsequent lifestyle? Paul has suffered from many other conditions besides alcoholism, but for now they have taken a back seat. After meeting with his psychiatrist in the Priory it was agreed that he should take a mild antidepressant. Paul felt okay about this, and agreed to try it.

Around a quarter of people entering treatment for alcoholism or drug dependency will have a co-occurring illness, such as an anxiety disorder, a mood disorder, a major depressive disorder or bipolar disorder. And according to studies, an alcoholic is six times more likely to have bipolar disorder than a non-alcoholic. Making an accurate diagnosis in primary treatment is very difficult. There are many issues to take into account before prescribing any psychotropic medication. Depression and bipolar disorder are particularly hard to spot in the early stages of recovery. That is because, by the time most people arrive for treatment, they are extremely low – or occasionally extremely high – as a result of their alcohol and drug intake.

There is a suggested abstinence of four to six weeks to allow each individual to come out of their addictive cycle and return to normal before any other diagnoses are made. It is essential that a thorough family history be taken to see if there have ever been any psychiatric illnesses in the family. This assessment should also cover a drink and drug history.

The main focus on Paul's treatment at the Priory was his alcoholism. It was not until much later that he would also be diagnosed with bipolar disorder.

After that first meeting in 1998, I was to see Paul roughly five or six times over the next nine months. He didn't attend many meetings and dropped his aftercare plan fairly quickly after leaving London. He eventually relapsed.

Paul

That was just the first of several visits to the Priory over the last eight years or so. I've lost count of how much money I've spent, which is just as well.

After that first twenty-day session in the Priory, I later did two other shorter ones, of ten days and three days. They were for different sorts of problems, not always drink, but for depression, anxiety and addiction to painkillers. That sort of thing. I don't do things by halves, do I?

I've also been a regular at AA meetings, but they're a bit hard if you're well known. I could understand why George Best didn't attend them very often. One of my fears is that you never know who is there, maybe planted by the press, or whether someone who looks and seems okay will then ring up a paper and flog a story for money.

I always kept in touch with Johnny throughout this period, looking upon him as a friend as much as a counsellor, going to see him for regular sessions. Well, to be honest, it was more like now and again, with a few longish gaps, but I still talked to him on the phone. And then I went to see him properly recently.

When I realised I was coming to the end of my football career, I began to dread it, thinking I would have nothing left to live for. That was all I had known, all I could do. And at football, I was a sort of genius. I had a talent, but with talent, so I'm told, there's a fine line between living normally and flipping. I think Robbie Williams is a massive talent, and he's had his share of problems in the past. Yes, I know there are people with talent who don't flip, but it does often go together.

I suppose, really, you are born with it, whether you are a so-called genius or not. It's there inside you, then slowly it sort of creeps up and takes over as you go through life.

I've also been to a clinic in Arizona called Cottonwood, three times so far. I've found it easier to go off to America to get away from everything, the press and other people, to a country where I'm not known.

The first time was when I was at Everton, in June 2001, and the second time after China in 2003, where I was trying to coach. At Everton, I'd got myself in a terrible state, partly because of lots of injuries, worrying about my career ending. I was getting hooked on diazepam as well as drinking heavily. So that didn't help. I also went in 2004. Just for two weeks. Not because I was drinking. I wasn't. I was totally sober then. Had been for a while. It was to do with Red Bull and a bit of gambling. I just needed to get myself sorted.

John

One day in 2001, about twelve months after I'd last seen Paul, I'd just come out of a training seminar at Guy's Hospital when I received a phone call from Bill Kenwright, the chairman of Everton Football Club. He had asked a mutual friend, Paul Roberts, for help concerning Paul Gascoigne, and my name came up. Bill wondered whether I was available to meet with him and Paul the following day to discuss how we could best help him to stop drinking. I agreed.

Bill was sticking his neck out because he didn't want Paul to be sacked from the club, and because he cared about him. He was very concerned, and shared with me that he was shocked at Paul's state of health and felt powerless to help. After meeting with Paul, I too was worried. It was agreed that we needed to talk to Walter Smith, the team manager, and discuss when would be a good time to refer Paul back into residential treatment. Walter agreed it had to be as soon as possible. Sheryl was also very supportive at this stage, and ten days later Paul was off to the Cottonwood de Tucson treatment centre in Arizona.

Paul returned to England on great form. He had spent a month in the desert focusing on getting better. He had learnt a lot from his stay and had been diagnosed with bipolar disorder as well as alcoholism. At the time Paul was very worried about this, but he was also relieved as it helped explain some of his past behaviour and vicious mood swings. Despite Paul being comfortable with this diagnosis, others were not so comfortable. He had been prescribed medication that would influence the way he trained and played, therefore affecting his standing in the first team.

The dilemmas that arise for friends and family and colleagues in such situations are commonplace. First of all, it is very difficult for a friend or colleague to accept that you're ill in the first place. They see you a lot and know you have been run-down, but think all you need is a rest and you'll be 'right as rain'. Furthermore, most friends, family and colleagues have never suffered from a psychiatric illness and therefore have no idea what it's like for you. So they don't help, because they say things like, 'Stop taking that medication, you don't need it!' How do they know? They're not trained to give out that type of advice, only a psychiatrist can.

This is what happened to Paul. Subsequently, over a period of time and with the help of his psychiatrist back in England, he came off his medication. It was a risk, but only time would tell.

His first team appearances were regular, but over the season Paul began to be disillusioned. He stayed focused on his recovery for a while but did not attend enough self-help meetings. He and I would meet on average once every three weeks to start with, but this also fell away again. Over the course of a nine-month period, Paul made a decision to try and drink only socially. He moved from Everton to Burnley. He eventually slipped back into his old pattern and we lost touch.

Then, in 2003, Paul went to China as a player-coach, preparing himself for when he would no longer actually be playing football. When Paul had been at Everton he'd had a great bunch of people around him on the staff. One of those was John Murtagh, who is now the head of Fulham's youth academy. He phoned me to say that Jimmy Gardner, Paul's oldest friend, nicknamed 'Jimmy Five Bellies', had called him as he was concerned that Paul was really struggling in China, and asked for John's help.

John gave me Paul's number. I called him in China and he told me he was in a terrible state. He'd been doing well for a while but was starting to encounter difficulties with the language, air quality, heat and the standard of football. He didn't want to quit but resented being there, and had started drinking. Once again his drinking got out of control very quickly and, as well as that, he was beginning to suffer regular panic attacks.

He was alone most of the time and this increased his need for a drink. I called his psychiatrist at the North London Priory, who suggested that as Paul wasn't able to get home, we send him a detoxification regime that would help with managing the alcohol intake and panic attacks. This helped Paul but in the end there was only ever going to be one conclusion – he would have to come back for help in order to get sober. Paul did return home during a break in the football season and, after some carefully planned tactics (such as not trying to stop drinking until he got to the clinic and could receive medical help), he flew back out to Cottonwood de Tucson for treatment.

Paul, despite the previous few months, felt more positive about his rehabilitation. He completed thirty-two days of treatment and returned on excellent form. He was back with Sheryl and this was going well. He attended regular meetings and would come for counselling every week. He wasn't playing football, but was working on his autobiography.

As time went by he became, in his own words, 'bored'. Life at home was also difficult and he and Sheryl decided that Paul would move out for a period and return to Newcastle. As far as I was concerned, Paul was in a stage of grieving. He was no longer doing the only thing he'd known for the previous twenty years – playing football. The game that he loved. For most of my life I'd played amateur football and if I ever had to miss it, because of injury or holiday, for more than a couple of weeks I would 'crack up'. So what was *he* going through?

At that time – unlike now – he wasn't interested in coaching full time. He still wanted to play but his body would no longer allow for the rigorous, punishing training regimes. He'd suffered many injuries and they had taken their toll. As well as this, Paul was starting to miss the spotlight. Would the fans still shout his name as he walked down the street? Would the football world miss him? This was, and still is, a massive issue for Paul, and I know many other famous people have experienced it too. And it is not just those in the limelight. I remembered reading some research that talked about the effects of redundancy on working-class men in the shipbuilding and coal-mining communities. I'd been shocked at the high proportion of workers who died within a few years of being made redundant, and at the high proportion turning to alcohol in order to cope with the loss of routine and identity. Paul could see that he needed to 'let go' of the idea of playing but couldn't do it. He was feeling unsure about the rest of his life. He shared with me in one session that he had bumped into Barry McGuigan, the former boxing champion of the world, and he'd told Paul about how he'd been struggling with the issue of not being in the limelight any more and that he'd had to seek help to get over the loss of his boxing career. It really helped Paul to hear that someone like Barry had experienced similar issues to himself.

As Paul was in Newcastle I wouldn't see him very regularly. He had split from Sheryl but was busy working on his book among other things.

But he hadn't really let go of football, and went off to train with Dave Jones at Wolverhampton Wanderers to work on his fitness and to see if perhaps he could still play at a high level. After about six weeks he decided it wasn't working out at Wolves, partly due to picking up an injury and partly because his depression had returned. He felt lonely and cut off. He was back living in a hotel environment.

Paul maintained his sobriety until unfortunately he got that injury through the *Strictly Ice Dancing* programme. Then he was back to the same situation – feeling ill and depressed, not knowing what to do with the rest of his life. Eventually he came to see me.

———————

Dear Paul

I hope that this has been a positive experience for you in Cottonwood and that you continue to use the tools you have learned here in your life back home. Best of luck – and we hope not to see you back here.

Best wishes

Greg

ChapterFour

Paul goes from the Algarve to Kettering

Paul

I played in the Premiership till 2002, when I left Everton, by which time I was thirty-five. So I'd had a good career at the very top, whatever some people might think. And I got 57 caps for England. I don't know whether football kept me going – helping me to overcome all my other problems because I was so obsessed by football – or not. I think but for football I would probably have been far worse.

I also don't know whether therapy and all the help I began to get towards the end of my career kept me going and able to play longer than I would otherwise have done. I'm sure it did, but who the fuck knows. You only go one way in life and never know which way the other road would have taken you.

In 2004, I joined Boston United, as a player-coach. I thought I'd be able to do some proper coaching, but that didn't quite work out, and I only stayed a few months.

Then, in the summer of 2005, I went out to Portugal to be coach of Algarve United. They'd just come up into the Portuguese league so it looked as if they were going places. I worked with them for two months. I tried very hard, but the proposed contract never appeared. It was all just verbal, or a shake of hands. I could see it wasn't getting anywhere.

Until around that time, I'd had two years not drinking. All the therapy and treatment and AA and stuff had worked, plus my own willpower. In my book, I suppose I did talk at the end, did boast I guess, about that, about being dry at last, but it was true. I'd stuck to it up to that point.

The book finished with me appearing to have got my life in order, that I was a success, which made some people think, 'Oh yeah, Gazza – he's sorted now. His life is rosy now, all right for him. He's got no probs.'

Which of course wasn't true. I was still getting myself in a state all the time for various reasons.

Anyway, it was in the Algarve I went back on the drink again. After I'd previously slipped at Christmas, as I've already told yous. I was stuck in a hotel, all on my own, with things not going well. Very like what happened in China, thousands of miles from home.

The Algarve was not quite as bad. For a start I was in a lovely place, Vilamoura, with all mod cons and luxuries and nice people but, all the same, I was on my own.

I decided to have a glass of wine. I took it for the same old reasons – I was depressed, anxious, desperate to change the way I was feeling. I still don't like the taste much, not even the best, most expensive wine. I take it to numb my pain.

Obviously I felt guilty. I was letting myself down, and other people. Once you're an alcoholic, always an alcoholic. You are never cured. And you always think, once you have one glass, you might as well go and get pissed. So I got pissed, twice. I hadn't talked to Johnny or been to the AA for ages. Hard to do all that, in the Algarve.

Chris Evans tried to help me escape from the press by letting me go to his villa, but I had a few drinks there as well. I admitted it to him, that

I'd had a relapse. I used to go for a ten-mile run, on my own, then I'd come back to the house and just sit there – and then I'd decide to have a drink.

I played golf a few times with Andy Townsend and Gary McAllister. They'd have a couple of drinks after we'd played. I'd pretend I wasn't drinking and say I would just have a Diet Coke, but behind their backs, I'd pour a couple of vodkas into the Diet Coke.

My dad and Carl, my brother, were planning on coming out for a bit of a holiday. I'd gone back to England to go see some tennis at Wimbledon and to do some filming for a DVD I was doing on my career. Well, I had a bit of a problem at the tennis. Had a few drinks. Then my dad, Carl and me were planning on flying out to Portugal together. Just a few days after the tennis final. Waiting at Gatwick Airport for the flight with the both of them, I again had a bit to drink. I caused a scene. I got into an argument with two cops who were called, fighting with them when they tried to restrain me. And giving them a bit of an earful. I know, I know, it was fucking stupid. I'm supposed to have shouted, 'Take your guns off and I'll have you as well!' I'm sure I didn't. I don't remember.

The upshot was that BA banned me from the flight, because of the state I was in. My dad was absolutely furious, shouting and screaming at me for being so stupid.

No, I didn't hit him, which one paper said I did, but I did have a row with him. He would have knocked me out if I'd hit him. I would never hit him anyway, even when drunk. I have too much respect for him. Anyway, he and Carl didn't go to Portugal. How could they? I wasn't going to be there. They went back on their own to Newcastle and I was left, crying my eyes out.

I rang Johnny and told him I'd had a relapse. He tried to talk me through what to do and I went off to the Priory for a few days. When I'd sobered up, things were a bit better. And the police in the end decided not to press any charges. That was good of them. Not that much had really happened. But even still.

Carl and me dad did eventually come out for a holiday, mind. But I was still drinking a bit. Behind my dad's back, I'd get Carl to get me a drink on the beach, but not to let me dad know. But he found out, of course. It is a difficult thing to hide.

He went mad at me. 'Look at the state you're in – go to fucking bed and sleep it off.' Which I did. Craving for a drink is like craving for a cigarette, only a hundred times worse. When I woke up, they'd both gone. Got an early flight home.

My battle with the bottle will be with me for the rest of my life. I know that. Every day when I wake up, I realise it's going to be a battle, just to get through the day without a drink.

The only people who understand these feelings are all the alcoholics. There are four million in Britain who admit it, who have come out, and another four million who have not admitted it – yet. But all of us have got to talk about it, face up to it. It's the only way.

During those two years not drinking, I wasn't sickened by other people getting drunk, spewing up in the streets in Newcastle. It didn't worry me. I've been there. Most of them won't turn into alcoholics. I know that. They won't get addicted. Lucky them.

The real alcoholics, I can easily spot them – by their faces, their shakes, the bulge of a bottle in their coat pocket. I often see them on the street and feel sorry for them.

I feel I can have two glasses of wine, then I'm shitting myself, wondering if I'll be able to stop. I know what I'm supposed to do – go for a walk, read a book, watch TV, or ring Johnny and talk it through. I can do all those things, but it's so hard.

I know I'll start playing the same old tricks. I might be with someone, having a chat, when I'll jump up and say I've got to make a phone call, or do something. But it won't be true. I'll be lying. Instead I'll jump in the car and go to the off-licence. After a quick swig, I'll brush my teeth, have some chewing gum, come back and pretend nothing has happened.

It might sound mad, but at the moment, now that the disappointment and loneliness of Portugal is behind me, I do feel I can control it, that two glasses will be enough for me. I don't see what's wrong with that, as long as I'm not hooked. But, of course, I'd rather not drink for the rest of my life, if I could.

Living in Britain, it's so hard. Everyone drinks. People are drinking, all around, wherever you go. I see people in pubs or at parties cradling a glass of wine – and then they leave it. You can see clearly that they've left half their glass. Only drinking half of their wine! Fucking hell. I wish I could do that. I wish I could leave half a glass. Even better, I wish I could just stick to Diet Coke.

So I went back to seeing Johnny, after that relapse in the Algarve – and then something even better than therapy came along to occupy my mind. I got a job.

Over the last couple of years, I've had various approaches from people saying they were going to buy so-and-so club and would put me in as manager. Some were quite good clubs, in the English First and Second Divisions, but nothing came of them. Usually when we looked into their finances, they were far worse than they'd led us to believe, with millions of debts we didn't know about.

While I was in the Algarve, I got a call one day from a friend, Ian Elliott, to say there was this guy wanting to meet me about buying a club, with me as manager. Sounded the usual fantasy stuff, but I agreed to go and see him.

He turned out to be a twenty-seven-year-old lad, Imraan Ladak, who had made a lot of money. He's a Spurs fan, basically, but he knew he was never going to be able to buy Spurs.

I had a three-hour meeting with him. It was strange, being interviewed by someone of twenty-seven, more than ten years younger than me. That hasn't happened to me before. I suppose it will happen more in the future, now I'm becoming an old fart.

I was struck by his enthusiasm and knowledge of football, so I agreed to go in with him, if he found a suitable place. That's when he came up with Kettering Town. I watched some videos, went to see them play, talked to some of their players, and I thought, 'Yeah, I could work with this lot.'

They are well down the non-league ratings – not even in the Conference, but the one below that, Conference North. That means they are six leagues below the Premiership. So yeah, they've got a long way to go. But they're an old club, 133 years old, who have so far never got into the Football League. So that's our challenge.

The news is now out and people have been quite surprised, asking me why I haven't started a bit higher up, then there would be less far to go to get to the Premiership. But you have to start somewhere. José Mourinho wasn't even a coach when he began, just working as a translator. I think it took him about six years to join a big club. So it can be done.

Kettering over the years has had some good people playing with them or managing them, such as Tommy Lawton and Derek Dougan. Ron Atkinson was with them at one time. So they're not a total backwater. The town is quite big in fact, about, I dunno, about 50,000, but their average gates were only around 500 when we arrived.

I have agreed to put some of my own money in, to show I am committed. I will own about a third of the club.

I'm letting Imraan do all the financial dealing, and the legal work. I'm just putting my mind to the football side. All the players are part time at the moment, doing ordinary jobs during the day, but my ambition is to get them full time – by the end of the season, if I can manage it.

To do this, I need to get in sponsors, which I've been working on, using my name and contacts, speaking to firms or people to sponsor our kit and get us some new balls. The balls we have are rubbish. I've approached about forty sponsors so far and most of them are really interested.

The players train on Mondays and Tuesdays, after their ordinary work. The reserves train on Wednesday evening. Yeah, there is a reserve team, so that's something.

Paul Davis, my friend who used to play for Arsenal and England, is a brilliant coach, with all the qualifications. He's my right-hand man. He takes the training sessions. I just watch, suggest things, keep an eye on progress. I'll be picking the team and deciding tactics, who comes off, who comes on as sub, but I rely on Paul's help.

There was a manager here, Kevin Wilson, who's done a good job with them, got them fifth in the league last season. Obviously he can't be the manager now I've arrived, as part owner as well, but he's agreed to become director of football. He's looking at players we can buy, when we get the money, and to scout the opposition. He's a good lad. He's taken it well. Of course at this stage, I don't know how it will work out.

So that's the position, as of now, at the end of October. We'll have to see how it goes, how I will cope.

I'm serious about it, in it for the long haul, whatever the cynics might think. I agree my track record as a coach hasn't been exactly brilliant so far. Two months has been my longest stint, but I promise you I'll be here for a long time, oh yes. The fucking bookies are taking bets that I'll be gone by Christmas, but what do they know? Fuck them, that's what I say.

I've been lost without football. I haven't found anything yet I love as much. That's been part of my problem. Whatever happens, it will be better than sitting around doing nothing, getting depressed. I suppose you could say football for me has always been a sort of therapy. Well it is now . . .

———————

Hey Freak

I know that it is going to be hard to recover from the devastation of losing to a girl in chess and battleships, but think of it as a learning experience.

I am not going to write anything cheesy in your book, so I am just going to mention that I am excited to receive and give the best. I am sure I can think of new things even for you! Heh heh heh. Also remember that you made two promises. It is bad luck to break them.

So see you in Cali. A chest of a man. Ready to have fun. Going to miss you, even your annoying tendencies. Loads of love. No explanation necessary . . .

Thank you

Tracey

ChapterFive

Paul managing to be a manager

Paul

It's now a month since I started at Kettering. After the first couple of weeks, finding my way around, I saw that I was doing far too much. I realised I had to set up certain ground rules. I didn't want people wandering around the club, into the directors' lounge, talking to players or whatever, without me knowing who they were and what they were doing.

I knew I couldn't do it all, although I've done most things apart from make the tea, but I wanted to know who were the people doing the various jobs. I had to know who the kit man was, the club secretary, the security man – then I could concentrate on being the manager.

I haven't seen Johnny for a while, as I've been so busy, and I've also taken on some outside commercial work, such as the DVD, and then gone on *Richard and Judy* to promote it.

I've been working eight days a week and now I'm unable to sleep. I was lying awake all last night thinking about what we'll do in training today, or who I'll pick for Saturday, or how am I going to get more money into the club to pay for things. Me and Paul are really up against it.

We started off quite well, won our first game, but got knocked out of the Cup. That didn't matter too much. I want to concentrate on getting out of this league. But since then we've only got five points out of a possible twelve in the league, which isn't quite good enough – especially as the last three games (all away) were against struggling teams. We should have got more than two draws and a loss.

I now feel for every manager I've worked for – which of course I didn't at the time, when I messed them around, went out on the piss, or got bloated and overweight. I want to apologise to them all for what I did. A bit late now, of course. At least I know the worst things players can do, the tricks they get up to. I did them all.

Almost all the sponsors I approached came on board, so that's been good. We've got new balls, new track suits. I've got the players drinking high-energy drinks and I make them eat pasta and also pizzas. Pizzas are good for carbohydrates. If the Italians eat pasta and pizza all the time, they can't be bad for you. They've won three World Cups after all.

A lot of pressure comes with being a manager, that's for sure. Especially if the results aren't going as well as you'd hoped. I've found myself getting uptight and frustrated, and I don't want to take that out on the players. That isn't good management. Probably time I saw Johnny again, even if I am busy. I can take it out on him. Sorry, Johnny.

One of the things about therapy is using it before it's too late. I have a rough idea of how to cope when things get on top of me, but Johnny always helps me to remember exactly what I need to do. I do try to take on board what he says.

When I feel a panic attack coming on, I have learned to do some deep breathing. Or I might read a book. I'm reading a book of poems, as it happens, propped up by my bedside. It's a collection of modern ones. One even mentions me in it. Ha.

And where is that bed? Good question. It's never easy pinning me down. Knowing where I am staying. As you know, I don't have a house or anything of my own. I'm staying at Champneys at the moment, at Henlow Grange, which isn't too far from Kettering, so that's good, but I've got Jimmy house-hunting in Kettering for me, either a flat or a house.

It's just a small room, here at Champneys, so I haven't got much stuff with me. It's all in Newcastle, or at me mam's. But it's all I need. The grounds are big. I can go for a walk. Use the gym and pool and all the health stuff.

When I'm here, in my room, I try to switch off my mobile phones, give me heed a rest. I have three mobiles, each with different ring tones. One's for Hunter, who's helping me with this book, one's for the club and football things, one's for family and friends and any girlfriends, hopefully. But if I'm in a state, I switch them all off and just listen to music.

Being a manager I've found it very hard to have time for myself. I'm thinking about others all the time, and their problems, or the team's problems, and, if I'm not careful, I let their problems take me over. So I need someone to listen to me – and that's where Johnny comes in.

In theory, I've got my heart's desire, with coming to Kettering. I'm back in football again, as a manager this time, not a coach, and with a stake in the club. I'm not liable, this time, to be messed around or carved up. I'm in charge of my own destiny for a change. I've got what I'd wanted in life, well, apart from the obvious.

I haven't got a relationship, not had one for years, not a proper one. Obviously, I'd like that, everyone would. There is one girl I took to the tennis at Wimbledon, to the women's final, in the summer, and that got in the papers, probably because I had had a few drinks – champagne – on the way there and at the tennis. I was gutted I did that. But I was nervous, even though she is just a girl I know. It's nothing serious. But it was a sort of date. And it had been a long time since I'd done that. So yeah, I was a bit uptight. Nervous like. But I shouldn't have had the champagne.

I don't have anybody. I have no love life. I still hope I will find a partner. I'd like to find someone and live with them, in an apartment or whatever, then buy a big house and start a family. That would be my fantasy. But of course it's harder now, with being a manager. I'm so preoccupied with that I haven't time for anything else, or any proper relationship.

But well, apart from that, I've got all I ever wanted. The trouble is, what I wanted is now causing me stress because of my relationship with the chairman, who I feel is stopping me from doing my job.

There's been something preying on my mind recently. Perhaps because of the stress of this manager job. And the other stuff that's going on behind the scenes. I don't know. Anyway, I keep thinking about a story that was run in the *Sun*, back in August. I'm upset about it again and I was then. Very. At the time I heard there was a story, supposedly by Bianca, that was accusing me of hitting Mason, Shel's son. When I heard it was going to appear in the *Sun*, I went to court to stop it.

I had to hire barristers and all that shit, which you have to do, to beat something like the *Sun*. I lost and it cost me thousands in legal fees. As I've said, the *Sun* ran it with the horrible headline 'Gazza Beat Up Family'. You can see why I was so upset, and still am. That's why I then told my version to the *Mirror*.

The truth is that I once did give Mason a smack – but just on his bottom, fully clothed, with my hand, and there was no injury as far as I was concerned.

I'd got drunk that evening and had gone to bed. Bad, I know, when you are a parent. I woke up when Shel hit me over the head with a shoe. She was trying to wake me up. I woke up, thinking 'Which fucker has been hitting me with a shoe?' and it was Shel.

She said Mason was out of control, she couldn't do anything with him, so why should I be lying in bed asleep leaving her to cope? Not unfair. It was my turn to go down and discipline him.

So I went down and told Mason to go to bed. He wouldn't, so I smacked his arse. That was all. I didn't touch Bianca, or anyone else, just Mason, cos he wouldn't go to bed.

I've smacked Regan, my son, as well, when he was playing up, speaking to us in a way he shouldn't have been. Mind you, Regan has always had me by the bollocks and can pretty much do anything with me.

We did have some good times, some great family outings and holidays. They used to say, 'Dad, I love you so much,' both Bianca and Mason often did. I bought Bianca a new car, and paid her insurance, which cost £12,000. I bought Mason about £10,000 worth of bling, which is what he wanted. Once they got that, it felt to me as though they turned. As if they hated me. I've even had a text saying, 'Wish you were dead.'

I haven't seen them for a while and I miss Regan so much. On the other hand, if I don't see them, they've got nothing to write about me. They can't sell any more stories about me.

In my mind, I've disowned them now, but of course I can't do that with Regan. I don't ever want to do that. He is my son. But whenever I do get to see him, Shel is on the phone to him twice a day.

Shel and I have moved on now, since I've paid her off. I don't know what will happen in the future. Anyway, I've got enough to worry about at present, without starting to think about Shel again. I remember I said, at the end of the paperback edition of my first book, that 'that was that'. I wasn't going to talk about Shel any more. And here I am again . . .

It's going brilliantly still. I couldn't ask for more, despite some of my misgivings about the chairman. I'm so happy being the manager. The lads have been excellent, couldn't have done more. I did get rid of three players and have brought in another three. Just had my seventh game – a win in the FA Trophy – and we've only been beaten once in the league and once in the Cup. I think we're nicely placed. Not a million miles behind the leaders. On Saturday we're playing Barrow at home. They're behind us, about middle of the table. So fingers crossed.

Before I took over, I spoke to various managers I respect, such as Terry Venables and Walter Smith. They all said go for it. Walter said it would be three times as hard as anything I might expect, but not to get downhearted. There will be bad days, sad days, but then good days and good results. I just had to try and treat them all the same and keep working hard.

Coaching badges? I haven't had time to worry about them at present. Anyway, you don't need them in non-league. You only need them in the Premiership. When that time comes, I'll have finished off my B badge. That's all you need anyway and I'm halfway through that.

All the players call me gaffer. Even the chairman calls me that. I didn't ask. They just did it. I feel a responsibility to them all. There are thirty at the club, including coaches and staff. Then I have my own family to look after – and Mason and Regan. I'm still paying money to support them. But not towards Bianca's upbringing any more. So all in all it means I have about forty-five people for whom I feel responsible.

I really want to make something of the job at Kettering. I'm giving it everything I've got. I'm committed to the team and I believe in the players. But I find it hard when we lose. As soon as we get one bad result, the superstition kicks in. I start having to change things around, things like furniture, towels, my wardrobe. Then I have to change them again. I worry that if things aren't arranged right we'll get another bad result. It's stressful and exhausting.

All right then, I have to admit I've started a bit of drinking again. But just the odd glass of wine, now and again, sometimes not for one or two weeks.

I like to think I am in control of it. It's not like when I would take cocaine and then get through four bottles of whisky. Cocaine always seemed to help me drink more. Don't know why. Now I'm not going out to the pub every night, just to get drunk, as I once did.

It's only now and again I have the odd glass to relax. I know I shouldn't. I'm tempting fate. We'll just have to see if I can cope. I have responsibilities, now, to the club and the players. So I have to try and not let them down, not just myself.

But, it has happened again, so I'll have to tell Johnny on my next session . . .

For Paul 'Ginger' Gascoigne

Your book is for a Transsexual! Madame Butterfly aka.

I enjoyed spending time with you at Cottonwood. Stay sober and let's get together soon.

Best wishes

Stefan

ChapterSix

Paul's second session: A look back at alcohol

John

In this session, we concentrate on looking at Paul's relationship with alcohol, both in the present and over his life up to now.

Paul talks to me about the various problems he's facing at Kettering, and how he's attempting to deal with them. Most of the issues he has revolve around relationships with personnel at the club. This is pertinent to our work together, because so often what triggers Paul to act out is his struggle with personal and professional relationships.

We then discuss Paul's cravings for alcohol during the week since we last met.

Paul

It's been a tough week, and I've had some cravings for a drink. After the game on Saturday the referee said to us I didn't seem in quite the right state to be on the line. I'm glad he said it because I'd just done a long counselling session, and my good friend George Best had just died, and then I rushed off to the game, *and* I was on medication. I'd taken Librium, the detox medication. So I was tired. I wasn't woozy or anything, and I was paying attention. We won that game, in the FA Trophy, but I wasn't quite on top of things the way I normally am. After that I was with one of the backroom staff at the club, and the cravings were driving us nuts, so I had a pint and a game of snooker.

On Sunday the cravings were driving me mad again, and I had to sign 1,700 photos. My dad picked us up, with Jimmy, and I went training. Later on, about 8 p.m., I was with Dad and Jimmy and they ordered wine. I knew if I started drinking with them I wouldn't stop. And I'd had a glass of wine already. Perhaps two, but no more. So I thought, 'Fuck, I need to get away.' I was upset about George and what was happening at Kettering. I got myself into a bit of a state. And I knew I needed to get away from the drink.

So I went out to the front door and ordered a minicab. I told him to drive. He said, 'Where?' and I said, 'Leeds.' It was the first place that came into my head. I did think about Newcastle, but decided that was too far. I just needed to get away, that was the first thing, then I needed to talk to someone who didn't know me.

I'd left two of my mobiles behind, just taking one, which had a low battery, but I managed to ring Jimmy in case they got worried – wondering where I'd gone, if I'd thrown myself under a train or been abducted by aliens. All I said was that I was in a cab, going to Leeds. Then I hung up.

I could have stayed and talked to them all night, but they know my problems. They know all my stories. They've heard it all before. I needed a stranger to talk to. With a stranger you can unburden yourself. They have no preconceptions, no idea if you're telling the truth. And you and they know you'll never meet again. So I talked to this poor fucking driver, all the way to Leeds.

To get away from the drink, I had to take that taxi. I paid him the £300 fare in cash, and then gave him a tip. I asked him to drop me at the railway station in Leeds. I then found the first B&B place and booked in for the night. I was shattered. I just collapsed. But at least I got away from the drink. That was the whole point. I woke up next morning, felt better and caught a train back again. All the way on the train I talked to a bloke I'd just met who asked me what I'd been doing in Leeds. I just said I'd had a meeting.

John

So Paul has suffered from cravings on and off all week, and each day he has had to take steps to get through them. We're going to look back over his drinking history, so that he can remind himself of what his relationship with alcohol has been over the years. Taking an honest look at this will help him build up a picture of what alcohol means to him, and what effect it has on his life.

Paul

I had my first drink aged fourteen. All the lads in the town were skinheads and all that, but not me, I was totally focused on my football. I was always out training. But that time they were all saying, 'Go on, have a drink!' So I had a triple vodka and I remember it hitting us straight away. CB radios had just come out, and we were going round all the houses talking to each other. I was paralytic. I went home and me mam cracked us over the back of the head and sent us up to bed. She threatened to tell me dad and I was terrified of him finding out. Anyway, next morning I had a stomping headache but me mam made me go to school like that to teach us a lesson.

The effect on me was massive. I didn't have another drink for four years. The next time was when I was playing for Newcastle in a tournament. I was eighteen, we were flying on to Fiji from New Zealand when the plane suddenly dropped 800 feet. I was terrified of flying after that. On the way back I was with Brian Clough, and I thought there was steam coming into the plane through the windows. It was just condensation on the inside, of course, but I panicked at the time. I knew we then had to fly another two hours on to Baltimore and then had a further ten-hour flight home and I was absolutely petrified, so I thought, 'Shit, I'm going to have a whisky.'

Only it wasn't just one. I had twelve, slept the whole way, and woke up twenty minutes before we landed. The lads carried me off through the airport. I don't remember much, but I remember being sick over one of them. Odd the things that stick in your mind. Mind you, I bet he remembers as well.

Anyway, the next day I had no headache, I remember that. I didn't touch whisky again though. But I *did* start drinking at that age – eighteen. I realised there was a buzz to it. I had a laugh, a *craic*. I was the centre of attention. I was already a joker, but I was that bit more confident with the drink.

Then for a couple of years I'd train and not drink all week because I had a game on Saturday. Then Saturday night I'd drink with the lads after the game, and Sundays I'd drink with me dad at working-men's clubs. I liked sweet drinks like piña colada cocktails; I didn't really drink pints. I didn't see drink as a problem back then, I took it in my stride.

Did I know anyone who had a drink problem? No. No one in particular. My brother sometimes got quite drunk. But it was just weekends. He didn't drink much – he wasn't that bothered. Me mam would hardly go out, and if she had anything back at home it would just be a Mackie stout which is a nothing drink – nothing else, she didn't have the money or the time. Me dad would have a beer now and then on a Saturday with the lads, but he also didn't have the money for anything more than that. So yeah, in the family it was only weekends. There weren't any problems in our house with regards to drinking.

But it wasn't that stable a period of my life. When I was seventeen I went through a phase of gambling. I'd bet all my money on slot machines. I was addicted. I remember one Saturday I'd lost all my money and I needed more to keep at it – so I stole money from my sister's purse and lost it. She cried her eyes out.

I love my sister and I didn't want to see her cry, so I didn't gamble for a long time after that. That's probably why I'm not a gambling man.

John

Over his life, Paul has dabbled with gambling on a handful of occasions, but it has never been his primary addiction. That's why he says he's not a 'gambling man'. It shows us, though, that even at seventeen the tendency to addictive behaviour was there.

I asked Paul when it was that his drinking became regular.

Paul

Drinking first became more regular when I moved to London. I was just twenty-one years old, and I went from earning £120 a week to around £2,500 a week. I'd train hard, then go to a big pub down the road with my mates Terry, Jed and Keith. I'd split up with my first girlfriend, Gail, so that was it, I was on my own in the bright lights of London, getting followed everywhere. For the first six months I stayed in a hotel – well, actually three I think. Got thrown out of two of them. I normally drank champagne – or a couple of pints and then moved on to champagne – because it was less fattening. Chris Waddle used to come round and we'd have a bottle of Asti Spumanti, which is another nothing drink, and then we'd drink champagne. I did eventually buy a house though.

It was a massive change for me, coming to London at that age. I didn't like living on my own, I really didn't like it. Jimmy came down now and then. But then my sister and her boyfriend came to live with me, and I'd sit in the house and have a drink with him. He could drink more than me.

I'd have a drink Saturday after the game, and Sunday, and if I had the day off on the Wednesday I'd have a drink Tuesday after training. I didn't have a problem with the drink then, or I never *seen* I had a problem with the drink. Then one time I was cleaning up the house and I came across some cans and bottles of drink around the place. I realised I didn't want to be around a whole load of alcohol in my own home. It didn't feel good to me. So I moved out. Back to a hotel.

All of a sudden I was living in the centre of London, and looking out of the window it looked like a party on every street corner. I had a lovely big suite with a nice big fridge and I started having a couple of beers after training – and I went back to drinking champagne. On Sundays I always seemed to get paralytic, because I'd get Monday off. I'd go without drinking Monday, Tuesday, Wednesday, and maybe have a little drink Thursday, nothing Friday and then drink Saturday after the game.

I'm not a big drinker. I can't drink a bottle of champagne and be sober. Ask any of me mates, they say, 'Gazza, I can't understand it because you're a shit drinker – a couple of drinks and you're pissed.' But I seem to stay that way for a while and then the next one really knocks us out.

No one was making complaints about my drinking or anything. I was getting followed by the press and getting caught having a drink or doing this or doing that, but it wasn't a problem because I'd say, 'See what he writes about me on Saturday after the game!' On the pitch I was scoring goals, getting Man of the Match, banging in hat-tricks and doing everything, so really there was no problem. In the two-and-a-half years at Tottenham I couldn't put a foot wrong on the football pitch, so I thought, 'If I can drink like that and play like that the drinking isn't a problem.'

The drinking started to be a bit less controlled from the time of the World Cup in 1990. The only way I could relax was to have a couple of drinks on the sly. I had a cocktail once, which Bobby Robson thought was a milkshake, and I had a triple Baileys and put the froth from a cappuccino on the top so they thought it was a cappuccino.

The other times I'd drink were when we were given a couple of days off.

Then, when I came back home from Italy, I suddenly got masses of media attention. I was getting followed everywhere. I thought, '*Fuck*'. They were outside my mam and dad's house, outside the hotel, outside my house. They were everywhere. That was when I went to a wine bar and got pissed, and met Sheryl. I fell for her straight away. All of a sudden I'd gone from being a single guy to a family man with Sheryl and her two kids, one aged one and one aged three.

Did I feel ready for that responsibility? No, probably not. But I loved Sheryl, and I decided to take it upon myself to take the kids on as mine, I didn't have a problem with that at all. My family didn't like it, and told me to be careful, and I ended up rowing with my family over Shel. I never wanted anything to come between me and my family. I stopped seeing my family, stopped seeing Jimmy, and was just with Sheryl. Then she split up with me. I'd got injured in the Cup final, making that daft challenge, and couldn't train, and I started drinking every night, getting pissed.

I wanted to get back with her, but it was Catch-22. She found photos of girls in a bag of mine, though I ripped them up to show I wanted to be with her. Then I went round her house and said I wanted to get back together. We got back together, but a few weeks later she said, 'I can't believe what I did. I've let you get so close to the kids they now think you're their dad.'

I was scared, but I didn't have a problem with looking after the kids. I don't know if that was emotional blackmail or what.

Then I was due to move to Italy, so I asked her to come with me. In Italy, I was trying to train really hard, get properly fit, get over the ligament injury and broken kneecap, and also be a family man and understand that role, and learn the Italian language. I was just under so much pressure. Shel always wanted to see more and more of me. I'd be training and I'd panic and have to rush home quickly for her, so I couldn't enjoy training. When I'd get home I'd be so wound up I'd have a few drinks to relax, and then we'd argue. Then she wanted to go back to the UK, but had nowhere to live, so I bought a house and she went back and lived in it. But then I was flying back and forth and all that and we still argued. Then we split up.

It all felt too much: the football, trying to learn the language, 100° heat, never having any peace, never having time off, just busy, busy, training, training, trying to fit in seeing Sheryl and the kids. The only way I could chill out was to have a drink. I'd have a couple of grappas, 100° proof.

At that point, I'd train first but drink afterwards with me mates. I always trained hard. It was on with Sheryl, off with Sheryl. Every time I got back with her I calmed down and trained hard and every time we split up I was back drinking again. For the first year and a half. The drink was an easy way out. Then Shel and my family came over, and my family didn't get on well with her so the atmosphere was unbelievable. Me mam was saying Sheryl wasn't right for me, and Sheryl was going on at me about me mam, and you could have cut the atmosphere with a knife. I was so angry, I went to training, and I just weighed in to a tackle and broke my leg straight through.

I moved my leg but my foot and ankle stayed on the ground, and I knew straight away I'd smashed it. I was screaming as they carried me off the pitch, but I wasn't bothered because all I wanted to do was get out of that atmosphere. I thought, 'Fuck me, I'm going to hospital, I'm going to be cared for, I'll get some morphine.' I'd first been given morphine after I broke my leg during the Cup final in 1991. I knew what it was like.

I thought, 'I'll be in hospital for a few weeks and I won't have to deal with anyone.' I flew back to England. To the Princess Grace. The doctor did a great job fixing it back together and I was given some morphine for the pain. But then the press came and sent flowers and all that, and Sheryl came and stayed in hospital with me for two weeks. Even then I was arguing with her and it was hard for her because she'd come to support us, but I just wanted to be alone. I felt like if it wasn't for all that pressure I may not have exploded into that tackle and broken my leg. I felt stressed again when she was there. I was trapped in the hospital with a broken leg still trying to sort out all these problems: money for the family, money for Sheryl. That was the first time I got a panic attack.

How did it feel? I remember losing my breath, I couldn't breathe. I tried to explain to Sheryl and the nurses that I couldn't get my breath, and I started panicking, but the more I was panicking the more I was losing my breath, and they thought I was joking. I calmed down and screamed at them to get out of my room right now. When they came back in they asked me, 'What was all that about?' It felt like all those flowers had taken all the oxygen, that's what I thought at the time because I just didn't know what had happened. I just couldn't breathe. It must have been my first anxiety attack – panic attack – but I never saw that at the time.

John

Getting that injury was actually a relief for Paul. The only way out of a quagmire of family responsibilities and emotions was for Paul to take out his anger on the football pitch in such a way that he got that terrible injury. Once again, it was easier to injure himself, this time physically, than honestly to confront the people in his life. Things had become so intense, and he felt so trapped by his intimate relationships, that a spell in hospital seemed like a break. For Paul, the awful irony was that even in hospital he didn't get any peace and, trapped in that bed, he couldn't run on to the pitch, he couldn't drink. There was no release. The result was his first panic attack. He was then faced with months of recovery time to get through – the legacy of a moment's passionate anger.

Paul

It is great to become famous but it's a nightmare once you *are* famous, and it all just got right on top of us. When I flew back with a broken leg the press were on the flight trying to take photos of us, and I thought, 'What the fuck is all this about? All I wanted to do was play football, what happened to my life?' I sat in a hospital in London. Then I lived with Shel with a broken leg for six months, and it was quite tough; I was frustrated and angry. I went on holiday with her and was drunk every day. She just thought that was a normal thing. While I was getting drunk I was a good, happy lad, but when I was pissed I was sometimes angry. So they would enjoy being with me, and then all of a sudden they'd be scared, and I knew they were but there was nothing I could do about it. I just wanted to get back to playing football because football was my life and I was frustrated. And we'd argue a lot.

John

Paul and Sheryl argued a lot during that time. I ask him what they argued about, whether any of it was jealousy on his part, and about how he balanced the relationship with Sheryl and the children against his other family and his friends.

Paul

I was jealous at times, yeah. Although I didn't really think there was anything to be jealous of, at the time. But that wasn't really the problem.

After a few weeks with Sheryl and the kids I wanted to be with my mates. Then after a few weeks with my mates I wanted to go back with Sheryl. I lived like that for about six years. Because Sheryl didn't get on with my family, the only way I could see my family was to have a row with Sheryl, split up, and then go and see my family.

John

This is an important pattern for Paul in his relationships – finding it difficult to state his needs.

JM: You felt having a row with Sheryl and splitting up was the only way you could see your own family?

PG: Yeah. Then after a couple of weeks I'd say to Sheryl, 'Let's get back together,' and I always did it drunk. And she'd take us back, we'd go on holiday, there'd be an argument and I'd think, 'I can't argue any more,' and go and see my mates.

JM: How did you eventually break out of that pattern?

PG: I went back to Italy, and split up with Sheryl for seven months. It took three months to get over it, drinking every day, but then I trained so hard and while I was training she was out of my head.

JM: So you dived right back into the football?

PG: Yeah, I quit drink for nine months. Trained five times a day, fit as fuck, enjoying life; my mates and Jimmy drank but I never did. Everything was fine. One day the manager called us in and said they had something to tell me, but they didn't want to tell me because I was doing so well. They said they'd seen a change and I was completely different, I was playing really well. I said, 'Please tell me, put me out of my misery.' So they told me Sheryl had called and wanted to speak to me, and asked me to get in touch with her. She'd called the club because she didn't have my new number.

JM: So even the club were worried about the effect your relationship with Sheryl had on you?

PG: Yes. So I called her and she was crying and wanted to get back together, but it wasn't what I wanted, so I said, 'No – but,' I said, 'if you stop crying I'll come home for a visit.' I remember going back to England, and I thought, 'No, getting back with Sheryl isn't what I want.' But eventually, I decided it was time to leave Italy and start afresh with Sheryl.

JM: Had that became more important to you than Lazio?

PG: Yeah.

JM: Was the drinking continuous throughout this period?

PG: Yes. Then Walter Smith came to see us, asked if I wanted to play for Glasgow Rangers, and I said straight away, 'Yes,' and I moved to Glasgow and saw it was a fresh start. Up there it was good, I was enjoying my football, back with Sheryl, it was great. But there was still the same situation between Sheryl and my family.

JM: Were you always stuck in the middle?

PG: Yes, I was. And then Sheryl got pregnant. I thought, '*Fuck me!*'

JM: So you didn't feel ready for the whole process of fatherhood?

PG: Right. No way I felt ready. But I asked Sheryl to live with me in Scotland and she refused unless we got married. She said I wouldn't see my child unless we were married. During that time Walter Smith was very supportive. Alan McLaren was great as well.

Then came Euro 96. Before that I'd split up with Sheryl. Regan had been born and I'd taken a couple of weeks before I'd gone to see him. I'd been drunk the night he was born and I was embarrassed and guilty about that. No excuse, mind. When I did see him for the first time, held him, I cried my eyes out. He was amazing. Then, before the Championships, we went on a warm-up tour to Hong Kong and China. I did that daft dentist's chair thing. You know, when you sit in a chair with your head tilted back and the barman pours booze down your throat. I was smashed out me head . Next day it was my birthday. I got roses and a card saying 'Happy Birthday Daddy, love Regan'. I cried my eyes out, Dennis Wise put his arms round me, and I got smashed out me head again. I came back and went to the health farm to sort myself out.

I then decided to get well, and that I was going to do well in the tournament, and I was buzzing. I asked Sheryl to marry me. So we started sorting out the wedding. And I thought, 'Am I doing the right thing?' But I'd made me decision and I stood by it. After the tournament she went mad with us and said, 'I just can't believe that *I* had to ask *you* to marry me!' She meant because of what she'd said before, that I wouldn't get to see my son unless we got married.

So I was distraught. Because in spite of what she said, I was getting married for the right reasons. I thought I should be a married man and settle down and look after the kids, and stuff like that. I had a great wedding, didn't really get drunk but had my first go on a joint which knocked us for six.

On honeymoon we argued all the time. We moved up to Scotland and bought a big house. It was just the same situation. Training; couldn't relax; racing to get back home; making sure she was okay; didn't want to argue; constant arguing. I said, 'Let's have a break,' so we went to Gleneagles with Bianca and the nanny. Went down for a meal and me and Sheryl had a row over family, and that was it. I was having champagne and I mixed it with whisky. I grabbed her and said, 'What are you doing this for?' She struggled to get free and I threw her on the floor and that's when she banged her face and her finger. I shit myself. I said, 'Sorry.' I didn't know what to say, I pulled her finger back in, got the doctor. We stayed together that night but the next day she'd gone. I couldn't tell Walter Smith, and went and played a couple of nights later. My head wasn't in it. At the Champions League game against Ajax I got sent off in the first half an hour. Then I said, 'I've fucking beat up my wife.' The next day, there was Sheryl, she'd rung up the *Daily Mirror* – or someone had for her – and got the paper to photograph her bandaged face.

I did beat her up and I was disgusted with myself. I'd behaved badly. Obviously I felt shit about what I'd done. Of course. She said she wasn't coming back and we needed to live separately for a while. In the end I felt massive relief that we'd split up. If we'd been together it would have just been the arguments all the same.

Walter was brilliant. I was always there at his place, playing snooker with his kids. I called her and begged to get back together. We both did that. It was fifty-fifty. I more or less lived with Walter Smith's kids for a year. I bought a speedboat, played the best two-and-a-half years in soccer. But the whole thing with Sheryl was off and on, off and on. And it went on to divorce.

John

Looking back over Paul's life, since a really early age he's had an enormous amount to deal with, and drink became a part of how he coped with that. To begin with it was just at weekends, and then slowly but surely it became more problematic. He didn't see it sneaking up on him.

In this session, I first asked Paul about his cravings and drinking at the current time. Although he did get the prescription for a seven-day home Librium detox that I had suggested in the first session, he still wasn't able to see the week through without a drink – though he did cut down on the intake of previous weeks. He was finding the balance between looking after himself and looking after other responsibilities difficult. This is, and has been, a huge issue in Paul's life. He's never been very good at looking after himself and has mastered the art of 'going with the flow'. Some may be surprised at that and even think of him as a selfish man, but that isn't the case.

Early on in this session we talked about the many aspects of running a football club. For the first time in his life Paul has a lot of responsibility: he's now part of management. He's gone from being picked to being the picker – a massive progression and one that brings with it many challenges. Together, we're now beginning to see a pattern that has contributed to Paul's relapse: his over-responsibility for others. This is one aspect of codependency.

In the rest of the session, I was trying to help Paul identify when it was that he started drinking, who and what influenced his drinking and how it progressed to being addictive. It is usual for clients who come to me for counselling to ask, 'Why *me*, how come *I* am an alcoholic and not my friends? Was I born like this, with this addictive personality?' It seems that Paul has always been an addict of one sort or another. Football was his first drug. He dedicated his whole life to it. It made him feel safe and it gave him everything he needed from an early age. A daily structure, a uniform, status, money, travel, a purpose in life and, I think most important of all, positive feedback. He belonged to something that he loved and that loved him. What more does anyone want? As he reports, he wasn't that interested in what the other kids did: he had found his niche and his surrogate family.

At the age of eighteen, there were expectations on Paul to perform at a very high level and, although most of the time he was able to deliver, he internalised this pressure. His career propelled him from Newcastle United's youth set-up, to the first team, to a move to the bright lights of London and Tottenham Hotspur, all within a relatively short time. A huge move for any young person to undertake. You can't compare that move to others that most young people make. For instance, if you go to university you know months in advance that you are leaving home, you're given time to settle in, you're amongst hundreds of others in the same boat, and there are many social choices available to you.

When any of us finds ourselves in a new situation, we rely on our past experiences to get us through. We can only call on what we've already experienced – the stuff that's in our database. We all have a kind of 'sat nav' system that gets us from one situation to another, which has been programmed over our lifetime from thousands of different situations. It also includes some of our parents' experiences – how they would navigate certain situations, both practically and emotionally. Most of these pre-programmed responses are subconscious, and because they're often effective we don't stop to question them.

Paul did what he knew best. He'd never learned how to live alone, and living with others brought its own difficulties: he'd moved out of his own house, making himself effectively homeless, rather than confront the situation that was unfolding – or upset anyone – which is one of his patterns. So he ended up a young lad living in a London hotel, playing top-class football with men mostly much older than him. It all started to get too much, and his drinking, which had progressed only slowly up to this point, became more regular. On the pitch he was faultless and as long as this continued he could do what he liked off it. In his words, 'I would let my football do the talking.'

The big problem was when he wasn't actually playing. Paul, like most young footballers, put training and practice before his education. Therefore he lacked some of the interpersonal skills needed to manage such a life-changing career. He learned from an early age to be a 'people-pleaser', and his pleasing other people has often been at the expense of his own needs or desires. When people put pressure on him he has bowed to it, so that at times he ended up in situations he didn't want to be in, and therefore became angry or resentful. One way of getting away from this pressure and relieving the resulting anger has been to drink.

When Paul moved to Lazio this pattern continued. As the pressure mounted, so did the need for an outlet. He had met his wife-to-be and, of course, that was a lovely change for him, and an escape. But it brought along many other pressures including children: two stepchildren and later his son, Regan. As Paul admits, he struggled to cope with this at times. Everyone wanted a bit of him: friends, family, the media, the clubs and the fans. To cap it all, his wife and family constantly argued. This contributed to one of his very serious injuries.

Then, while in hospital, Paul rediscovered morphine. He liked the calming feeling it gave him, and found it enabled him temporarily to switch off from the world. The morphine would soon lead him back to the drink.

Paul returned to the UK to play football at Rangers. He was relieved to be home and for a short period his first love, football, kept him on track. He was happy. But by this time his relationship with his best friend – alcohol – was well established. Each time Paul had a good run of sobriety and football, some big life-event – an injury, marriage, bad press – came along that he wasn't able to handle without drink. Alcohol interferes with blood-sugar levels and the balance of chemicals in the brain. Moods swing wildly, and a sudden attack of rage can lead to violence. Paul's drinking was now having catastrophic consequences on his life which were proving harder and harder to recover from.

Paul's pattern of drinking increases in parallel with his responsibilities. It's important that, as well as looking at Paul's life as it is today, we also cover the past. My job is to help Paul see the link between his past and his present: at the moment, history is repeating itself. This feeling of powerlessness links in with his childhood experiences.

When Paul drinks alcohol, instead of standing up for himself he loses control – the opposite of what he wants to happen. He's hoping to feel relaxed, less overwhelmed and more in control. Instead, he relinquishes his personal power and ends up becoming a victim. When this happens all sorts of feelings arise – anger, resentment and even a desire to self-sabotage. He presses the 'fuck it' switch: a self-destruct button. Some in my field would describe this phenomenon as a 'death wish'. This is the most dangerous aspect of addiction and can lead to death through many routes such as alcohol poisoning, drink-driving accidents and violence.

As a manager, Paul's in a new situation which any footballer would initially struggle with, and he needs the key skills of patience and negotiation for the job. He needs to stop drinking before anything else can change. Once Paul starts drinking, even if it's initially moderately, his alcoholism takes over. Rational thought goes out of the window, and denial kicks in. If he doesn't stop, it will eventually get the better of him and bring him to 'rock bottom'. He cannot use alcohol to cope with pressure, no matter how big the pressures are.

Hey Gazza

A true honor, not only to have met you, but to experience the romantic gifts you left us all with your sugar-free 'tablets'. Bring some back from Jimmy for me will ya. Hell . . . fuckin hell . . . bear with me a while.

I get serious for a minute a'rite Gazza . . . you are an absolutely amazing individual Paul and I'm sure you've heard it all before. I just want you to know that I truly respect you . . . and look up to you, for your character and your attitude and the strength you have shown to beat the demons of alcoholism.

Don't just tell the little bastard on your shoulder to fuck off . . . give him a swift kick to the clems and make him wish he was born a woman, a'rite . . . fucking hell . . . a'rite man . . .

Cheers ya wanker. Ha! All my love – keep in touch, stay funny.

Jim

Chapter Seven

Paul's personal problems

Paul

I never discuss football with Johnny and I never discuss my personal problems with Paul Davis. I keep them separate.

There was one thing, though, I don't think I mentioned to Johnny in that last session. It just didn't come out. It's to do with my weight which I've always been obsessed about. When I was playing, it always ballooned up in the close season when I'd binge on ice cream and sweet drinks or cocktails. It wasn't really junk food like burgers and kebabs that did it, but drink and ice cream, that's what put the weight on.

I can't remember when I first started bringing it all up – and by that I don't mean talking about it – or when I first heard about bulimia, and how you did it. It must have been when I was about seventeen. Funnily enough, my sister Anna was in a TV series at the time, acting the part of a bulimic. So that's when I might have first learned about it.

I've done it regularly over the years, but then I might not do it for a year or two. The last time was two weeks ago. Yeah, here at Champneys. I did it three days running. That's what I haven't told Johnny.

I haven't been going to the dining room since I moved in here, which was before I got the Kettering job. I usually just have room service, snacks and stuff. I love their toasted bagels. This evening I kept on eating them, ordering more and more, plus I had chocolate and milkshakes and cakes from the shop. I was bored, stuck in my room on my own after training, worrying about the team, worrying about Imraan, full of nerves, so I just kept on bingeing, knowing what I was going to do.

When I'd really had enough, I went to the bathroom, put my fingers down my throat, and up it all came, straight away, down into the toilet pan.

I don't do it because I like doing it. I hate the feeling. But if I know I'm going to go on an eating binge, I keep on eating, knowing I can sick it up. That way I won't put on weight. It is a proper eating disorder, I know that. And I know it's bad for you. It brings up the acid and can burn a hole in your stomach.

It's an addiction, like all the others I have. Like drink and drugs. But right now, I feel in control. All right, I'm drinking again, but I feel a couple of glasses of wine a few times a week is okay. What harm can it do?

I've been here at Champneys for two months, thanks to the owner, Steve Perdew, who's a friend of mine. He's let me stay for free. But now I have to get out, as they are filling up for the Christmas season. Anyway, I want to move into somewhere handier for the ground and training.

What I'm going to do is move into the Kettering Park Hotel for two weeks, then I'm going into an apartment near the ground. Jimmy saw a big five-bedroom house he thought I'd like, but I looked at it and didn't fancy it. Too big. I just need a two- or three-bedroom apartment at this stage, as handy for the club as possible.

I've been living out of a suitcase for years, so I'm used to it. I'm not bothered, not really. If I did meet a woman, and bought a house and moved into it with her, she'd take it from me if we split. I lost about £4 million, all down the drain, being married to Shel. I'm afraid of that happening again.

Lots of my stuff is in storage. The clothes will be out of date I guess. And I like to be fashionable. Ha! You've seen some of my haircuts. That proves it.

As you know, I did tell Johnny about going to Leeds. One of my obsessions has always been talking to strangers, telling them about myself. Like that taxi driver. He had to listen. He couldn't escape. And that bloke on the train on the way back. I love it on trains when I get talking to someone who doesn't know me. I can just rabbit.

A few months ago I went up to Newcastle on the train and I found myself beside this old woman, must have been about seventy, and we chatted all the way. She was a brilliant listener, listened to all my problems. After talking to her for two hours, I felt so much better. When we got to Newcastle, I got out some paper and wrote a little thank-you letter: 'With much love, Paul Gazza Gascoigne.' As I walked away down the platform, I could see her looking at it, a bit puzzled. But I think, watching her from afar, it did begin to dawn on her who I might be. I travel a lot on trains. I don't like to fly if I can help it. That's another one of the things that mess me up.

When I started having therapy, I never hid it from anyone. I wasn't ashamed. After that first trip to the Priory, I'd tell all the lads in the Boro dressing room about all the things I had to do, making them laugh. But I also told them about the serious therapy, that I had a therapist, Johnny. And also about going to AA meetings.

I've always talked about what's on my mind, holding very little back. All the teams I played with knew about me. I wasn't ashamed. They never took the piss out of me because I'd revealed something. I think they just felt sorry, or perhaps they just thought that was me, daft Gazza. They probably got fed up with me in the end, when I was hyperactive or was endlessly talking, rabbiting on.

I don't think in my football career I ever heard about any other players having therapy. Not that they told me. But most players are a mass of superstitions – about putting their boots on a certain way, or their shorts, being last out on the pitch, eating certain things, driving a certain way to the ground – and they believe these things. They worry they'll play badly or get beat if they don't do it. With me, I never went in for those sorts of superstitions and lucky charms. I had enough other things going on inside me heed.

I always had obsessions, for as long as I can remember, which I suppose are a sort of superstition. As a kid, I had to tie the right lace on my right shoe last. I always had to have my knife and fork laid out the right way, all my drawers had to be arranged just so, socks in a certain place. I would go mad if anyone ever mixed them up. It scared me. What would happen if I didn't have things always in the right way? It would take me twenty minutes to leave the house, because I always had to go back and close all the doors, over and over again.

Before an important game at Spurs, once, I got in a state because I thought I hadn't locked my front door. I'd just moved into this new house, still getting used to it. It went round and round in my mind as I tried to think back, go over what I'd done. In the end, I rang the next-door neighbour and persuaded him to go round and check the front door. He rang me back to say I had locked it. Only then could I concentrate on the game.

When I was in that house, I had a gas fire, a big one with pretend logs, really good, really hot, but I would often sit in front of it freezing because I worried that, when I went out, I might forget to turn it off. I knew when I did go out, whether I had turned it off or not, that it would dwell on my mind. I'd be wondering all the time. So, I thought, best not to turn it on at all.

For years, I had numbers which I considered as bad or evil, such as 13. Even a combination, like a 6 and 7 equals 13, or 9 and 4, would make me panic, convinced something bad was going to happen. I would change my hotel room number, if I didn't like the number, or my mobile phone. The wrong number would absolutely throw me.

Even now, if I'm doing a text message, and it says I have 13 letters left, I will add something, saying goodbye instead of bye, just to make the text longer, not leave a gap of 13 letters.

In hotels and hospitals, where I've spent half my adult life, if my coat hangers got messed up and were hanging at a different angle from how I left them, I'd go mad. I felt sure something bad would happen. Still do to some extent. But nowhere near as bad. I think David Beckham has a little bit of this. He believes certain signs are bad ones. I saw somewhere, recently, that he's admitted to being a bit compulsive in his behaviour. Like having to have everything in a straight line or in pairs, wanting everything to match, all his cans of soft drinks to be in a certain formation, no untidy magazines or leaflets or books mucking up his room. Some of the lads at Manchester United, apparently, used to deliberately rearrange his stuff in his hotel room, just to annoy him, knowing that it would. It would have upset me.

I remember seeing that Jack Nicholson film, *As Good as It Gets*, and I thought to myself, 'Jack Nicholson, you fucker, you've been watching me.' I understood exactly all the little rituals he had to do each day, otherwise he panicked.

They have tried to treat me for this when I've been in the Priory or Cottonwood. They teach you to blank it out, to divert yourself by going for a walk. I didn't find that sort of thing helped much. What has helped me has been medication they prescribed at Cottonwood. I take Depakote for panic attacks and Seroquel for anxiety attacks. And I do think they have helped. I've been on both of them for two years. I have improved. I could come off them now, so the doctors say, but I'd rather stick with them. I don't want to go back to where I was before.

I don't have the twitches I used to have as a lad. When I was playing football, people did comment on it, how my neck used to twitch, or my mouth. For many years I used to twitch my right shoulder, sort of stretching it out and twitching it. I didn't know I was doing any of these things. They didn't bother me personally, till people pointed them out or wrote about them. When I was at Newcastle, I had this habit of kicking my toe in the ground when I ran. That was just a nervous habit, which I did under pressure. Now, I seem to have grown out of most of my twitches, which is good. Age, perhaps.

Pill popping – I started that when I was at Boro. When I couldn't sleep, I used to get some sleeping pills prescribed but I never had enough, so I would buy them from people, people who had them on prescription, or mates of mine got them for me. It was things like Zimovane and diazepam. I'd take one and find it didn't work, so I'd then take seven or eight. Daft and dangerous, I know.

It was also to lose weight. By 8 p.m. I'd be starving. I'd take all these sleeping pills so I'd fall asleep without having eaten and I'd wake up two pounds lighter. At Rangers, I used to break into the medical room and steal sleeping tablets, just to knock me out, stop the depressions.

I'm still on lots of pills these days, three a day, which the doctors prescribe and Johnny knows about.

Look at the table in front of me now, at my three mobile phones, all lined up in the same way, at the exact angle. I'm not even aware of arranging them like that, till now, looking at them. Now, it doesn't worry me as much if they get messed up. I no longer believe it's a sign something bad will happen. But I still find I have to have all my things in a certain order.

Hold on, there's a text message coming through from Chris Waddle. I'd better read it . . . 'I don't want you to get upset,' it reads, 'but I thought I'd better tell you something. I know you won't like it and you'll only get depressed, but I thought I should let you know about it before anyone else . . .'

What the fuck is he on about? Now he's really got me scared. If the fucking *Sun* has got another story about me I'll go . . .

'Don't ring me back, when you've read what I'm going to tell you, as I know you'll want to. I just feel this is the best way to inform you . . . THERE IS NO FUCKING SANTA CLAUS!'

The bastard! Very funny.

He's got me at a bad moment. Scrolling through his text, I really was shaking. I was thinking something awful was about to come out in the papers, just when I'm getting myself in a state about other things. I was sure it was the press. I do live in fear of them all the time.

That bastard Waddler. I'll get my own back on him some time . . .

Heh Man, what's up

It's been great having you in primary group and getting to know you. You are such an awesome funny guy. Thanks for always listening to me in the group and supporting me.

Good luck staying sober. I know you can do it!

Lil

Chapter Eight

Paul KO'd at Kettering

Paul

I'm a bit worried about Imraan. I hadn't realised he was going to be so involved. He's there all the time, at all the training sessions as well as games. The other day he came into my little office, the one I share with Paul Davis, to do his paperwork, working on contracts for new players. Me and Paul were trying to get on with our own paperwork, so I didn't want him to be there. I asked if he'd leave, but he didn't. I wasn't happy.

Paul Davis told me that Imraan asked him to help get him through his FA coaching badge. 'Are you serious?', I said to Paul. I couldn't believe it. He can't even do keepy-uppies, so what's he thinking about, wanting to take his coaching badge. Then he told Paul his ambition is to be a manager. Fucking hell.

He's also been playing cards with the players on the team coach, which I'm not happy about. All football players do this on the team coach, always have done, but most managers have an absolute ban on players playing for money. They know what can happen – you lose £1,000, or £10,000, on the way to a game, and it preys on your mind. With us, it would only be £20 or £50 max. But it's the same thing. Playing for money causes problems. So I told him to stop. I wasn't happy with it. He is the chairman after all. I've never heard of chairmen playing cards with the team. Have you?

When he is around he's not always in what I'd call appropriate gear. It's got me thinking, mind. When we have a bit of money, or the right sort of sponsorship, what about having special suits, or perhaps just blazers, for the whole team, and the coaches? I might even pay for them myself. I met someone on a train the other day who was in the clothing business. He said he'd do me a deal. I'll even buy a suit for the chairman.

Apart from that, we're all getting on okay. I love being the manager, every minute of it.

We got beaten by Barrow, 3–1 at home on 3 December. It was only our second league defeat since I became the manager. But we're sixth in the league, so still in a good position to go up.

Imraan gets me afterwards and asks me why I played so and so, why I had done this, done that.

He said, 'Forget about our friendship Paul, I just want to know why you played so and so in that position?' I said, 'I'm the manager, I pick the team, that's my job.' He went on and on about it, really pissing me off.

If we'd lost *nine* games in a row, I could have understood the chairman asking questions, getting worried.

We'd already had words about the reserve team. He'd signed two new players and wanted them played, but I'd got two new players on trial who I wanted to play, one of them an Under-19 England player. He told the reserve-team manager to play his players. I told him not to, but to play my two – one in the first half, one in the second. I wanted to test one of them as soon as possible, because I knew other clubs were after him.

So after the Barrow game, and those words with Imraan, I came back to my hotel in Kettering, and yes, I did have some wine. I then sent him a text saying I thought he'd become a control freak. I'm the manager and I pick the team. If he doesn't like what I'm doing, he can sack me.

I just didn't think it was right, the way he was going on. He'd also said the gates had recently dropped down to 1,400. Fucking hell. They were only about 600 when I joined.

I didn't hear anything, till Andy Billingham, who was also at Kettering, rang me. He said Imraan had asked him to tell me I'd been sacked. He never told me personally, not face to face, not even on the phone.

So I texted him, told him what I really thought. I said I thought it was a disgrace, treating me like that. After everything I'd done for the club. And how could he sack me anyway? I'd never had a contract. So I resigned.

At the very beginning, I said I'd never walk away from the club, whatever happened. And I meant it. But fucking hell, I didn't know I'd have a chairman like that, did I?

The next day, the Sunday, I went up to Birmingham, to stay over with Andy. I was due in Liverpool on Monday to go to a do, for a charity that Johnny's involved with which is opening a day centre for drug and alcohol treatment. It was a fund-raising thing and I'd agreed to be there as the chief guest, do a question-and-answer session, auction some stuff.

After I got the sack on the Saturday night, I told Johnny my head wasn't right and I might not make the do. But then I thought, 'No, I won't back out, I don't want to let them down. I'll go all the same. I've got to stay strong.'

So on the Monday I went on to Liverpool and booked into a hotel in Hope Street, near where the charity do was taking place.

I sneaked a couple of glasses of wine at the event, but that was all. Of course there was drink there. Don't be daft. The fact that it's an alcohol charity is beside the point. If you go to a do which is to help disabled children, you don't have to be disabled to be there, do you? So of course they provide wine for all the guests. And I sneaked a couple of glasses. That was all.

I spent two hours at the do, did all they wanted, did the question-

and-answer thing. I put on an England shirt then I took it off and signed it for the auction. I couldn't have done all that, if I'd been drunk, could I?

I realised I'd left my mobile in the hotel so, during the do, I nipped out to my hotel to pick it up — and there were two paparazzi who insisted on following me. They took dozens of photos. I put up with them at first, wasn't too bothered. Then they followed me all the way back to the event, which was in this restaurant. Later I popped out again to buy some cigarettes, and they followed me down the street again.

I then made a bad mistake. I had agreed to be interviewed by Sky TV about Johnny's charity but then it ended up being about getting the sack at Kettering. Everyone knew about it by then. Jane, my agent, had advised me to say nothing. I don't know why I got sucked into it. I suppose I was still all wound up and emotional and angry about what happened.

But I wasn't drunk. People later said that I was drunk during the interview, they could tell it by the way I was shaky and slurring, but I tell you, that's just not true. I'd only had two or three glasses of wine. The reason I was in an emotional state and shaking was because I was on lots of medication and just one drink on top of it can make you shot. And it was made worse by having had the sack, unfairly, so I think.

I know when I'm drunk. I'm an alcoholic. And I wasn't drunk, whatever people might think. But I was in a state, which might have looked to some people as if I had been drinking.

After the do was over and I was walking back to my hotel, there they were again, snapping away. This time I said, 'That's it guys, you've got more than enough pictures, now just leave me alone.'

One of them was really winding me up, sticking his camera right in my face. I was with a friend from Everton who couldn't believe it, what I was having to put up with. I told him I'd had to put up with this sort of shit for twenty years.

Anyway, I gave this pap a shove. I can't believe I hurt him. I just pushed him away. Perhaps he fell, or bashed himself on his own camera. Anyway, I didn't look. I just walked on, and then into my hotel.

Not long afterwards, two cops, a man and woman, arrive and tell me

I'm under arrest. They put me in their police car and drove me away. The police were fine. No problems with them, no complaints. They knew who I was, right enough, but they explained they had to treat everyone the same, which they did.

At the police station, one of the things they asked me was had I ever been up for assault before. I said, 'Yes, many years ago.' This was in Newcastle, when this bloke attacked my sister and I gave him a punch. They asked me when it had happened. I knew it was 1991, but I wasn't sure when. They looked up my records – and, fucking hell, I couldn't believe it. It was on 5 December! The same date as that day. Incredible coincidence.

I said, 'That's it then. For the rest of my life, I'll never be going out anywhere on 5 December.'

At the police station, they said I could make a phone call, so I tried to ring Robin, my lawyer, in Newcastle. But this was late at night and I failed to get him. I couldn't think who else to ring for help. I needed a solicitor. I knew enough not to make any statements about what had happened until I had a proper lawyer. So I rang my financial advisor, Dave McGhee. I don't know why. Just couldn't think of anyone else. I got his wife out of bed and then Dave comes on the line. I said, 'I'm in a police cell for the night.' He said he'd try to get some help.

I also rang Jimmy, to tell him what happened, and also my brother Carl. I told them to tell me mam and dad that I was okay. I knew it would be in the papers and on TV in the morning – that I was in a police cell. I told them not to worry. It would all be sorted out. I was fine. And I was *not* drunk.

Round about 11.30 at night, I was put in a police cell. Just a little cell, with a bed on the floor and a potty. They took my clothes away for forensic testing. I dunno why. Because of any blood stains, I suppose. They gave me paper pyjamas. I looked like Wurzel Gummidge.

I couldn't sleep. I never do anyway, wherever I am, but this time I was also getting claustrophobia, stuck in that titchy little cell. In the morning, they offered me some breakfast. I said no. I ate nothing.

That's going to be my new phone number – 80 80 80 – eight nothing, eight nothing, eight nothing. Gerrit? Yeah, I can joke about it now, a week later, but it wasn't funny, not then.

In the morning, I pleaded with them not to put me back in the cell, cos of my claustrophobia. They were very good about it. So while I waited for a lawyer to come, they put me in an ordinary little room and left the door open. I then felt a bit better.

Jimmy had eventually got through to Robin at his home about 7.30 that morning, the Tuesday. He then managed to contact a lawyer friend in Liverpool who eventually appeared. I left the police station about 1.30 p.m. The police had to smuggle me out and take me to a meeting place where Andy and Johnny picked me up.

Imraan came out with his twopence worth and was reported as saying that I'd been drunk for thirty-seven days out of the thirty-nine I was at Kettering. What bollocks. He only saw me three times a week for six weeks, which comes to eighteen times max – so how could he have seen me drunk thirty-seven times?

The only time I got near it was after George Best died, my old friend. I rang his son Calum to sympathise. Then I had a couple of brandies with Paul Davis. This was before our Cup game – which we won. That's the only time I had a drink before a game. And I repeat, I wasn't drunk then. I just might have looked it.

I met the sponsors, met the directors from the other club, talked to their chairman. I couldn't have been drunk to do all that. The trouble with me is that, because of all the medication I take all the time, I can appear drunk when I'm not. And also when you've been dry for two years, as I had been, then a couple of brandies can go straight to your head.

But drunk thirty-seven times in six weeks, that's a fucking joke.

I was furious and bitter at the time but now, as I'm sitting here, a few days after it all and looking back, I'm just sad. No, I don't regret getting involved with Kettering. I loved the lads and the team and every moment of being manager. I loved watching Paul Davis do the coaching.

I've learned from it – and what I've learned is not to get involved with a chairman who it seems really wants to be a manager. Next time I want a chairman who takes a back seat with the team and lets the manager and coaches get on with it.

I never got paid, during those six weeks, not a penny, not even my expenses or petrol. I'm going to get my lawyer on to that.

I've spoken since to a few managers about what went on. I mentioned to some of them how I hadn't been paid and how I thought the chairman was a control freak. They said I should have walked away. They said you should never work for no money, not even for one week.

I never did become part owner. The plan was to put £50,000 of my own money into Kettering. That was the deal. It was to show I was serious and had no intention of walking away.

I was always asking Imraan, over and over, 'Where's the contract?' I saw one once, but then he took it back. Said it needed to be changed, but it never reappeared. He always said he was so busy. So I paid out nothing in the end. In that sense, I haven't lost any money. But I wanted to invest.

I don't know whatever happened to that contract.

I feel used, stitched up. I never said a bad word about him to anybody, all the time I was there, never criticised him or said in public how he was interfering. Though I knew he was. I just kept quiet.

Then he sacks me and comes out with this bollocks about being drunk for thirty-seven days. Two players also said a few things about me afterwards – but they were two players I had to drop because *he* wanted them dropped. They don't know that, but it was all his doing, not mine. I took the can. I won't make the same mistake again. Don't say it. I'll probably make different mistakes next time . . .

But honestly, I don't regret it. I'll bounce back. It's made me more determined to succeed next time.

I know I've had a series of jobs that have led nowhere, but there's always been a reason, like China or Boston. People want me involved for my name, for the publicity, to get attention for themselves, to put the gates up, all those sorts of reasons. Then, when they've had all that, they change, lose interest.

I could just try to be a junior coach, with a youth team, perhaps in a higher league, where I wouldn't have the worries and responsibilities of managing a first team. I'd be able to get home at a decent time of night and sleep well – but I don't want that. I want to be a manager. That's the only thing in life I want to be.

The size of the club doesn't matter, though I don't intend to go any further down in the divisions than Kettering. I'm already getting one or two approaches. We'll have to see. But I'm not giving up. I know I'm going to try even harder next time, but first I'll check out the chairman properly.

As for the court case, the photographer has now dropped the charges. In his statement he denies harassing me – but at the same time he says he'd only taken seventy-five photos of me. Seventy-five! Bloody hell. If that isn't harassment I don't know what is. So, no charges will be issued. It's all been dropped, but I have to report back to the Liverpool police station on 15 Feb. I dunno why. That's just what I was told.

The press reaction to me getting the sack, and supposedly being drunk on thirty-seven occasions, was phenomenal, well over the top.

They believed all that Imraan had said, so they all had a go at me. I did think about going away straight afterwards, somewhere abroad, but they'd still find me and hound me. There's no escape. The press want to crucify me.

I really believe they won't be happy till I'm dead. One of the posh papers, the *Independent*, had a headline, 'We won't be happy until Gazza is dead.' It was written by Janet Street-Porter. She repeated all the stuff about being drunk for thirty-seven days without knowing the truth, knowing my version. But what she was also saying was that it was time all those journalists stopped doing to me what they did to George. She said the press should leave me in peace. That was good of her. To understand that.

They didn't, of course. Leave me in peace that is. And they don't get things right either.

The Times is supposed to be a decent paper, isn't it? Yet they had a big piece about me after I got the sack. They used it as an excuse to go over my life. In it, they said, 'his father died of a brain haemorrhage when Paul was 11.' I have the cutting here, 7 December 2005. How could they have got that so wrong? I didn't correct it. I'd spend the rest of my life correcting things, once I started. But it will go in the cuttings and other papers will repeat it, just because it was in *The Times*. To be fair, the journalist did send me an apology.

Then David Mellor in the *Evening Standard* said I was back living with my dad in his 'two up, two down'. Wrong on both counts. I'm not living with him and, anyway, my dad lives in a very nice semi-detached house in a nice area. I know, cos I bought it for him.

I'll bet Mellor just lifted something from another paper and used it. I felt it was a bit sneery. Not a very important mistake, not as bad as saying my dad was dead, but it's typical of what they do. Lots of these columnists don't bother to check things. They believe everything they've read, then add a bit of their own. And so it goes on. And if they can make up stuff like someone's dead, of course they make up that you've been seen out drinking, getting up to this or that.

I'm now back at Champneys. After the police let me go, I decided to come here. No point in staying in that hotel in Kettering any more, when I'd had the sack. Steve, the owner of Champneys, rang and said I could come back.

Some people have said I'll now be going into rehab, to the Priory or to Cottonwood to dry out, after being drunk for thirty-seven days. But I'm not. Why should I, I wasn't drunk. So I don't need to go away and hide.

Yes, I'm an alcoholic, but I still feel in control at the moment. I'm still just drinking the odd glass of wine, that's all. It would mean Imraan had won, if I had to go away and be dried out.

I know what it's like to be drunk, and I wasn't. And I'm not now. I'm just going to chill out, keep my head down for a bit.

One thing I am planning on is to go and see Johnny. Talk to him about what's been happening, then perhaps have a bit of a holiday, go home to Gateshead for Christmas to be with the family . . .

———————

Me Clems!

Hello Mr Gazza. It's been a pleasure getting to know you. You are a genuine person I will never forget. Take care.

Love

Cath

At fifteen I decided I was going to support my family for the rest of my life. Breaking into the Newcastle first team helped me fulfil that promise.

I loved my time at Spurs. I sometimes wonder why I didn't stay longer. I'm celebrating a goal against Sunderland here, by the way, not the fact that I'd eventually got that damn fat pigeon ... I never managed that.

1990 World Cup semi-final. Taking on Augenthaler with the final still in our grasp ...

... and then it was all over. Tears again. Because we weren't winners. And I have always wanted to be the winner. At everything.

Playing for Lazio was great, but the coaches really came down heavy, ha, if I put on any weight.

At Heathrow after smashing my leg at Lazio. I was frustrated and angry cos I wasn't playing football. And the press followed me everywhere. Mind you, maybe it was the fashion photographers, looking for some tips.

THE Sun

Friday, May 31, 1996   27p   Thought: Wasted talent

DISGRACEFOOL

Look at Gazza.. a drunk oaf with no pride

WORLD PICTURE EXCLUSIVE

By EUGENE HENDERSON

THIS is the photo that shows shamed Paul Gascoigne "in training" for the biggest soccer tournament in England since the 1966 World Cup.

Grinning drunkenly, his shirt torn to shreds and a beer bottle in his hand, Gazza looks more like a soccer yob than a £20,000-a-week superstar.

The oaf knocked back cocktail after cocktail in a Hong Kong club as he led a huge binge with England team-mates including Teddy Sheringham and Steve McManaman.

Early today it was reported that on the flight home Gascoigne tried to force his way into the cockpit of the Cathay

Continued on Page Two

YOU THE JURY

DO you think Gazza should play for England in Euro 96?
YES: 0891 400698
NO: 0891 400699

Calls cost 4p extra than 10p

Guzzla ... Gascoigne, his shirt torn to shreds, sinks another beer with Steve McManaman (left) and Teddy Sheringham

The night of the dentist's chair.

Euro '96. Another semi-final against the Germans. I scored my penalty, but again we were out.

Champions League against Ajax. October 1996. A red mist came over me and I kicked out at Winston Bogarde. And was off. I hadn't told Walter Smith what had happened at Gleneagles a couple of days earlier.

Happier times at Rangers. Coisty is keeping tight hold of the Coca-Cola Cup. Probably worried I'll go off with it and rearrange all the Rangers trophies in a nice, neat order. Just like I did to the tin cans in his kitchen.

Bryan Robson has been amazing to me. It was Bryan who first took me to the Priory when I was in a terrible state. Not that I was admitting it then. This is my first public appearance after I came out. I promised, promised, promised Bryan I would never touch drink again...

Chapter Nine

Paul's third session: Crisis

Paul

I can't believe that last Friday I was a manager, and by this Monday I'd been sacked and was locked up in a cell. I just can't believe it. On Saturday we lost, and I had it out with Imraan, and he wasn't happy. By Monday I'd been to three cities in three days. Got beaten, got sacked, then the next minute I'm locked up in the cells.

It wasn't very nice in there. I was banged up for nearly ten hours without my medication and, as you know, suffering from claustrophobia. They took all my belongings away from me. It was quite scary. Since it happened I've been trying to get myself back on track again, but the papers have been disgusting. It was Kate Moss's turn not so long ago, now it's my turn . . . But I'm not happy with myself.

I think, 'Right, I won't drink,' and then I get bored and I eat too much. Then I look in the mirror and think, 'Fuck me, I'm putting on weight!' I've got a battle on me hands. I want to stop drinking, but I just want to enjoy

Christmas and New Year and give up afterwards, on 2nd January. But if it gets bad, really bad, I know I'll have to fuck off to the clinic and get a fresh start because, when I get back from the clinic, I'm happy, the sparkle is back in my eyes. But why should I do it just because the press are saying it?

John

I'm keen to explore with Paul this statement he made about not being happy with himself.

For the moment, we need to concentrate on what is blocking Paul from doing the right thing for his health. Paul's stuck because the press are saying he needs to get his drinking sorted out, and he doesn't like being told what to do.

Paul

All my life I've been told what to do: at school by teachers, by me parents, as a player by the coach, the managers, as a coach by other coaches. Now the press.

The press say this and that and I think, 'No.' I can go five days without a drink. But then I get cravings. It's boring *with* a drink, fuck knows what it's going to be like *without* a drink!

I do think I've been depressed. When I'm sober, all the things come back to me that I have to battle with. Obsessions with food, the gym, Red Bull . . . And it's like the press just won't let go.

Do I feel persecuted by them? Yes, but I know I can't ever get rid of the press – it's all about how I deal with them.

But I just think, 'Why should I let them dictate to me what I should do and what I shouldn't do with my life?' You've seen what they've done to Princess Diana and you've seen what they've done to George Best. He wasn't left alone to sort out his own problems. But I *have* to do it, I have to get sober. I can *get* sober, it's *staying* sober that's hard.

John

Paul's very concerned about being told what to do by the press, so I'm interested in how we can get him out of that thought cycle – knowing that he needs to get help with the drink but not wanting to get help because then the press will have won. I wonder if he could look at it another way: if he does get help he'll get himself back, and then *he'll* have 'won'.

We talk about what worked for him last time he got sober and stayed sober for over two years. Paul needs to take responsibility for getting himself back on track. I want to support him in reaching a place psychologically where he's able to say to himself, 'I'm going to get sober, and I'm going to do it for me.'

Paul

I've got this thing focused in my head, get Christmas over and knuckle down to getting myself sorted out after that. I know a lot of friends are worried for me. I'm worried for myself. I'm feeling sorry for myself.

Yes, when I get sober it's going to have to be for me, but at the moment I feel it's for everybody else. After Christmas I'll start afresh. It'll be a bigger battle after Christmas even than it would be now, because I'll want to have a great Christmas. Christmas Day, Boxing Day, New Year's Eve – I know I'm going to drink those three days anyway, so why stay sober now?

John

Another part of Paul's resistance right now is the idea that Christmas is around the corner and he doesn't want to spend it having a miserable time, trying to give up alcohol, or in a clinic. He's more or less made the decision that he's going to drink until after Christmas and New Year. What worries me is what he said about wanting a good Christmas. I ask him to watch out for thinking, 'This is my last party before I get sober,' and going out with a bang.

We go back to this feeling Paul has of being controlled. One of the first times we met, he was feeling trapped and controlled by the football club. I suggest that what seems to happen is that he has a good run, even getting away with drinking for a while, but then one way or another alcohol seems to get in the way of his life. Then when he loses control because of the alcohol, people around him rush in and try to control him, telling him what to do, and he feels manipulated and controlled again.

Paul

It's been that way my whole life. Everybody's trying to tell me what I should do. And I've had a drink problem, cocaine problem, food problem, so many problems to deal with. I'm not forty yet, I'm going to live a long time, I've got to battle these problems every day. What sort of life is this? So then I just want a glass of wine.

But the drinking doesn't even bring me relief, because as soon as I have one glass I think, 'Fuck me, what have I done that for?' I'm even regretting it as it enters my mouth.

It's a battle I find hard to fight. If I can see sense again, or light at the end of the tunnel . . . But at the moment I feel like I've just entered the tunnel and it's very dark and dull, and there's a long way to go.

I thought there was hope when I took the Kettering job. But I've had that man Imraan breathing down my neck every single day for six weeks: trying to pick the team, trying to pick the reserve team, trying to sack the reserve-team manager, getting rid of players, making *me* get rid of players and then the papers having a go at me for getting rid of them and not reporting when they were injured. My two top strikers were out injured and no one said anything about it in the papers when the results didn't go our way.

John

The analogy of the tunnel is a good way of describing the feeling of powerlessness. Everything that's happened has led to Paul starting to lose hope. The whole job experience has been really hard, and he's still feeling it.

I think it's important that Paul tries not to sabotage himself. He got the job he wanted at Kettering, the drink sneaked in and that was okay for a while, but then it turned. I ask him for a minute to forget about Imraan's behaviour. Here was something he really wanted, and yet the drinking crept in almost unknowingly. Then it increased to the point where he'd given his power away, because when Paul's boss felt he couldn't control him he was able to blame the drinking, and he was able to list issues and events, whether there were thirty-seven of them or not. Looking at Paul's process, it's as if he gives his good things away – things are going well, then something in him says, 'I'm going to fuck this up.'

Paul

I don't know where he got those thirty-seven incidents from. I wouldn't drink for six days, then I'd be feeling pissed off and want a drink. I'd have a couple of glasses of wine, then not drink again for two days. I can't remember the last time I was drunk. You know what it's like, Johnny, I have to hide my drinking. So it's not easy, fun. I think, 'Why am I doing this? Why can't I just sit there and relax and enjoy it?'

But I know what the problem is. I'm an alcoholic so I can't be like others, social drinkers. I have to do it myself. I rang Eric Clapton up the other day, to ask him about his clinic. But the thought of two hours of group therapy every day ... And they take everything off you, mobiles, everything. And I have to spend a fortune. How many times have I got to keep on going to clinics?

There's no way I'm going into a clinic over Christmas. But that doesn't mean I'm going to get drunk every day until New Year. No way am I going to do that.

I'm so fucked off about the job. Now I've got nothing to look forward to when I wake up in the morning, nothing to get up for. I do want to get back into management, I enjoy it. If I prepare myself properly I'm hopeful I can crack it once I get myself sorted out. That job was a mad rush. I had the players ringing me up distraught. I was still trying to help the players even though I'd been sacked and there was no one to help and support me. Just Paul Davis and Andy.

John

A lot of people have to go to treatment for alcoholism and addiction a lot of times. People even have to go nine or ten times before they get it. I know Paul resists that idea. Most importantly we need to do what's right for Paul, and never mind what other people think. But at the moment he's angry and hurt by his boss and by the media, and the injuries to Kettering players he feels haven't been made public, and being made to drop players he didn't want to drop. In public he's been blamed for the whole thing, so he doesn't want to be proved wrong by going to a clinic so that everything can be blamed on his alcoholism, and no one else has to take responsibility for their own behaviour. When we drink we set ourselves up to be blamed for everything, whether it's all our fault or not.

We talk about how he'll get sober in January. I've suggested going to a clinic, but if he doesn't want to go he'll need a lot of support at home, going to AA meetings and arranging his life so that it supports not drinking.

Paul

I'm not good at getting support. I've got Jimmy, and in the past I've belonged to football clubs. But apart from them I've always managed alone.

I hate being an alcoholic. People don't understand the illness. And you can't get away from alcohol – adverts, billboards, mates at the pub, off-licences – everywhere you look, alcohol is there.

John

On the football field, fighting to win is everything. When it comes to our health and well-being, trying to 'win' can be our downfall.

JM: I want to go back to one thing. The way you were brought up was to fight and to win. You've won so much but, with this, you can't win, you can't beat it.

PG: This is one battle I can't win.

JM: I think that's where your pride comes in because, really, the only way to beat it is to give in – to stop, isn't it?

PG: Yeah.

JM: We need to put a plan in place. We've tried different strategies. We talked last time about cravings: how to ignore the thoughts. And it's important to talk about it and that's the good thing about AA, hearing people talking about being angry about having to stop. Why are you an alcoholic and someone else isn't? It's not fair is it?

PG: No, it's not fair. I have to face the fucking fact that I can't drink. I wish there was an injection for it.

JM: Is that how painful it is for you right now?

PG: I just can't believe it; one minute manager, the next minute in the cells. If I thought I deserved it I'd hold my hands up, but I don't think I deserved it.

JM: You know now and then when something reminds you of your own life? A friend of mine broke his neck playing football. I was injured that week so I wasn't at the game. He went up for a ball and fell awkwardly and he's been in a wheelchair ever since. He was a good footballer, but he's had to accept he can never get out of that chair. Remembering that helps me put things in perspective: it could have been me. This is not to take anything away from your feelings at the moment, they're valid, but maybe you need, finally, to have that acceptance that you can't drink. Whatever your desires and dreams, you can't drink, and you have to accept it.

PG: I understand. I can't win. It brings out the child in me. The fact that I can stay sober for six months, then have just one drink and that's it, I'm away again.

JM: Maybe you have to accept this is the battle you'll never win. You can't be too stubborn, it'll kill you, like George, your friend.

PG: I don't want it to end that way. It's going to take time. I'm slowly slipping into this depression. I've got to get through these two-and-a-half weeks. I wish it was 2nd January now, I really do.

JM: I know you've said you won't get sober before 2nd January, but I want you to reserve the right to change your mind. I want you to get to that point where you say, 'I'm ready to put down the drink.'

PG: I will be, 2nd January.

John

I found this session difficult. I'm very concerned for Paul and don't know what will happen over the next few weeks. He's in a corner and knows he has a fight on his hands. It's an either-or situation: either he surrenders and asks for help, but then feels weak – not strong enough to cope on his own – and gets judged by the media for going back into rehab; or he continues to drink and takes the risk that he won't get through to January without losing control and inviting further condemnation from the press as a 'no-good alky'. He knows how powerful his illness is. By drinking, he ended up giving control to others, something that he hates doing. He is, and has been, a victim of his own success and he needs to take some control back before he can feel okay about himself; the only way to do that is to get the help he needs.

Paul is in denial. I want him to explore other situations in which the old pattern of feeling controlled and helpless has led to sabotage. Paul's refusal to see his part in the self-sabotage is obvious, yet there are valid grievances against people who want to control and dominate him. Taking responsibility is all that Paul or anyone can ever do – he can only look at his own part in what's happened, and see how the drinking has set him up to be caught out by anyone who might want him out of the way.

The paradox of the addictive personality is that the illness leads the addict on into battle with the disease – they try to 'beat' it, by proving that they can control it. But to beat it they need to accept that *it* has beaten *them*. By pitting their will against the object of their desire they come crashing down again and again: every time they set foot in a bar with the intention of having 'just one', they end up drinking all night. Small successes further encourage the addicted person to believe in their own willpower. Paul talks about how long he can go without a drink, or the times when he only had 'a couple of glasses of wine'. Alcoholics talk about these occasions as proof of their ability to control their intake. And at times and for a while they can. But while you might not drink anything for a week, or even a month, you're safe in the knowledge that you'll be having a drink on Friday night, or at the end of January, and some part of you is looking forward or holding on to that, even if it's subconsciously.

Accepting that they need to abstain is a massive leap for most people, and they'll look for every other way around the problem before coming exhaustedly to that point.

Over the last few days I have been in regular contact with Paul and his close friend Jimmy. Paul's moods are at an all-time low and he hasn't managed to stop drinking. The good news is, he's now considering entering treatment before Christmas.

My role as an addictions counsellor is very different from my role as a psychotherapist. One aspect of the addictions role is to make clinical interventions outside of the consulting room. This can include planning the best way to get someone into treatment, if that's what they need. It involves talking to family members, friends and colleagues: anyone who'll help.

I was in daily contact with Jimmy, discussing how we could get Paul back into treatment and getting a report on how Paul was. He was looking after Paul, ensuring that he didn't get too drunk and would get home okay after going out drinking. Jimmy acted as liaison officer, talking to John, Paul's father, and the rest of the family. My main aim was to persuade Paul that now was the right time to go and get help. The longer he left it, the worse he would get.

This stage is probably the most frightening for the family and friends of alcoholics because it's so unpredictable. There's just no way of knowing what will happen. I could not tell you how many times I have heard, 'Will he get drunk tonight and not come home?'; 'Will he crash his car?'; 'I think she's sleeping with other men!' I have worked with many family members who need counselling in order to cope with this stress. Research says that for every alcoholic drinking, there are at least four family members or friends suffering as a direct effect, whether that be emotionally, physically or financially.

In the run-up to Christmas I was on stand-by, not knowing what would happen from one day to the next, hoping that Paul would make that call for help. Then, out of the blue, Jimmy called me and asked if I could get Paul on a flight to the USA. I thought it would be better if he could get Paul to fly to London so that I could meet him at Heathrow for a time before he flew out to Arizona. Paul then called me and said that he had had enough. He was sick and tired of being sick and tired, and was ready to ask for help. He arrived at Heathrow the next day. We talked about the treatment and I told him I thought he was showing great courage in going for help. He felt shame and guilt about the last few weeks but had enough courage and humility to admit defeat. The ability to do that can mean the difference between life and death.

I suggested that Paul concentrate all his energy at the clinic on getting better, staying in touch with me only now and then as the need arose. I would catch up with him again in around a month's time.

Dear Paul

Ya cheeky Bastard. Wishing you the best in this new chapter of your life. Thanks for the Psycho Drama and the advice. I am going to attach myself to winners and stay on this like you said. I appreciate your wit, sense of humor but not your colon. Take care. Rock out with your c..k out. I hear voices in my head . . .

Vince

Chapter Ten

Paul's connections and responsibilities

John

I always worry, before a session with Paul, that I might make him feel worse. This does happen with some clients. When you get deep into stuff, they can become furious and angry. I have had to stop certain people coming to see me at nine in the morning – because I know they'll leave angry, go to work, sack people, do things they regret.

Sometimes you have to allow them to get angry. Jokes and being matey are all right, but don't actually get you very far or uncover stuff.

In that first session with him, back in the early autumn, when I let him do all the talking, I didn't want to engage on too deep a level and be disruptive. That wouldn't be helpful. At that point, I wasn't trying to get in touch with his core pain – to use the jargon.

He talked a lot about his accidents and injuries – and there's no doubt they spark off his mental problems. He was in hospital for his neck, then he got a blood clot and had to be on warfarin. Then he developed pneumonia while in hospital. So he was in a mentally as well as physically bad state for weeks.

He managed to work out for himself what the accident he had while skating, which hurt his neck and gave him such agony, had led to. He was prescribed morphine for the pain, even though he knew that in the past he had been addicted to morphine. The doctor had to give him this sort of painkiller because the other sort might have affected his stomach – and he has had a history of stomach ulcers.

I think going back on painkillers, and the fact that he was cut off from support, did trigger the relapse he had into alcoholism over the summer and into the Kettering period.

I encourage people to make the links between what has happened to them and how they felt and behaved, so they can understand the causes. He gets addicted to painkillers: he knows he's having to take them to relieve the pain, but worries about being addicted to painkillers, so has a drink to escape it all . . .

The big thing about Paul these days is that he knows where he is going, where it might lead. That's progress. When he had the major relapse in China back in 2003, and went on an alcohol binge, the fact that he was able to take himself off to Cottonwood showed he is able to check himself. It is always good when I hear him being so honest.

One of the things I was trying to get across to Paul when he was at Kettering was that he was now like a father – he had a responsibility to his players. He's not a kid any more. Which is hard, when he's had years of acting and being treated like a kid.

But I could see he was soon aware that he wouldn't get love and caring as a manager. He had to give all of the time, not take. He must have been thinking, 'What about Paul Gascoigne?'

There is a lot of shame in the way people like Paul think. They feel weak, yet they know they have been indulged.

I know Paul has always found it hard in the past to ask for help, so we have to work on what blocks him.

As a child, I think he didn't get much help. He looked after the family when he was still quite young, assuming financial responsibility for them when he started earning money – for his parents, and his sisters and brother. He assumed the financial load – and it's stuck. He sees himself as a provider.

He has also always seen himself as an entertainer. He puts his tongue out at a serious moment and we all laugh. He wants to make people feel better. It's part of being a provider. He is providing light relief, entertainment, although I'm not sure he's always realised it, not in those terms.

So what happens when he's depressed? Who is providing for him? He has, of course, not got a relationship of his own, where someone is caring and providing for him. He is totally on his own, physically and emotionally.

I know a lot of people rubbish therapists when they start on about the influence of parents, but in my experience it's very hard to avoid a link between how you yourself relate to and attract people, and how your parents related.

Paul's parents had rows, lived apart, his dad worked away from home, then they eventually got divorced. His two sisters are both divorced. The same has happened to Paul.

I'm not saying his ex-wife Sheryl was anything like his mother, but nevertheless there is a pattern. For whatever reason, she would appear not able to give Paul the love he needed – and he probably didn't give it to her.

That sort of love was not there to go around when he was growing up either. He didn't receive it, and was thus unable to give it out.

We rarely, of course, receive the kind of love we would like in life, but coming from Paul's sort of background makes it even more difficult.

The more people talk consciously, the more it disturbs the unconscious. By talking, you can make connections you might not have made before.

With Paul, I think he has been able to look back at events and perhaps now make connections he has not made before. I have tried to get him to talk about his brother Carl's drinking and I think he has thought about that and sees it in relation to his parents. Some things pop into your mind immediately. Others take time.

I think he can now see the stages he went through in his drinking, how he was emotionally going up and down till he crossed a line, which all alcoholics cross, where it doesn't alter whether you feel happy or sad – you just want to drink anyway.

At Newcastle, he was contained by the club, having been with them from a young boy. At Spurs, he didn't feel part of a family. Then there was a lot of stress when Sheryl came along because she didn't like his family, and vice versa. That was a very revealing moment when he said that he deliberately had a row with Sheryl in order that he could leave and therefore go home and see his family.

In the early days, he was pleased that Sheryl's children saw him as a father, and called him Dad, but of course that gave him more commitments. Don't forget, he was very young.

It takes time to build a picture, to track things back, but I think he is aware of the stresses and strains he has had in his life, and how ill-prepared he was to cope with them. But I hope eventually to get him to look at his own part in his problems.

I haven't been particularly tough on him so far. With all addicts, you have to make it safe for them. From the first minute they come into your room, the therapy is starting, even if you appear to be doing nothing. You are settling them down, putting them at ease.

Because we missed a few months, I had to get Paul used to sessions again, so I might not have appeared earlier on to have been pushing him very much. I tend to say. 'Yeah, that must have been hard,' rather than criticise or suggest, just to encourage him to come out with it all.

With someone like Paul, you have to nurture them so space opens up and you can get beneath what they are saying. Most of the addicts I deal with are much more stable than Paul, despite all their problems. Paul has got few internal foundations to fall back on. He's been without a home of his own for five years and has no partner in his life – but you could say he's been like that for *all* of his life.

It is amazing, with alcoholics, how some of them do find a way round to asking or crying out for help. It's often not obvious or straightforward, and they don't know themselves why they are doing it. I have had clients coming to see me drunk – as a sort of statement, a defiance, to let me see what's happened, but in reality they are asking for help. Getting drunk was a way of saying what they couldn't put in words.

It was hard to get across the notion of self-sabotage. I'm not sure Paul accepted it. But in his career, it's noticeable how often things go wrong – just when they are going well. He did love being at Kettering, and there was no real need to start drinking again, so why did he do it? It's as if he can't cope with success. There are people like that. They don't believe they deserve success. It's not always happened with Paul, but often enough to suggest an underlying pattern.

I did vaguely try to suggest it but I don't think he quite grasped it. It's a form of masochism which all goes back to his lack of an internal structure. If he was more comfortable with himself, had secure foundations in his life, he would be able to step back and analyse what happened when things go wrong, rather than immediately see himself as a victim, which is what he often does. There's an old joke they use at AA meetings. 'Poor me, poor me, pour me another drink . . .'

At the same time, there were specific causes for his recent problems, which led him to start drinking again in the summer. That accident during the ice dancing did trigger off certain events which have had a bad effect on him.

When people relapse, there are real causes, proper triggers, but of course the main thing which has to be done is get the person to face up to them, to accept that ultimately they are responsible.

I'm very pleased he did agree in the end to get away and get treatment and is now at Cottonwood.

———————

Dear Paul

'I'd do anything, for you dear, anything, for you mean everything, to me.

You know that I'd go anywhere for your smile, anywhere, for your smile everywhere I see'

Ha Ha Ha

Wow am I going to miss you pal. I never thought I would laugh my ass off so much in rehab.

I would love to see you in California. You are a great guy with a great heart. Your stories are truly amazing and I love listening to every one of them.

I don't have a cell yet but I'll make sure I get it to you as soon as I do.

Love

Jaz

PS Every time I eat sugar-free Mentoes I'll think of you and fart. Ha ha!

ChapterEleven

Paul gets help in the desert

Paul

Well I'm back from Cottonwood now. It's mid-January. Getting there was a nightmare. I flew first class to Phoenix where a driver from the clinic was supposed to pick me up but I somehow missed him. So I hired a taxi at the airport and told him I wanted to go to Arizona Cottonwood. Took four hours, before we both realised I should have asked for Cottonwood de Tucson. There's more than one Cottonwood clinic, just as there's more than one Priory or more than one Champneys. We had to drive back two hours. He charged me $860 – then asked for an extra $50 for petrol, cheeky bastard.

I should have arrived at the clinic at seven in the evening but didn't get there till one in the morning – after a ten-hour flight, plus six hours in a car. Fucking hell. What a state I was in.

And all the way there I was thinking, 'I don't want to be here, it's a waste of time, I'm only going because I've been talked into it' – by Jimmy,

Johnny, and my agent Jane. But most of all, I blamed the press. They'd been going on that I was gonna die unless I got treatment. After the Kettering shambles and all the allegations about being drunk, some of the tabloids were putting out a warning under my photo: 'Don't serve this man a drink.' I knew that even if I went to a pub with Jimmy and stuck to water it would appear in the papers that I'd been drinking champagne.

But I honestly didn't think I needed help anyway, not all that much. I know when I've been on a bender. In the past I've been on binges that have lasted three months – that's when you definitely need detoxing. This time, okay I'd been drinking again, but just three days on, three days off, nothing that five days going to AA meetings every day wouldn't have sorted. That's all I thought I needed – one week detox, max. But, what the hell, just to keep the peace, make everyone happy, keep the press at bay, I agreed to go. And then I ended up with this fucking nightmare journey.

Cottonwood is in the desert, miles from anywhere. It's all fairly new, not in an old building like the Priory. There's a group of single-storey buildings, round a sort of square. A bit like a prison, really, with all the different units – but that might give the wrong impression. It's an attractive building, in a wild but really beautiful area.

The first thing they do is take your photo. They want a record of how you looked when you arrived – in other words, like shit. Then they take another photo when you leave. You get to keep both of them – as a warning.

They test your blood for alcohol, drugs, all sorts. They do a body search the moment you get there, and they take away things like your mobile phone and any credit cards. Not because there's any way you can use a card to buy things – but in case you slash your arms with it. It has happened.

They also take away your aftershave and any mouthwash, anything with the slightest hint of alcohol, any stuff you might start drinking if you get desperate.

On the first full day I had an AIDS test, tests for hepatitis C, liver and kidney tests. They were all okay – even my liver – no problems. That proved what I thought – that I had not been on a right binge, not like the old days.

I suppose the real reason I agreed to go was that I was depressed. I just felt fed up. My head was taking a beating after that mess at Kettering. I'd had enough. I couldn't trust myself not to do something really stupid.

For the first five days I was in the detox unit. This is a sort of big ward divided into little single rooms. You have privacy in each room, but each one is very small, with one window, just really a bed and bathroom.

The bed has plastic sheets, which is part of the treatment, to keep you sweating, night and day. They give you tablets to stop your shakes – yeah, the shakes had started before I left England. I admit it. They also give you vitamin B tablets and tablets to help you sweat.

At any one time there's up to fifty people staying at Cottonwood – people come and go so for a few days it can go down to nearer thirty, but it's normally about fifty. There was also a small unit for adolescent girls, aged from fourteen to seventeen, but they were kept separate. I never saw them. They used the same pool, but on different days.

Over the weeks, I got to know all of the fifty. You mix with them, though basically you are put into groups of eight. You stay with this group, and the same therapist, all the time you are there.

I got put into my eight after my five days of detox. We had a woman therapist looking after us, Elaine. She was quite young, probably just over thirty.

Almost all therapists have had first-hand experience of some sort of addiction – either suffering it themselves or they've been brought up in homes where one or both of the parents have been addicted. I don't know her background, but she was good. I liked her.

Once I joined my group, I moved out of the detox ward and shared a room with three other blokes. All of them like me – alcoholics. In each group of eight, there are both women and men, and they can be suffering from all sorts of addictions, such as drugs and gambling. There were two sex addicts while I was there, but not in my group.

I suppose the average age of all the fifty patients was about my age – mid to late thirties. But there were a couple much younger, about nineteen.

You don't know who they are, what they do. That only comes out in passing, if you've made a particular friend and get talking to them. Otherwise you don't know any personal details. It doesn't matter. You are all equal, trying to struggle together.

They were all American in my group, which is how I wanted it. I didn't want to be with any English people. There were a few Brits when I was there, in other groups, and a couple did recognise me eventually and told some of the Americans. But I didn't get bothered cos I still didn't mean anything to them . . . That's really why I prefer Cottonwood to the Priory. I can be really anonymous.

I didn't mind sharing the bedroom with three others – except for one thing. All my life I've slept with the light on, since I was a kid. I can't go to sleep otherwise. This time, I had to have the light off, because the others wanted it off. But I managed. When we got to bed, we were all so tired. You're on the go all day long.

Once at least during the night someone comes round and shines a torch on your bed – to make sure you haven't scarpered or topped yourself, I suppose.

I'd get off okay, but then didn't actually sleep much. Three hours max. I was always up by four o'clock. I'd just wander around or go outside into the desert and watch the sun rise, or listen to the coyotes. I liked sitting in the sun for that first hour after it rises. It was hot, up to 90°, even early in the morning.

I never had breakfast. I couldn't be bothered. I didn't feel hungry. Perhaps later in the morning, I might grab a handful of cereal, but that was about all. I'd just have a coffee and wait for the medications to come round. They started at seven in the morning, along with various medical tests.

After my first five days of detox had finished, I felt much better – and I wanted to come home. The shakes had gone. I didn't fancy starting all the rehab stuff and the therapy sessions. This was my third time here, after all.

I did think of booking myself out, but I remembered that Jane – my agent – had warned me not to. She said the papers would find out and it would be held against me again. I had to do it – to show the world I could, that I could stick to it.

So I started all the therapies. You have to do them, really. The place is full of doctors and psychiatrists and specialists and they have you down for shitloads, doing things all day long, while there's usually someone sitting monitoring you, writing endless notes.

I specially didn't want to go to anger management. I'd done that twice already. I don't consider I get angry any more, not in the old way. First time I was there, I did cause a few scenes in the anger-management sessions.

This bloke was telling us to count to ten when we feel anger coming on. So I says to him, 'Someone smacks you in the fucking face so you then count to ten? Fuck off.' He said, 'Yes, that's what you must try to do.' 'By that time,' I told him, 'you're on the ground and he's kicking your fucking heed in . . .'

But they said I had to go. At the first session, the bloke told us how he used to lose his temper when driving, now he thinks to himself, 'Why am I in a hurry? Do I need to get there at a certain time? Who is being harmed most by me losing my temper?'

I know, I know. All very sensible. But I know all that. I haven't actually lost my temper for some years. So after two sessions, I didn't bother to turn up to anger management any more.

All the same, I was still on the go all the time, with other sessions. You start with your own group every morning, from 9 to 11. You have to begin your bit by saying, 'My name is Paul, I'm an alcoholic and OCD.' Everyone starts off like that. 'My name is Jake, I'm a drug addict,' or whatever . . .

Then you have to tell the group how you are feeling today. There are big signs on the wall with the words written in large letters, like ANGRY HAPPY DEPRESSED SAD UPSET GRATEFUL GRIEVING etc. It's to help you describe how you feel, which one applies to you that day. If you stand up and say right away that you are sad or grieving, then the others know not to take the piss or joke with you. If you are happy, then they know it'll be okay to tease you.

You then try to explain *exactly* how you feel – and they all listen. Perhaps some might ask you questions. Then the next person describes how they feel. The therapist is mainly taking notes, watching how everyone behaves and reacts. It's being with the others, hearing them, that's the main point and, yeah, I think it does help. By listening to others, you do identify with a lot of what they are saying and going through.

One of the sessions was psycho-drama. You play out dramas or little scenes from your life, incidents and events which matter to you. I didn't do any scenes from my life, not this time. Instead I helped others.

What happens is that you tell everyone about this real drama from your life, then the other patients take the parts. You explain what was said, how you felt, the rows and shouts and arguments or whatever, and they have to act it out.

I took one part as a bloke when he was aged two. Yeah, not exactly a hard role. I didn't have much to do. I just had to sit in a corner and shake. That was his memory of his childhood.

In previous sessions at Cottonwood, I had played out bits from my own life. I had someone sitting in a chair as Steven, aged eight, the little boy who got killed. I apologised to him, said how sorry I was, blaming myself, saying I was responsible for his death, and would he ever forgive me. And in the psycho-drama, he did forgive me.

Another time I described some of the scenes with Shel, how I used to shout at her, how she shouted back, what we argued about and why. The person who acted Shel did it so well I felt battered afterwards. She'd won, once again.

They do have family-therapy groups as well, real ones, where your wife or husband or children are invited to come along. When I went out there while I was at Everton it was arranged that Shel would come over to Arizona, and join in a family-therapy group. She'd agreed. And it was all fixed for her to travel. Then I changed my mind. I cancelled it. I just couldn't face it.

No, I've never thought of inviting my parents to any family-therapy sessions, either here or America. Why should I? I am responsible for my drinking. Not them. And I never will. I don't see any point.

Dinner at Cottonwood was early, about five o'clock. For lunch and dinner, for the whole five weeks, I ate the same thing – bagel salad. Cos I liked it, that's why. At seven o'clock in the morning and evening, you have the medications coming round.

On Friday and Saturday, we had a movie show. We would be given a list of movies and we'd each have a vote, then one would be chosen. You're not allowed anything violent, or about drugs, drink or sex. Bit of a limited choice then. They were rather soft, but I went to them all. Something to do. They give you popcorn as well.

One Saturday we saw *Finding Nemo*, which is a cartoon. We also saw *Seabiscuit*, which is about horses. Strictly speaking, we shouldn't have seen that, as there's some gambling in it and one of our group was a gambling addict.

In the evenings, I just rested or read or wrote. I wrote about how I felt, moaning on really, saying to myself, 'What the fuck am I doing here? What is the point?' The thing I wrote most was 'I hate myself for being here again.' I kept going over how I'd put myself in the situation of needing to be there.

One of the things I did was fill in a Body Map. Yous'll see it in this book. Bit scary, eh? What you do is you have to lie down on the floor on a big sheet of brown paper. Someone then draws round the shape of your body. Then you slowly fill in all the parts of your body that you have damaged through your drinking or drugs or whatever – not just the liver and stuff, but injuries and brain damage and obsessions. One time I was in there, I did that Life Line, the Path to Recovery, which was used in my autobiography.

When you've finished your Body Map, you hold it up and talk to the group about it, talk them through it, explain what damage you have done to yourself over the years.

About three times a week, there's a Community Meeting. That was when all the patients, all fifty of us, met together.

When you first arrive, you're known as one of the 'peers', that's the name they use when you're a newcomer who's just checked in. As the weeks go on, you become a senior peer. At the beginning of every Community Meeting, you elect from the senior peers, by a vote of hands, who will be the chairman and secretary for that meeting.

I made it to senior peer quite early. I'd been acting like one from almost the beginning, as I'd been there before, helping new people to acclimatise. I would take people round, show them the building, explain what would happen, make them feel at home.

I always said to them, 'Cry if you want to, say anything you like to anyone. You'll never see me again, or any of them. So don't be scared or embarrassed. Just show your feelings.'

I explained to them that feedback from the other people would help them. It had helped me. I told them to have faith, that they would feel better when they left. They had to give it a proper chance.

At the meeting, jobs would be given out, such as cleaning out the ash-trays in the smoking areas, which were outside. Or you might have the job of raising and lowering the Stars and Stripes flag, in the morning and evening. One job I got was bell-ringing. You had to go round ringing a bell to tell them it's five minutes to go to the next session. I quite enjoyed that.

In the third week, I got made chairman for one meeting. Fucking hell. There was a lump in my throat, having to address all of them. But I think I managed okay.

One of the things the chairman has to do is go round the room and ask everyone if they have any problems. They might, for example, have a problem with one of the therapists, or a doctor or psychiatrist. As chairman, you encourage them to speak out, if they want to, and name the person they have a problem with, if they want to.

In the first week or so I was there, many of them did have trouble with my accent. Mind you, I have had the same problem in England, especially when I came to London for Spurs. But as the weeks went on, they did get used to it. By the time I was chairman, I think most of them could manage to work out what I was saying. Just about anyway.

If you didn't want to speak out, you could write out something and put it in the God Box. This was just a wooden box, where you shoved any notes. They can be good or bad. It's called the God Box because the idea is you are addressing God, up in the sky, and only He can hear or read what you've written. At the end of every week, the contents of the box are burned, so no one ever knows what it was you wrote. It got things off your chest. The note I put most in the God Box was: 'God, please get rid of my OCD.'

But you still can stand up and say it aloud, to everyone, even if you have already written it in the God Box. This way the other patients get a chance to react – meanwhile the therapists are all making frantic notes.

When I was acting as chairman, this woman stood up and said she had put a note in the God Box, but now she wanted to share it. I asked her what it was she had written.

'Thank you God, for getting me through all this.' That was what she said.

'You're welcome,' I replied.

They all laughed. In fact it brought the house down . . .

Every week we had an outing, such as to a church. You could join in the service, if you wanted to. I made friends with a Jewish bloke. He took me to a Jewish synagogue and I wore the skull cap at the service.

I also made friends with a girl there. She challenged me to play chess. I pretended I'd only just learned to play since coming to Cottonwood. That wasn't true. I learned years ago. Anyway, I hammered her 3–0 and she was furious. I went round telling everyone, of course, that I'd only just learned and yet I'd beaten her. She did eventually beat me – and of course she went round telling everyone this time.

I did play quite a bit of chess and draughts, as well as a game called battleships. They also had some horses and you could go and wander amongst them, and do a bit of riding if you wanted.

After twenty-nine days, I did feel better. It had helped me to be healthier and cleaner but, really, I still felt I need never have bothered. Five days detoxing at the Priory, who use the same sort of methods, would have done me as much good. I wasn't in desperate need of all the therapies and group sessions. But I suppose they helped. I was glad to be away, out of England. I felt secure, which I never feel in England.

I was thinking of George Best a lot. He never stuck at such things. Then I'd think, 'But it's my fucking life. If I want to drink, I'll drink. Fuck them all.'

Then I'd think, 'No, I don't want to drink. I have no wish to start drinking again, ever.'

One of the things we all did at the end of Cottonwood was get people to sign your book. You could buy a book in the Cottonwood shop, just a simple little notebook, or a more elaborate, expensive one if you wanted. I bought a fancy one, with thick leather binding and a clasp thing. That's just cos I'm flash, I guess.

You ask all the patients who've been there with you to write in it, anything they like. And you do the same in their books. It's like the class books or year books they have at American high schools.

You just leave it out when you're about to leave, on a table, with all the other books. People sign if they want. You can write anything, good or bad, you'll be gone very soon and you'll probably never see any of them again.

A lot of people wrote in my book. That's what those messages are at the end of all the chapters. I thought you'd like to see them. See what other people thought of me. Not as Gazza. As Paul. They were all American, so they didn't use words like 'wanker', which was one of the words I taught them. I also introduced them to 'clems', which means balls. I think it's a Geordie phrase, one my father uses. They've got no fucking idea what a Geordie is of course. A lot of them used my words when writing in my book, just as a joke, or wrote about things we'd laughed at during my stay.

One or two of the people who wrote in my book were staff members, but mainly they were my fellow patients – alcoholics, drug addicts, manic depressives, sex addicts, all sorts.

The reference to the Mentoes mints was because I loved them. I'd never come across sugar-free ones before. They were on sale in the

Cottonwood shop. I bought the whole lot – a carton containing something like fifteen packets. I got through about two packets a day, until I finished them. What I didn't know was that they made you fart. So that's why people were writing remarks about farting. I gave some to a girl, and she started farting as well. It was a running joke.

I don't understand why some of them went on about me being rude and obscene. They didn't see nothing, not like the old days, when I was playing football. I'd get drunk, then go around flashing my arse. I never do that sort of thing these days, and I'm sure I didn't do anything rude at Cottonwood. I never showed my cock or my bum. You wouldn't dare anyway, not with sex addicts around!

Did you read that one from the girl, who wrote out the *Oliver* song, 'I'd do anything . . .'? She had arrived very depressed and wouldn't talk to anyone. Instead of talking to her, I sang that song to her – and she immediately started smiling. From then on, every time I met her, she sang the song to me.

The reference to being a transsexual, that was because of my fancy book, 'decorated like a tart's diary', so this bloke said. It was his little joke.

They all gave their addresses or emails, asked me to look them up if I ever get to America again. I have texted a few of them.

I sometimes open the book and read their remarks again. They saw me as a winner and someone who was trying to make them winners. So I have to try not to let myself down, for their sake as well as my own . . .

On the other hand, when I read their comments, I think, 'Who was helping me?' I needed help as well, but all I seemed to do at Cottonwood was give. But then that often seems to be the case with me . . .

———————

Dear Paul

I've loved our chats and sidebar conversations. I have appreciated your insight and humor. I may not have lasted as long here without you . . .

Jen

Chapter Twelve

Paul's fourth session: Back from Cottonwood

John

It's been just over five weeks since I've seen Paul, although he called me a few times while he was away in Arizona, and he seemed to be engaging well with the treatment process and working hard to get better. Today we started by discussing his three-month 'aftercare plan', which details the support Paul needs in order to continue the process begun in the clinic. This includes self-help meetings, counselling, healthy eating and keeping a balance in his work life.

One of the big issues for Paul is that of codependency. There's a link between when he's feeling manipulated or controlled by people and his finding it hard to tell people when to back off, i.e. laying down a healthy boundary. When we suffer from codependency we put other people before ourselves more often and to a greater extent than is balanced – or 'healthy'. At some stage we then feel angry about this – we feel taken advantage of – and this anger may be swallowed down as resentment; it may be acted out in a row or a fight; or it may lead us to use an addictive substance or behaviour. Codependency is therefore a cycle of behaviour that is very destructive.

We began the session by talking about this, and how things had gone generally at Cottonwood.

Paul

The treatment at Cottonwood was good. The first ten days in the clinic, I didn't do much. I did the meetings, the groups, spending two hours with the same eight or nine people each day – that was enough. I felt quite comfortable. It was nice. I could be relaxed and get some of my shit off. I talked about when I got worried when George died. Oh, yeah – I've been asked to say a little bit about George at a memorial dinner. It's nice to be asked to do that. Anyway, so I talked about George, and about being harassed by that photographer, and about the sacking, and feeling harassed by the chairman at Kettering. And, of course, about the drinking.

They said in the clinic I was codependent. Codependency is like not setting rules, not having boundaries.

I like to be a happy and fun person. Easy-going. I've enjoyed my life. I've done things and I hate saying 'No' to anybody. They were laughing in the clinic: I can't say 'No' without saying 'Fuck off'. If someone asks me to do something and I can't do it, instead of saying 'No, I'm really sorry, can I do it another day?', I'll say 'Yeah', and try and squeeze the two things in the one day. Then I'll be tired and then I'll be angry and end up saying 'Fuck off' to someone. They were laughing at us when I talked about it, and kept asking why so many people asked us to do things for them. They couldn't understand it until some English person told them I played professional soccer.

How do I get myself some peace back here? It's difficult. When I wake up I've got to deal with bipolar, alcoholism, OCD, food – all these things before I even walk out of the house. I take a mood stabiliser every morning. My OCD's more under control. I'm not touching things, I'm walking away from them. I'm enjoying myself again. I enjoy sobriety. I try and live for the moment and, if it's a good moment, then great. I've got AA. I'm not going to think to myself that I'm missing football on TV because I'm stuck in a room full of alcoholics, which I have thought in the past. I'm not going to think like that. What I get from AA is, not just to stay sober, but to get confidence back. I realise I'm not the only one with this problem. I'm lucky: I've got football – I mean going to matches – I can write this book about my problems, I can get counselling. But there are people who live on the streets and have to go through what I go through without any money or anywhere to live or anything, and I feel sorry for them. I hope this book will help some of them.

You know, it was a relief being away for Christmas and New Year. I didn't have to be round people who were drinking. Anyone who's an alcoholic and says it's easy being around drinkers at Christmas and New Year – I don't know! But I've got no wish ever to drink. I'm tired of being tired. Never say never, but if I relapsed again I'd have to find a different clinic. It's embarrassing when you get a discount at the clinic! I've been four times.

John

Paul showed me some of his Cottonwood book the previous night, and people had written lovely messages of appreciation for him. He touched people in a deep way – there's something in him that comes alive in those environments, and he gives good feedback to people. Paul doesn't see that side of his character himself. I'd like to stay with this point, so I suggest to Paul he doesn't recognise this caring and insightful person. I ask him if he can appreciate that people mean it when they say these good things about him.

Paul

When people say anything nice to me I push it away because I think there's something nasty round the corner. Maybe because of what the press say about me. The press never give me a chance to start enjoying sobriety. Most people believe what they read. I get scared of taking too much praise. When I played football and I scored a hat-trick or got Man of the Match it was nice, but I got worried that then I'd get followed for the next few days so they could see what I was up to. I got hammered by the press and it's not nice.

So it's true that, for me, it feels like to do well will bring trouble. Every time I had a good tournament or went on holiday to relax, I was getting cameras up my arse. It's a nightmare. It doesn't matter how strong a person you are, mentally and physically, these people do get to you and you can't escape it.

I've been back from the clinic a week. I'm feeling good. But there is pressure. Off-licences, cameras – you know. If you walk into a pub with a friend to get a soft drink, because of what's happened in the past you get paranoid about what might be said, and think some guy in there's a reporter, when in fact he's a really nice guy just minding his own business.

It's sad that the media don't recognise this illness, considering there are so many people dying on the streets in this country because they haven't got any support with it. If I see an alcoholic on the street, I give him a drink and some money. I know some of them haven't got long to live. There's no help for them, so I buy them a drink.

John

I'd like us to think about how Paul can maintain his health in order to work towards his aims for the future.

JM: I think any therapy has to look at trying to find happiness. Keeping in mind what we've discussed about what you want to do – go back into management – the next few months need to be about stability, sobriety, self-care and self-management in order to prepare for that.

PG: I know what I want and I know what I have to do to be happy. I've done it before for two years. I've got to change the people and places around me. I can do that – it's no problem. I'm taking up fishing again. Going to meetings. I don't want to go every day – I'll go every other day. Until I feel secure in myself. The good thing is, if I'm somewhere and I'm not happy I can leave, but when I was drinking I couldn't leave because I had to stay for one more.

JM: It's also crucial that when you're not happy with something, you express it and set boundaries. Talk honestly to me, talk to your friends, family and the people you work with. In the past, because you didn't like letting people down, you ended up in situations that made you angry and resentful and thinking, 'What about me?' I'm worried that if you can't say 'No' to people, that pattern will establish itself again.

PG: It's boundaries, I've got to set boundaries for myself instead of changing my mind at the last second. I've got to stick with my decision. I've said 'Yes' for so long that people aren't used to 'No', and they keep pushing and pushing and then I think, 'Fuck it, I'll do it.'

JM: I know you've done it with me. It's important to say 'No, I can't', and if people are offended, then they'll have to deal with it. There are so many charities and good causes, but together they'll all suck you dry.

PG: I need to have a structure each morning and stick to it and not change it, and if I do that I'll be okay. That's what I've got from the clinic, apart from sobering up. Sometimes I get worried hearing stuff in these clinics, about the effects of drugs and stuff. I remember when I was thirty-five, after I left Burnley, I thought, 'I won't drink but I'll take cocaine.' Now I think, 'But how much damage did that do to me?' And I was only on it for six weeks. What about these people who've been on it for years? They don't realise the damage they've done to themselves.

You have to look at Danniella Westbrook and how courageous she was, she's come forward and told her story. She took cocaine as a social drug and look what happened to her. In the clinic someone spoke about the damage opium can do, and I thought, 'What the fuck's opium? Opium's a perfume for women!' It's good to go to a clinic and find out the facts about addictive drugs. That wasn't the first time I've been a bit naive about drugs. I remember one time, when I was on tour with Newcastle in Holland. Must have been about seventeen or eighteen. A kid comes up to us and says, 'Do you fancy some grass?' I looked at him and I said, 'Are you fucking daft? I'm playing on a field of it, aren't I?' That's how green I was back then!

Every day I say, 'Fuck me, I've put on weight.' I eat more, and then I start training. I love training. But it's like with the fishing. Once I go fishing on a Monday, I'll go Tuesday, Wednesday, Thursday. Same with golf. And once I go to the gym, I'll go every single day. Same with my diet. Having an addictive personality is terrible. Once I put my mind to something, I just stick to that one thing for weeks. That's why people said I was a great trainer, because once I start training I put everything into it. But it gets out of hand. I train every day. I mustn't do that, but I wish I could.

John

Part of Paul's life now is finding a balance. Working the recovery programme and being aware of himself, but not feeling like a victim of it either, and balancing that with having fun, relaxing and training. These are issues that over the last few years have pulled him back towards drinking. It's about setting up a structure that works for him, that he can maintain. And it's tough to have the acceptance to learn to say, 'Yes, I'd like a drink, but no, I know I can't.' I remind Paul that he's managed to do it before.

Paul

I have done it before. Sometimes I did go out and enjoy myself without having a drink. I'd get myself ready, be prepared. Then if the thought came: 'I don't want a Diet Coke, fuck this!', I'd know temptation was coming on. I'd get ready for it. So I got quite comfortable doing it. My structure is, if I'm going out, I'll go to an early AA meeting first or speak to you, Johnny, if I'm feeling I need to.

John

Putting together the right structure and training the mind can be done, and Paul has shown that he can do it.

That 'fuck it' voice has to be watched, because addiction is like a split personality. There are two voices. One says, 'I can have a drink tonight,' and the other says, 'Hang on, no I can't, I'm an alcoholic and I know what having a drink could lead to.' If you don't look after yourself properly and keep balanced, the addictive voice wins — and that's what being an alcoholic is.

Paul

That voice is murder, saying, 'Have a drink, have a drink.' It creeps up on you and won't go away unless you give in to it. But if you have a good habit, a way of working round it, you can fuck it off in a few minutes. If I've relapsed in the past, it's because for three or four days I've had that voice in my head and it wouldn't fuck off because it knew it would have us in the end. Somehow I had lost whatever good habit I had got into before — that managed to get rid of the voice. We were laughing in the clinic about some bloke whose friend got addicted, but they wouldn't give him money or serve him. He just went out on to this airfield and started a jet, flew it until it got to Mexico and ran out of gas, sold it to the mafia for $10,000 when it was worth, like, $10 million, spent the $10,000 in two days and got a boat back. Mad.

I did three or four lines of cocaine one night — during that six-week session — and then bought nine Harley Davidsons. The bloke who delivered them to us checked the house to see if I had loads of mates! I spent over £100,000. Then the next night there I am taking more cocaine.

People ask why you do that mad thing a second time. It's because you're powerless. It's got a grip of you. And I was thirty-five and coming to the end of my career. I really wanted to get fit and have one more season. Not take more cocaine.

John

Paul has mentioned coming to the end of his playing career. Letting go of the past is an important aspect of Paul's life at the moment. We talk about how much letting go he's had to do over the last couple of years. Alcohol, Sheryl and, of course, football — twenty years of his life. That was his identity – that was what he did. He lost the family he had for a while with Sheryl. And he talks about giving up booze as another loss.

Paul

I've got to deal with it the rest of my life. I can't keep battling for the rest of my life. I'll just give in and stop drinking.

The reason I'm doing this book is because I want people to see where I'm coming from, with all these illnesses. I'm actually coming forward and saying, 'Yes, I'm eating too much, I'm codependent . . .' With the co-dependency, this is the first time I've worked on it in the clinic because I've always blanked it, because I knew what it meant – I can't tell people 'No'. I cried my eyes out with it, and I explained to them I'd rather relapse than tell somebody 'No'.

Going to the clinic and getting away from all that is kind of like a holiday. Like a man said in the clinic, 'Taking heroin or cocaine is like a holiday from that voice in your head.'

John

People know that Paul's an extremely generous person, with his time and energy as well as his money. But if he's saying 'Yes' all the time there's no space for himself. That's one reason why he likes being away: the demands on him aren't there in the same way. Practising laying down healthy boundaries and being honest with people is one of the key ways we've been working on Paul's codependency.

We talk again about that 'voice in the head' his friend in the clinic mentioned. It's important to make sure it doesn't get listened to. Paul tells me that voice has gone away for the time being. We end the session by talking about being in the right environment for recovery, where the voice is less likely to pipe up.

PG: That voice has gone out for the time being. I won't go clubbing, I won't put myself in dangerous situations. If there's a match on TV I'll go out and watch it, but that's it.

JM: As you said, it's important to be in the right environment for recovery.

PG: I think for the next few months I've got to be selfish.

JM: That is music to my ears, because of the need to use your time well for yourself. Self-care is so important for you, you don't have to justify it. People will move their arrangements if you're not up to something that day. You can say 'No'.

I can see now, you're thinking about it, the idea of saying 'No' feels difficult, doesn't it?

PG: Yes. I've said 'Yes' all my life. People will think I'm being a bit of a prick.

JM: Well, they might not be used to it, but they will get used to it.

John

It's good seeing Paul back and looking well. He clearly worked hard when he was away and, as well as breaking the very important cycle of drinking, he was able to look at the issue of codependency. He recognises the need to set a structure for himself that works for him. This includes attending self-help support groups and getting regular but moderate exercise.

It's imperative that he has control of his agenda. I've always known how difficult he found setting boundaries with people. This has to change if he's to be happy. We'll be going on to explore where this codependent behaviour originated. It usually stems from our very early relationships with our parents and siblings.

As well as seeing how well Paul has done, I've also been reminded of how delicate he is at the moment. In fact it's normal for anyone returning from treatment to be like this: sensitive, raw and vulnerable. Spending time in a recovery treatment centre can't be compared with anything else. You're turned inside-out – you *have* to be in order for the programme to be beneficial. Therefore it's important that at the moment Paul should be surrounded by people who understand 'where he is at' – those who know what a tough job it is to combat alcoholism and his other, related, conditions.

I don't like to say this but it needs to be said: not everyone makes it. Rehab is a very important stage but it does not guarantee anything – nothing can. As Paul said in the session, many people die of these conditions. We can't count on a happy-ever-after ending. What Paul is dealing with is massive. I was fortunate enough to receive the right support in order to deal with my problems early on in life. There is alcoholism and bipolar disorder in my family and it has caused much pain and anguish. It doesn't go away; all we can do is continue to treat it. Self-awareness, a supportive lifestyle and, for some, the right medication will help. But it takes maintenance and hard work.

Paul will need to work really hard on all of his issues and, as he said, understand that this has to come first. The next few weeks are paramount as he needs to consolidate what he's taken from his time in rehab. We'll be focusing on this over the next few weeks: helping Paul to help himself, helping him understand that now he has more information he needs to put it into practice and to watch out for that old cry of, 'It's not fair.'

With Paul now back from Cottonwood, and having heard what he felt about the treatment he received, it's interesting to look at what they're trying to achieve there, and how they go about it. There are many different types of rehabilitation programme. Most aim to help the addict build a life away from drinking and taking drugs. Behavioural modification programmes examine the underlying reasons for the addicted person leaning towards a life involving dependency on drink and drugs, and aim to change that learned behaviour. The most popular programmes use the 'disease model', which classifies addiction as an illness. The majority of private-treatment programmes in the UK and the USA are based on the Minnesota model of treatment, which is a version of the disease model. This method of treatment was formulated in Minnesota in the 1950s and incorporates the 'Twelve Steps' of Alcoholics Anonymous. The first step says: 'We admitted we were powerless over alcohol, that our lives had become unmanageable.' Minnesota is a very successful model of treatment and has helped millions of people to overcome addiction.

Paul has been in two treatment centres (sometimes referred to as clinics): the Priory Hospital in London, and Cottonwood de Tucson, in the USA; both use the disease concept as the model of treatment.

It's a pretty busy schedule – you may be surprised by how much there is to do. While one or two groups are optional, it's strongly suggested that you attend all sessions. When you arrive you're assigned a focal counsellor, the person who will be working with you in many of the groups and with whom you will be having one-to-one counselling. You will be part of that primary group of around eight to ten people who will be in treatment for many different reasons, ranging from drug addiction, alcoholism, depression and bipolar disorder, to food disorders and codependency. The treatment team decide which group is appropriate for you, taking into consideration many factors.

Cottonwood, like many treatment centres, has a policy of room-sharing. This can be a shock for some people initially, but most actually prefer it as time goes on. The reason for the sharing is to promote interaction and communication at all times. It's easy to isolate yourself, especially during the first few days when you're feeling nervous and unsure of yourself, and sharing helps you to settle in and make contact with others at the centre. Another benefit of sharing is that it's a leveller – no one is more special than anyone else: there is only one class of room. Recovery in treatment centres depends on unity and identification. It doesn't matter what you do or don't do for a job, where you're from, how much money you do or don't have, or what your race or sexuality is. These are important issues in everyday life, but they're not why you are ill, and this will be brought home to you.

During the first few days you'll see several specialists, from psychiatrists to nutritionists. You'll be weighed and have blood taken for many tests. Your physical, mental and emotional states will be assessed and you'll also be treated on all three levels. Most patients need a medical detoxification and this can last up to fourteen days, depending on your addiction. But this doesn't mean that you lie around all day in bed. You're expected to get to work straight away on your first assignment, which is usually a written life story. You will be expected to complete various assignments throughout your stay including drawing out a 'timeline' (see Paul's Path to Recovery in his first book).

The Cottonwood day starts early, with a brief meditation at around 8 a.m., and ends with a look back over the day at 8.30 p.m. There are group therapy sessions that give you the chance to open up and explore some of the issues that have been bothering you throughout life. It's also a time when you can exchange feedback with your peers about everyday events, and find out how they perceive you and you them. This can be invaluable since such opportunities don't normally occur in our day-to-day lives.

There are assignment groups, for which specific time is set aside in a structured way to allow you to share your written work. Each assignment is designed to help you go deeply into a certain area, such as the consequences of your alcoholism on you and your family. As there is a focus on the 'Twelve Step' programme of Alcoholics Anonymous, a typical assignment might be to look at the first three steps and complete some written work about them. There may well be a need to focus on past traumas, such as grief and loss or physical or sexual abuse.

There are also educational lectures and the psycho-dramas that Paul mentioned. It's a non-stop programme: if you're not sharing your own life experiences in a group or a one-to-one session, you'll be listening to someone else's.

Cottonwood has an excellent five-day family programme for the families of all patients. As you come to the end of your stay it's strongly recommended that you invite your loved ones in for the family programme since it's not only helpful for you but extremely educational and supportive for them. However, not all families will be in a position to attend or engage with this process.

Your one-to-one counsellor will help you focus on what you need to work on. Most counselling staff have themselves battled with addiction problems or have experienced some of the traumas you have been through. They are trained to a high level and can spot denial at fifty paces. The relationship between patient and counsellor is key to a successful outcome.

The minimum stay is twenty-eight days, but it's usually suggested that you stay for longer to give yourself the best chance you can. About 25 per cent of patients leaving primary treatment will move on to secondary care for another three to six months. This is what we call 'half-way house'. It's less structured than primary care but allows you to develop your recovery in a safe and supportive environment. The other 75 per cent or so return home, and for these a comprehensive aftercare plan is put together by their counsellors so that when they wake up back in their own beds, they have a plan for how to get on with their new lives.

———————

Dear Paul

Just remember to strip away all that exterior shit. You still are a fucking great guy. I haven't got much to offer but what I have is yours. Call me if you need anything. Much love. Keep it real.

Peter

Chapter Thirteen

Paul takes a break

Paul

After I'd been to Cottonwood, and had a session with Johnny, I decided to have a holiday. I went to Dubai, with Jimmy and my younger sister Lindsay. She's divorced – in fact both my sisters are divorced – and has a little boy called Cameron who came with us. He's great at football. I thought she needed a break. I felt I needed one as well. And of course Jimmy is my best friend, who has always stood by me, so I had to take him too, didn't I?

I enjoyed it, the sun and swimming, but I've come back a bit depressed. It was fucking hard, during those two weeks away. Jimmy and Lindsay were drinking, naturally enough, as it was their holiday. But I couldn't. It got so bad I could hardly talk to them, as I was so down.

Then, when we left, I realised I had put on ten pounds in the two weeks, with sitting around eating all the time, no training or going to the gym. So that made me more depressed.

On the way home, on the plane, I hardly dare say it, I had a drink. For the same old reason. I'm shit scared of flying.

I thought, I can't cut myself off totally for the rest of my life from drinking, not be able to go into bars when Jimmy goes or any of my other friends. What will I do with myself?

Then when I got home, I got a text from Jimmy saying that Bianca (my stepdaughter) had been on TV, a week or so before I got back, slagging me off again – the old so-called abuse story that I'd hit them as kids. I asked him if anything bad had been said and it had, it was nasty. I just wish she and Shel could stop using the name Gascoigne. If they hate me so much, why doesn't she go back to her old surname, or her maiden name? Bianca's real name is Bianca Failes. The way they all keep on using my name I think I'll have to be the one to change. I'll no longer be Gascoigne. That might be the only way round it. I just don't understand it. I was never nasty to the children. I wish they'd move on – why don't they move on? I wouldn't mind if what they were saying was actually true.

I'm fed up anyway being Gazza. I can't keep that up seven days a week. I want to be Paul John Gascoigne.

I know people think I'm a nutcase, but I'm not. I just have violent mood swings, and the rest. And I'm getting better all the time.

The therapy sessions *do* do me good, even if I may relapse and have the odd drink, like on that plane. I might hate the session at the time, but I feel better afterwards. I know I have to get rid of all the shit in my head, get it all off my chest.

For the five days after I got back from Dubai, I didn't answer my phones at all, even though I knew my friends had been ringing and texting me. I was just too depressed. I knew I would just moan at them, give them all the shit in my head. They don't want that. No one wants that.

But now that I've gone and done some gym work and had another session with Johnny, I feel I can talk to my friends, be normal, like. My head feels cleared. I can have jokes and laughs, not make them as depressed as I am.

There's no real cure for alcoholism of course – AA is the best thing. I have this little book I read – *A Day at a Time* – which has little sayings and stories for every day of the year. They're meant to make you feel positive. And they do, for a few moments at least.

I'm bipolar. That's what Johnny calls it. It's called that because you go between two extremes, two opposite poles, all the time. In one state, you're manic, your speech gets all speeded up, you rush around, can't sleep, are full of ideas and excitement. Then you go to the other extreme when you are down and depressed. When you are up, on a high, you have so much energy and ideas, you feel on great form – even if other people don't think so. The flip side is when you go down and get depressed.

They used to call it manic depression. I dunno why they changed it. Bipolar is the new term, that's the one Johnny uses all the time. I suppose it sounds better than manic depression. Being a manic-depressive makes you sound really mad. Being bipolar doesn't sound as bad, does it?

Too much coffee and caffeine can get me on a high, or drinking all those Red Bulls I used to drink. And cocaine could cause it, of course.

I've now given up Red Bull and I know not to have more than two cups of coffee a day and none at all in the evening. I'm also still taking my medication, which has helped. I don't think I'm as bad as I was. Just as I don't think my OCD is as bad, thanks to all the therapy and medications. So, really, alcohol is my biggest problem.

My other problems are a bit easier, so I like to think. Being in that police cell, forced to stay all night in that fucking little cell, did help ease my claustrophobia. I managed to calm myself and got through it. It sounds mad, I know, but thank you, cops.

When I went to a clinic for the very first time, it was a revelation. I had never heard addicts talk before about their addictions. I hadn't realised that people were going through what I was going through. It does help, to hear others. You find out you are not quite as bad as some people. Mind you, it does scare me a bit – when I see the trouble some people are in, the damage they have done to themselves. That does affect me.

A lot of the people at Cottonwood were in a far worse state than me because they had no friends at all, no family, no money. I'm lucky that I have all those things.

They weren't all rich people. A lot of them were on health insurance, taken out a long time ago, perhaps through their work. They didn't have much money themselves. My stay there cost me, let's see, I did get 10 per cent discount as it was my fourth visit. All in all, with flights, the cost probably came to £23,000, which I paid for myself. Good job I'm a best-selling author, ha ha.

When I'm in a clinic, I do find myself not thinking so much about my own problems, because I'm so busy cheering up others. But you do learn to be a bit ruthless. You want to stick with the winners.

On my first visit to Cottonwood, there was an English guy there who greeted me and took me around. 'You'll really love this place,' he said. 'I've been here nine times ...'

I thought, 'Fucking hell. What chance have I got? I'm not coming back here, again. Once will be enough.'

What you need is willpower. You need the willpower to win and, even more important, the willpower to want to win. I think I read that somewhere, in one of my little books ...

I don't know about God. If he's so fantastic, why did he let little Steven die? That thought bugged me for years.

A lot of people who go to clinics do end up finding God, and good luck to them, but it hasn't happened to me. I can't see myself as a Bible-basher.

But I do believe in God. I know I'm shit scared of dying, because I'm probably frightened of hell. He is probably up there, somewhere, watching us all. He must exist. For me to be still alive, it proves there is a God ...

But nah, I've never had any spiritual awakenings. At Cottonwood, that last time, I did have about three hours once when I felt sort of light-headed. I was sitting on this rock, at the edge of the desert, and I suddenly felt at peace. It was actually a bit scary. Then it passed and I forgot about it. Don't know if that was some sort of religious experience. Might just have been the sun ...

About a year ago, up in Newcastle, I had a panic attack one day when I felt really suicidal. At the time I was in Dunston, near Gateshead, where I come from, visiting me mam and dad.

I suddenly felt I needed help – at once – so I knocked on the door of a local vicar's house. I knew a vicar lived there, though I'd never met him or been to his church. When he opened the door, I said, 'I know it's a bit stupid, but can I come in for a chat?' I stayed for an hour. He made me a cup of tea and I told him how I'd felt suicidal. I was much better afterwards.

I do pray, now and again. Just the Lord's Prayer, Our Father and all that. But I don't go searching for him. I don't want to. I don't feel I have to. But you never know, he might search me out one day . . .

Yeah, I do seem to have this nurturing side. I do like helping others, in clinics and elsewhere. That's why I was always an entertainer. I liked to cheer people up, make them laugh.

But at the same time, I know I am a spoiled, selfish, arrogant bastard. All alcoholics are like that. We drink because we are self-centred. We believe we are the centre of our universe. We believe we are God.

I made them laugh once at Cottonwood – I said that God thinks he's Gazza.

It's strange, though. While I know I'm selfish and self-centred, I do have a genuine need to help others. I believe I am a caring person.

'There's no rules for loving and sharing,
But hearts beat faster when someone is caring . . .'

Don't know where I got that from either. A pity I haven't got someone to share things with and to love. I know that's a huge lack in my life and filling it would help me a lot.

But I'd never like to do any proper caring work. I couldn't go from being an addict to being a therapist, the way so many have done. I only like doing it when it's fun, when it just sort of happens, not when it's all planned. When people come my way, I try to do what I can for them.

Hold on, just got a text from my old friend, Archie Knox. He was the assistant manager when I was at Rangers, under Walter Smith. He's always stayed a close friend, helped me and given me advice when I needed it. Oh, he seems to want some help from me now, according to his text . . .

'Dear Gazza, I want to know if you can do me a big favour. I know people are always on at you for favours, but this is important. I am in London at the moment so could you ring me on . . .'

I'd better do it now, see if I can help him. I'll just dial that number.

Oh fucking hell, just listen to this message . . .

'This is Buckingham Palace. You could have received a hoax message asking you to ring this number, in which case hang up. But if you have a valid reason for ringing Buckingham Palace, then please hold on for an operator . . .'

Bloody hell, Archie, bastard. I'll get him back . . . Just like Waddler.

———

Dear Paulie

I loved beating you time and time again in sokky. You are one funny son of a bitch. You made my stay here so much easier and I am thankful I met you. I will never forget your dirty mind.

I hope you continue with your sobriety and good luck in all you do.

I love you ME CLEMS!!!

Claire – one third of Paulie's Angels

Chapter Fourteen

Paul's fifth session: Making links – food, exercise and having to be happy

John

Talking about ourselves in a counselling session is a process. We don't usually get to the crux of the matter straight away. We talk around the subject, test out the sound of what we're saying, then move on to talk about something else for a while. A lot of the issues we talk about link up with each other in some way, but at first we're not conscious of how. We might dart all over the place from topic to topic but we are, in fact, gradually homing in on what's really eating us. The counsellor hopes that, as we talk, both during an individual session and over a number of sessions, we'll begin to recognise the links and get braver about looking into ourselves. And we'll come back to issues we've brought up early on in the session, or in previous sessions, and perhaps look at them in a different light.

It's towards the end of February and Paul came back from his two-week holiday a few days ago. Now he's come in to see me. We spend a long time going over what happened to him while he was away, how it feels for him at the moment, post-holiday and post-clinic, his depression, his food and exercise, and especially his relationships with people and his tendency to isolate. Paul manages to recognise some links between his current behaviour and thought patterns and his early experiences as a child and young adult.

Paul tells me, and I can see, how low he is at the moment. We discuss Paul's medication, and we decide to contact his psychiatrist to talk about reducing the amount he takes so that his mood isn't so depressed. Getting the right kind of medication at the right level can be an on-going process.

Paul tells me about his holiday. After all that work in the clinic, he wanted a break, but he found it much more difficult than he thought he would. He was still raw, having just spent thirty-three days getting himself sober and back together in a safe setting, with daily support. Out there in Dubai, he had no structure and no support at all. He tells me about two occasions on which he drank.

Paul

While I was on holiday with my sister, Cameron and Jimmy, it was tough. Going out there, I was frightened of flying, so I took a brandy. There were rumours in the papers that I was back drinking and I thought, 'I'm never going to win. Every time I go out they're going to say I'm drinking whether I am or not, so I may as well have a drink.' But I didn't drink while I was out there.

It was tough, because in the evenings people were hanging out, chilling out, drinking, and I didn't want to be in that situation. There was a forty-day music ban because one of the princes had died, so I couldn't listen to music to switch off, and that made not drinking harder. I was eating and eating, and then I panicked and started obsessing about putting on too much weight. I really wanted to drink, but I didn't. You said it wasn't a good time to go on holiday, right after coming out of the clinic, and maybe it's true, maybe it wasn't the right time. Sometimes it was okay, and I kept myself busy during the day. I took a boat out with Cameron and we went fishing, and I played around with him in the pool. But then I hurt my neck in the pool, and I panicked and after that I stopped going in the water. I've had so many injuries, I can't get injured again.

I thought if I went there on holiday I'd lose weight quickly. I'd put some pounds on in the clinic. I knew it would be easier to lose weight in the heat, and in England it was -2°C. But it didn't work. While I was there it was a matter of just eating so as not to drink. I didn't drink out there but, on the flight back, I had fear of flying again, and someone said there were going to be bad storms, so I took a tablet and had a couple of drinks to get through it.

When I got back from Dubai, I thought I needed to get properly fit so I went to Champneys. I just wanted to lose weight and feel good. The place is stuck out a little bit in the middle of nowhere and I haven't got my friends around or meetings to go to. But it's good because, when I train, that's when I'm at my happiest. Before I went there I was really depressed and worried.

I was worried about work – not the money, but what I'm going to do with the rest of my life, to keep myself busy. There's stuff I can do at the moment, but there are also certain things I feel uncomfortable doing, such as talks, dinners and travelling. I get embarrassed being paid for doing after-dinner talks as a footballer. You should be doing that in your fifties not in your thirties. But I'm forced to do them in order to pay Sheryl the maintenance for the kids. But something will come up, some football job. In the meantime, I'm just concentrating on doing my counselling and the book. It's nice to do a follow-up to my last book.

I have lost weight. I've lost half a stone in four or five days, but I'm still feeling down. There's a chance of meeting up with Chris Evans. I'd like to, but I don't feel up to seeing people, anyone. I don't know why I'm feeling down.

José Mourinho kindly invited me to Chelsea for a couple of months, to watch the lads training; it's a great opportunity. I could watch the way he works. But I'd be no good like this – feeling low. I could learn a lot from José Mourinho, I know that, but I don't know if I want to come to London or go to Newcastle. I feel lonely. I just feel like I'm battling all the time. Others seem to me to be enjoying themselves, seem happy.

I do feel alone, it doesn't matter how many people I talk to, I still feel it inside. Everyone thinks I'm a happy-go-lucky lad. I come off holiday and try to cheer myself up and then get stepped all over. I was fine until that business with Sheryl's daughter being on telly.

I'm really pushing myself with the training. I wake up, do my training. I'm happy when I've finished it, then after an hour I'm bored and lonely. I have a salad for lunch. I lie there and worry about what I'm going to do in a month's time when I'm fit. I worry about the future. So I look forward to six o'clock when I start training again. Then if there's no football on TV I'm fucked.

When I'm down like this there's nothing I want to do. I just want to lock myself in a room. When the football on the TV finishes, then what am I going to do? I can't go and train again because I'm already killing myself. My moods are terrible at the moment.

Right now, I'm hardly taking any phone calls, I can't be bothered to text anybody. People think I'm blanking them. I'm not, I've just got fuck all to say to them at the moment. And I can't be honest with them, so I say I'm feeling great. If I said to me mates, 'I'm really down at the moment. I need a bit of company, a bit of help,' I know they'd come, but then I think I'd be shit company.

If I started telling people what I'm really feeling they would stop calling me because they'd think, 'He's always down.' I do think they'd care for me – but what could they say?

John

How many times have any of us hidden away at home when we've been feeling down? The thing is, we feel pressure to be on good form when we see people:

JM: I think you've got this view of yourself that people will only accept you if you're on good form or behaving a certain way, and I think you think they won't like you as much or they'll reject you if you're not those things. Is that what you think?

PG: Yeah, of course it is.

JM: I think we've got to challenge that thinking. People will care for you no matter what mood you're in. Everyone suffers from time to time.

PG: Trouble is, I was brought up as a fighter. They get upset when they see us upset because they're not used to seeing us upset.

JM: You hide your feelings a lot. What do you think that does to you – hiding them?

PG: It makes me want to just give in. Thing is, everyone shakes my hand and says they want an autograph, and it's great for me to do things like that, but it's hard. You walk out on Chelsea or Everton football ground, and both sets of fans are cheering, it's great. But two hours later I think, 'I used to have that every week, but I don't have that any more.' I feel like I'm training to get back playing again. But I'm not. I've got depression and mood swings.

JM: Some of your friends, perhaps only a few, do understand what you go through. But a lot of people just know the happy-go-lucky, funny, generous Gazza. Few people know who Paul Gascoigne is.

PG: People haven't ever seen Paul Gascoigne.

JM: I really want to help you with that because that's the next stage in your life.

Paul

Something that's affecting me a lot is not seeing my son. I want to see my son, and I miss him. It hurts. I've got my own family, but I haven't got my son. They say, if you want to speak to him call the house. So I call the house to speak to him, and the next thing I get the lawyer on the phone saying I'm getting done for harassment. I send him cards, texts. I suspect he's not got them. So I sort of give in and think, 'Well, I'll have to wait till he's older.' I'm happy then I'm sad and then I'm all right – my mood swings.

I've been invited to a football club to start learning with the coach, but I'm not ready for that yet. It feels like laziness, but it isn't. I don't like having to be patient. Having to wait for the right time to get on with my life. It's a nightmare. I start thinking negative. I get bored. Sometimes I think positive – come May things will pick up for me – but February, March, April, I have to get through them first.

Thanks to the health farm I keep myself busy. I've got company. There are people there I know. There's lots happening all the time. That's good. I want to get myself fit.

I have had these problems for eighteen years. Some days I deal with them really well and some days it's hard.

The thing with this book, the people that read it are going to be the ones with the same sorts of problems, and they're the ones who are my friends. They understand my illnesses. But only I can pull it round. If I can come through after all of thirty-odd operations, I've got the determination to pull this one round. If I break my leg I've got to get my leg fixed and that's it. This time I feel like I've got to fix about six things. What woman is going to want to be with a guy who's had all these problems?

It's true, I do judge myself for being ill. I can be my own worst enemy. I feel like I'm forced to train really hard. I've only just been back training since Monday. It's Thursday now and I've done seven sessions in three days – and I'm in agony. I have to tell myself to rest – rest tonight and train tomorrow morning, but I feel like I've got to train tonight. I feel like I have to do it because if I don't then I'm going to put on weight. My hips are sore, my calves are sore, my arms are going into cramp all the time because I've started doing weights on them.

John

I've seen Paul punishing himself through rigorous exercise. I ask him about that.

JM: Why are you so hard on yourself?

PG: Fuck knows.

JM: What might it be?

PG: I feel I have to prove to people all the time — I can do this, I can do that. But I've got nothing to prove.

JM: Can you say that again?

PG: I've got nothing to prove.

JM: They're so important, those words. You've proved your abilities beyond the ordinary. People know what you've been capable of. But of course none of us can sustain that level throughout our lives — partly because of our physical bodies. And yet there's that voice somewhere in your head that says, 'I've got to keep proving that I'm okay.' Most people who know you say, 'I wish he'd just relax a bit more, we love him as he is.'

PG: I have to keep proving to the outside world that I'm fine. While really, I *am* fine.

JM: You are fine.

PG: But I have to keep on proving it. You know Archie called me and said, 'What are you doing in the gym? Don't go killing yourself!' Too late Archie — I've already fucking done it!

JM: What would help you slow down a bit? What would help you believe what other people say — 'We love you as you are, you don't have to prove anything any more, you're good enough?'

PG: I wish I could answer that.

JM: We need to work on that, because it's a massive issue for you.

PG: Chris Evans has been in contact with me. I do want to meet up with him — and Danny Baker — but I said I'd see them when I come out of the health farm. It's a shame because I think the world of Chris and Danny. They're great people to be around, but I don't think I am at the moment. I said I'd look after myself this year. I thought last year was a tough battle but I've got another tough battle this year. It's too easy for me to relapse and go back to drinking. They made me look at things other than alcohol in the clinic. Being myself without a drink. The other thing that was worrying me was it was too easy to relapse and go back to drinking.

JM: Treatment gets harder. It's never the same as it was the first time.

PG: You do the detox, then you've got another twenty-four days to get through. I do now have a good support system back here: yourself, my sponsor (a sponsor is a friend in AA who is like a big brother – a mentor and guide), AA meetings. But I don't like other people seeing me upset.

JM: I want you to keep reminding yourself that you judge yourself too harshly. If you're seeing Chris he doesn't have to see Gazza, he wants to see Paul. Danny can be a comedian, but he's not like that all the time, is he?

PG: No, and they'll tell you when *they're* pissed off as well. Chris knows me well enough to know when I'm down. When I've got a miserable face.

JM: So what if you've got a sulk on your face? So what if you're not happy? People will have to deal with it, won't they? How many people do you see who are happy all the time? Can you tell me any?

PG: None.

John

There's a link between Paul's punishing exercise regime coupled with not allowing himself to eat properly, and feeling that he has to prove himself: that he's not good enough as he is. During the remainder of the session we also have a look at where some of his beliefs might have originated. I ask him about his exercise routine now, and whether he got the feeling of always having to fight and battle from his family background.

Paul

I can enjoy half an hour's run but I push myself until I'm exhausted. I do push myself because I've done it all my life, I really don't know any different.

Mum and dad worked really hard to make ends meet, and of course argued a lot because things were so difficult – we had an outside toilet, and a tin bath, you know. I've said it before but that does affect you. I think it's just something that doesn't go away until you let go and I never seem to let go. I carried it on into my football career. I know things will get better, I know they will, I'm confident of that, but I do need to let go.

I was always up to mischief, mucking about – me and my sisters. It's true that that was when I first learned to cheer people up. I just wanted to be in a happy family and we did have great times. Even now I still go back to that accident when I was ten. It still affects me, that young boy dying, seeing his lips move . . . I was looking after him, we only had a quarter of a mile to go to the boys' club, but that happened.

John

I suggest to Paul that the accident and that whole period of his life could be where his problems started. To deal with that kind of trauma at that age takes a lot of help and support.

A lot of us have had difficult childhoods. Things can go wrong in life, and they do. But it's learning how to deal with the situations and accompanying feelings that's key to how we develop as adults. Paul believes he had enough support after that accident, and after the other deaths and situations that occurred while he was growing up.

I suggest to Paul that if such an accident happened to a child of ten today, there would be a lot more awareness about trauma, and the support to go with it. And I ask him if it's right that, because there wasn't the right support, back then when he was ten, he buried something. It was no one's fault, it's not about that, but that was the effect on him.

Paul

I guess there would be much more support nowadays if something like the accident happened to a kid. The support nowadays is fantastic, the number of people in America who see psychiatrists and therapists is phenomenal, whereas we tend more to blank it. Even when I mentioned the OCD in the first book, the amount of letters I got was encouraging. It helped me. And it helped me that a lot of people also had OCD when I went in the clinic.

After the accident I got nervous twitches, made nervous noises, and got kicked out of the classroom for it, because I was making noises and the other kids couldn't concentrate on their work. Noises like clicking or gulping.

Sometimes when I played for Tottenham I got twitches – until I actually watched myself on TV doing it, and then I stopped. Even the smoking is like a nervous thing. I started smoking when I was twenty-nine, and I've thought, maybe I should give that up, but it actually feels like one of the things that calms me down.

I buried loads of stuff when I was young. Had to. My dad was working away in Germany trying to make money to make ends meet, and my mum was left with us four kids, and she had masses of other things on her mind so she couldn't just concentrate on my needs and my support. She had to work, feed us all, keep the house going, look after the other children. So I kept loads of stuff hidden.

And she had to look after my brother when he got into some trouble. He ended up in a care home for a bit. So she had him, me with nervous twitches, and we nearly lost my sister three times. My sister Lindsay got run over by a car and we nearly lost her, she got clipped on her head. Then she got stung by a wasp and the poison nearly went to her heart. Then when she was on a swing in the woods a huge branch snapped and fractured her skull. My mum had all that, and then my sister was leaving school, looking for work, my brother would come home and we'd be arguing, and I had an obsession with the slot machines, and I stole that money from my sister's purse. All stuff like that.

Yeah, it was tough. And I said I was going to support my family for the rest of my life.

John

I ask Paul to say again what he's just told us: that he decided to support his family from then onwards. That was a huge decision to make. He actually made that conscious decision and determined to stick to it. He took responsibility for his family upon his shoulders. I ask him what age he was at that time.

Paul

I was fifteen when I decided I was going to be the one to support my family for the rest of my life. My mum had three jobs: cleaning cars in the morning, cleaning offices in the afternoon, working in the fish shop at night. My dad was in hospital, it was fifty-fifty whether he was going to live or not; my sister was looking for work; and it must have been really hard for my younger sister seeing all of that because she was only seven. Getting into a tin bath in front of the fire, finding wood and newspapers to burn to keep us warm; I saw football as a way of helping them all for the rest of their lives. When I packed in football, it felt like suddenly everyone hated me.

John

Before we move on from this topic, I recap this moment at which Paul made such a big commitment. At fifteen, there were all the stresses he mentioned – the deaths, then soon after that his father's brain tumour, and all of his mother's anxieties about the children. And so he made the decision, at that age, that he wasn't going to let that struggle go on for his family; he was going to become a professional footballer and look after everybody. He seemed to feel that he had to hold it all together. As if he thinks to himself, 'I can't afford to break down, I can't afford to have depression, I can't afford to be myself. I've got to look after this one, look after that one.' That's a pattern that's continued all throughout his life right up until today, and he now has another family to support financially as well.

So, he has massive responsibilities, which contribute to him thinking he's got to keep it all together. And yet what happens sometimes is that he does fall apart because, if he's drinking, he gets anxious and he gets ill and he can't look after everything. It will destroy any of us, this stuff, not because we're not brave or because we don't care or try hard, but because that's what having this illness means.

Paul feels how hard that truth is, and how hard it is to keep going. I think one of the powerful things for Paul about doing this book is that it's given him a chance to go back over everything again, and remind himself about how much he's taken upon himself. And I suggest to him that now it's time for him to concentrate on sorting himself out – that now it's time for Paul to be Paul.

Paul

I need to just drill that into my head.

Sometimes when I played football and played well and got Man of the Match and there were 50,000 people applauding, I still went home sad. It was job done, now back to the real world again. Pleasing others.

It felt like all that applause wasn't really for me. It was me making others happy, but I was still sad. I'd go home and sit in the house and wouldn't go out. Jimmy's a witness to that. He'd say to me, 'Why don't you go out?' It's weird, I know. I felt like all those cheers and everything weren't real, for me anyway. And yet I miss football more than anything because I still love it. There's a massive cloud above my head, and it's just not clearing.

That's the way I am at the moment. The other day I had a workout, and a lovely steam afterwards, and I ended up with this massive headache. What's all that about? It's not normal.

John

The headaches could possibly be linked to the balance of food and exercise. Over-exercising can cause headaches. If you push yourself working out, and then steam, you sweat a lot and sweating takes salt out of the body and can dehydrate you. If you're not drinking enough water and not eating, you're not putting the salts back, and that can cause headaches. I suggest Paul needs to drink lots more water and needs to eat properly, especially while he's training.

Part of the solution at the moment is to say, 'I'm not going to punish myself.' Even Archie – and Paul's mentioned how tough a trainer Archie is – asked Paul what on earth he was up to doing so much in the gym. I ask Paul where he thinks the punishing voice comes from.

Paul

I think it comes from all the operations, saying to myself afterwards, 'I've got to get fit, I've got to get fit.' In 1991 I had a year to get fit at Lazio otherwise I'd be off, so I pushed myself hard. Ever since then, every time I've had an operation I've pushed myself. That's stuck with me for fifteen years.

John

An important thing for us to do is practising and strengthening that voice that says, 'I'm all right at the moment. I don't need to abuse myself or punish myself. I don't have to be together.'

Paul

I don't like being overweight, it takes away my confidence and self-esteem. There's a negative voice that says, 'I'm not good enough, I'm overweight, I'm not confident with people.' If I feel I've let someone down I get depressed. It's when I say to someone I'm going to talk to them tomorrow and I don't, and I leave it a couple of weeks, and by then I'm too embarrassed to contact them. I hate it.

But I can't always be in a good mood, or contact people straight away when they need something. I've got to find a balance. I've done it before, so I know I can do it.

JM: Yes you can. And I'd like to go back to the way you made a decision to support your family financially, as you still do today, and suggest it's your turn now to have some peace. When you train so hard and push yourself so much, are you on some level still trying to please your parents?

PG: They don't expect it.

JM: They don't expect it, exactly.

PG: They don't put us under pressure.

JM: They love you as you are, don't they? They don't want to see you getting stressed and anxious. They both told me that. They just want you to be happy. So can you say to yourself, 'Who am I trying to please? I'm not trying to please my parents and family any more.' And try bringing it back to Paul. Can I get comfortable with Paul, feel all right about Paul? Does that makes sense?

PG: Definitely, yes.

JM: Because you deserve it.

PG: I've done it before so I can do it again, I know I can. I don't feel like it at the moment. I know I'm depressed, and my mood swings are all over the place at the moment, and I need to knock the food and the exercise on the head again.

JM: And obviously keep talking. If you meet up with Chris, can you be yourself? Because the people who care about you, they don't mind what mood you're in.

PG: Hmmm.

JM: They don't. They'd rather see the real you, than see someone pretending that he's fine when they know you're not.

Paul

People have been so good, and I'm lucky like that. Richard and Judy texted me, the amount of help offered is unbelievable, José Mourinho, Alex Ferguson, David Moyes, Paul Jewell, they've all phoned me. Terry Venables. Bobby Robson even called us: 'How are you doing, what are you up to, do you want to come round?' Dave Seaman texted me. Shearer's been fantastic. The help I've got is amazing. Maybe taking some of the help is what's hard.

John

I tell Paul that this is genuine care, these are genuine offers. These are people who don't want anything from him other than just to see him. They have problems too, everybody does. It's all right to be himself with them, he doesn't have to be entertaining.

Of course he doesn't want to see people all the time, and feel overwhelmed, but I think it's important that he just allows a bit more care into his life. And he says he'll take that step, and try it.

We've reached the end of talking for today, and we've looked at his early life. It's as if he felt he couldn't afford to fall apart, he couldn't afford to show his mum and dad that he wasn't well because they couldn't take that pressure at the time. And so he decided he was going to push it down and suppress it, and those noises or tics or the OCD came out. I myself know those noises he talked about, because it's something I used to do, funnily enough. If stresses are stuffed down, the anxiety has to come out, and that's how it sometimes does it.

So he's had to hide that pressure all his life, while he's achieved amazing things on the football pitch. But off it he's an ordinary man who needs the same love and care we all need.

———————————

Dear Paul

It has been such a special time getting to know you. You brighten my day every time I see you. Be strong and stay sober. I'm gonna read your book and if I'm ever on your side of the world, I will visit. Much love

Kerry

Chapter Fifteen

Paul receives some good news

Paul

I've just had some good news from the doc, from my surgeon. He's the one who operated on my neck, after I buggered it practising for that BBC ice-skating show. He now says I can start football training again. I've done ten sessions in the last five days in the gym at Champneys, which is too much really, one a day at this stage would be enough, but that's me. I take everything to excess.

I'm just doing fitness work at the moment, on my body and legs. I can't start actually football training till 15 March, because of my neck. But if all goes well, I can do full football training from 1 May, including heading the ball. I've been very touched because I know that both Alex Ferguson and José Mourinho would let me go and train at their place, if I wanted.

The reason for wanting to get football fit is that I've agreed to play some six-a-sides and some charity games and a testimonial. The testimonial is for Ted McMinn, at Derby. He used to play for them, and Rangers. He got some sort of infection – and lost part of his leg. Terrible. The charity match is on 27 May. A sort of World Cup warm-up – England against Rest of the World, which will have celebs as well as football legends playing. Ha, I wonder which one of those I'm meant to be playing in! It will be at Old Trafford and will be live on ITV. All profits go to UNICEF.

So, I've taken on quite a lot, considering I haven't played for about a year, but I'm looking forward to all the games. It will get me fit again, concentrate my mind and body.

After all that, who knows? I might have another job as a manager or coach lined up by then. But I don't see myself playing football professionally again. Those days are finished. I'll just do it for testimonials or charity. You do get offered expenses but, if it's for a testimonial, I never take any. I pay all my own expenses. If of course it's an event with a TV deal, then you get a fee for that.

After all that, I will have the Big Decision to make – where am I going to live?

I'm still at Champneys, this time at Tring, and it suits me champion, but I know I should start looking for something permanent for myself. Johnny has been on at me, saying I need some stability in my life.

I suppose I should buy something, but I can't decide whether to find something down here, near London, which will be handy for most things, or back up in Newcastle, where I feel at home.

I don't mind living in one small room, where I am now, and having all my stuff shoved in storage. I'm used to it.

If you're in a hotel or health farm, you don't feel lonely, at least I never do. You can walk into the corridor and there will be people to talk to, round the hotel, in the gym or the restaurant.

The thing about hotels and health farms is that if you have to, you can hide inside all the time, yet still be with other people – but the paparazzi can't stake you out. If you have your own house, they get to know it. If there's some stupid story in the papers about you, they'll sit outside your front door all day long, waiting for you to go the pub and get smashed.

David Beckham has gangs of them outside his house in Madrid, all the time.

In hotels, I might go to the bar, and have a Coke, and just talk to anyone who happens to be there. In Dubai on holiday, in our hotel, I went to the bar one afternoon and there was this woman sitting there – reading my book.

'Do you like it?' I says to the woman.

'He's a fucking idiot,' she replies.

'Do you know him?'

'No,' she says.

'Well you do now . . .'

I got up off the bar stool and walked out of the bar.

As I left, I could hear her screaming, 'Ohmygod, Ohmygod . . .'

Another time, one evening when the bar was quite crowded, a bloke nearby had heard my accent and he leans over and asks where I'm from. I told him I was from Newcastle.

'Oh aye,' he says, 'that's Gazzaland, where that fat bastard comes from . . .'

I didn't say who I was, but wound him up for ages. Talking about Gazza and Newcastle and all that stuff. Then another bloke comes over to me and says, 'Hiya Gazza, will you sign an autograph for me?' 'Certainly,' I said, 'no problem.'

The first bloke then turns and stares at me. 'You bastard. You didn't tell me who you was . . .'

My gym work is still going well, in fact I've now just done twenty sessions in the last ten days. I know I said before that was too much – and stupid. It still is, but I'm so desperate to get in shape to play football again. My day revolves round getting fit, that's all I seem to do.

Here at Champneys, I usually get out of bed about 7 a.m. I don't have any breakfast, except a couple of cups of coffee, with no sugar, plus usually two ciggies. Then I'm in the gym from 8.30 till 10. I usually do forty-five minutes on the bike and fifteen minutes on the running machine, or the other way round. I also do 1,000 sit-ups and I lift 400 light weights.

I don't usually have any lunch or dinner, perhaps a bagel salad in the evening if I haven't had one at lunch time. So no, I'm not eating much. Just one bagel salad a day.

In the old days when I woke up I would say to myself, 'I want a drink. I want a drink.' Now when I wake up, my mind is racing all the time with the words, 'What shall I eat today, what shall I eat today?'

It's become my major obsession, just when I thought I was getting to grips with all the others. It's worse than thinking about the alcohol. Since Cottonwood, that's been under control. Now I seem to be in the grip of this eating disorder. I've been doing my best to eat sensibly but I can't eat three meals a day, as Johnny suggested I do when we first got together again, this time round.

What's happened is that I'm scared to put on weight and so, in order to be fit for the football games, I don't eat, and yet I know I'm losing too much weight – but I can't help myself. And I want to lose more while I'm here.

I've had eating disorders since I was seventeen. I remember when Jack Charlton arrived as manager at Newcastle he could see I was overweight, with all the junk food I was eating.

He calls me into his office and asks me, 'How long's your contract?'

'I've got another two years, boss.'

'Two weeks,' he says. 'You've got only two weeks to get that weight off, or you're out . . .'

I was in a panic. Went running all the time, wearing plastic bags, trying to sweat it off. I did some training with Brendan Foster which helped.

That was about when I first learned to stick my fingers down my throat, after I'd stuffed my face with burgers and sweets and stuff.

That's how it all began. Since then, for the last twenty years, I've usually had some sort of fight with eating.

I've told Johnny all about it and he's trying to train my mind to fight it. I managed it for quite long spells, but now I'm back on it again.

I've battled against OCD and now I don't really worry about that as much, but I can't conquer the food problem. There was a girl at Cottonwood with the same problem. She was in tears all the time. I suppose it's a bit like anorexia. You get it into your mind that you're getting fat and you're scared to eat.

After my first lot of training in the morning, I come back and sit in my room, watch TV, do nothing really. At the moment I'm not answering the phone or texts from my friends. I feel too depressed, too obsessed. I don't want to moan on to them.

Yesterday I did think of having a salt beef bagel at lunch time. I really fancied one, then I decided not to. I do have some salted popcorn in my room. I eat a bit of that, now and again. It's fat free, so that's something. I always check the fat content before I eat anything.

Of course people still think I'm a fat bastard, stuffing my face with burgers all the time. I was in this minicab the other day and picked up the driver's paper, the *Daily Star* I think it was. The headline said 'Kebabs can kill you'.

Before I'd read the first paragraph, I turned to the driver.

'I bet I'm in this story,' I said to him. And I was.

They dragged out that 1998 story when I got photographed having a late-night kebab with Chris Evans and then later I got chucked out of the England squad by Glenn Hoddle. Eight years later, and that story is still following me around. And it's balls. I haven't eaten that sort of stuff for years. I wish I could.

I do my second training session between about 5 and 7 p.m., and then just go to my room again, watch TV, do nothing really, perhaps read one of my therapy books, thought for the day, that sort of stuff.

Two days a week I come to London. I see Johnny at his place.

I've been reading all these stories in the newspapers about obesity, about these overweight kids we're now breeding. I do feel sorry for them. They're in a far worse state than I am – as they're getting no help. I'd love to try and help them, to work with some of these obese kids, try and get them to eat fat-free stuff, as I do. But of course I wouldn't want them to go the other way and get obsessed.

I keep telling myself I can't eat, because if I eat, I'll get fat and won't be able to train. I just can't break that cycle of thought. Then I tell myself it will just be till the end of this summer. Once the various testimonial and charity games are over, I'll sit down and look at the rest of my life. I'll try to work out a different routine, not worrying about being fit to play football. I'll get involved in other things and try to have some stability in my life. But in the meantime, that's all I think about – not putting on weight and getting fit.

During those two years not drinking, I would often have a glass of wine sitting on the table in front of me. It was to prove to myself I was strong enough not to touch it.

Now that I'm obsessed by food, I'm doing a similar thing. I've just been to Tesco and bought some tomato ketchup and some bags of sweets, six packets of jelly babies and other stuff. I have them in my room, here at Champneys.

I know they're here, in the room, tempting me, but chances are that when I leave, they'll still be here, lying in the wardrobe. I've done that sort of thing for years – been in hotels or apartments and, when I've gone, there's loads of stuff left behind. I feel good, leaving them behind. I've risen to the challenge and won. Of course sometimes I don't – then I stick my fingers down me throat.

I know what I should be doing. No need to tell me. I should not be worried about my weight at all. I know I'm not remotely fat. I'm probably at least a stone underweight. I should be striking the right balance between a decent healthy diet, with three meals a day, while keeping fit. I know all fucking that. But I can't do it. I wake up each day and my head is going round, 'What shall I eat today, what shall I eat today?'

I wish I could jump out of bed every day and shout, 'I'm really happy, I'm really happy today.' That's what I'd like to do. But I'm so down at the moment. There's no fucking chance.

Then I tell myself how well I've done. My OCD is under control. I'm not drinking. I just have to hang on in there and, after this summer, I'll have beaten the eating problems. I'm sure I will. I'll then have started a new life, I dunno what or where, but things will be much better. That's what keeps me going . . .

Who can say what causes all this shit? Search me. I dunno. But I don't blame it on my parents, or my family.

Me mam and dad, they were never alcoholics, nor my sisters, so I didn't get it from them. None of my family has OCD. None of them had twitches or the sort of mood swings I have. You can't blame it on them and say that was the way I was born, inheriting stuff through their genes or whatever.

It was events that did it, that's what caused it all, like when Steven got killed. That still hangs over me, all these years later. It's always coming out when I'm talking to Johnny. I know I've mentioned it a few times already in this book. That was what led to the twitches. No question. I never had them till he got killed. That's a fact.

Then I became a crowd pleaser, always acting the fool, being the joker. I don't know why. I just did. I wanted to amuse people.

When I started football, that's when my real obsessions took over. I was obsessed by football, just as for a time I was obsessed by tennis. I loved tennis. I did think I might like to be a professional tennis player, till football took over.

I often think what would have happened if I'd played pro tennis not pro football. In tennis, you are on your own, one against one, you don't rely on anyone else. In football, you have to be part of the team. In tennis, I might not have become the team joker. I would just have been playing on my own, not in a group.

But for football, would I be in a worse state today? Who knows? My stealing might have got worse and I could have ended up in jail – but then again I did anyway, if just for one night.

I might not have become an alcoholic because I wouldn't have had the money I earned in football to pay for drink. I would have been like most of my mates from Newcastle, not able to go out for a drink till the weekend. By the time I was drinking heavily, when I was at Rangers, I had the money to drink every evening, and all afternoon after training, which for a time I did.

Playing football gave me a lot of money, so I've been able to pay for a lot of help with my problems – for clinics and therapy that I couldn't have afforded otherwise. On the other hand, I might not have needed all that help. I do think the pressures of football made things worse.

I often think it would have been nice to have had an ordinary job, been an ordinary person, unknown, able to go anywhere without being pestered.

God knows what my ordinary job would have been. A carpenter, perhaps. I quite liked woodwork at school. But perhaps I might not have managed a trade. I'd have been like my dad, a hodman, a labourer. Yeah, perhaps that's it – I would have ended up like me dad, doing odd jobs. Nothing wrong with that. He's a good lad. And he's not an alcoholic or a manic-depressive and he's certainly not got an eating disorder.

But, all things considered, I am glad I became a footballer. I did enjoy it. I might be more relaxed today, as a person, if I'd done something ordinary, but no, I don't regret what I did. I'm glad what happened to me happened to me.

———————

Paul my love

Oh Paul. If I wasn't single I'd marry you! No but seriously you have meant and will always mean so much to me and I wish I could have shown you that. Unfortunately I'm terrible when it comes to that kind of stuff.

You made me laugh when I could think of nothing but crying – and there have been few in my life who could do that.

I wish you would stick around forever, then life would never go wrong again. You were the first person here that asked me how I was doing and made me stop dead in my tracks because I just know that you were genuine and you actually wanted to know. You have changed so many lives here for the better.

Now I know what kind of guy I need to marry. Hee hee. Enough of this mushy crap. I wish you all the love and best of luck in your recovery. You deserve it . . .

Rachel

Chapter Sixteen

Paul's sixth session: Where to go next?

John

Paul and I start by following up on the previous session, when we talked about his daily structure, and about what it was like for him when he first arrived back in the UK after Cottonwood. Paul had said that he probably shouldn't have gone on holiday at the time he did, given the stage he was at, and in some ways against the advice he was given, bearing in mind how vulnerable he was.

Paul looked at the treatment options available after the thirty-three-day stay in Cottonwood. One of these being to go into three months of aftercare in California. This would form a transition stage, involving support and a period of adjustment to ease people back into a more normal routine. But this wasn't really an option for Paul: he felt he needed to get back home.

We need to talk about what's going to help Paul, first of all in the short term, to continue moving in the right direction – to keep his feet on the ground, keep talking about how he's feeling rather than reacting to it, carry on taking the right steps to keep himself on track, and continue to monitor himself. A key factor is to maintain balance – not to overdo anything: not caffeine, sugar, exercise, isolating himself, obsessive thinking, or anything that can tip him off balance.

One of the suggestions I keep making is that Paul goes back to AA meetings again. These are good for support, for being with people who totally understand without having to have anything explained to them. Attending such self-help groups is good for discipline, routine and for building up a strong inner reserve so that, when temptation strikes, you're ready for it. They're also a very powerful way of dealing with the 'addict' inside, which will so often emerge in a different way, like food or gambling, if the feelings aren't dealt with. When he's in Newcastle, there are a lot of the old temptations around such as Paul's old drinking friends and haunts. Although there are AA meetings in Newcastle, it's not so likely that he'll go to them because he's got so many other distractions.

Paul

When I've been in a clinic just a week, I know exactly what I need to do to live well and be happy; and then, when I come out of the clinic, for the first month I'm really down. When I'm in the clinic I'm away from everybody who's part of my everyday life. Instead I'm with people who understand. Unfortunately, there aren't many people in this country who do understand.

I want to do the training. I've trained for the last twenty years. I don't want to stop now and I don't want to be uncomfortable in my body and in my clothes. I want a good level of fitness, because that's when I feel good; I don't want to turn forty and be out of shape.

I could go and join a football club for training any time I want, and that's a nice feeling. To feel still wanted. I'm in two minds: I don't know whether to live in London or stay in Newcastle.

I hate the traffic in London, and I can't go fly fishing, though there are some lakes outside London, but you have to travel. I think, 'What else is there in London apart from meetings?' There are great meetings, but I don't want to live my life somewhere just because there are great AA meetings!

I know living in London would only be a short-term thing; you've suggested I move to London for three to six months because of the support here, but I'm in a situation where, when I wake up, I must take my medication, and if I forget, it ruins my training in the gym. Instead of enjoying it, I'm thinking, 'I've got to take my meds' and if I've got to go to a meeting, then as well as remembering the meds, I've got to remember to go to a meeting. I have to keep saying to myself, 'Don't forget the meds, don't forget the meeting', and that's what's really pissing me off. Having to remember all this stuff.

I do hate feeling trapped and being told what to do. I know I've said it before, but it really gets to me. I started off getting told what to do by my mum and dad, then my teachers, then captains and coaches, then managers, and now you, my counsellor, are telling me what to do, to come to live in London, and it's pissing me off.

I know the meetings are important. It's true I have got good friends in London, and I could live with them. I like the people in London, but it's an expensive place to live. I haven't got a job at the moment. I could bring my stuff down, and if I hate it I could go back. If a job comes up, a manager's job up north, then I'll go up there. I can head Gateshead Football Club, I've been offered it, but owning a football club doesn't appeal to me.

John

I tell Paul the reason I recommend meetings is that in a group environment where people do understand him, and identify with his problems, he thrives, he can be honest. There's something dangerous for him about not being free to say how he's really feeling. In meetings he's more free to talk about his 'demons'.

One of the problems for Paul is that he's so popular with people, and of course there's a tradition in self-help groups for people to be friendly and give you their phone numbers. With Paul, he might get overwhelmed by this and, as we've discussed before, he can have problems saying 'No' to people. In the past, he's taken too many phone numbers and felt obliged to ring them all. He felt he was constantly on the phone, which of course isn't the idea – those people are there to call only if and when you really need to, there's no pressure. It's another area of learning for Paul about his recovery.

Paul talks a lot about getting his body into shape through training. The work of recovering is about training the mind, just like training the body. This is something Paul resists. He really needs to make the decision to train his mind, just as he trains his body, because his mind can work against him. That part of his mind that is associated with 'the addict' works against him. It might say, for example: 'I have to be a stone lighter than this in order to feel okay about myself, so I have to train three times a day, once isn't good enough; I have to lose x stone in y days; why shouldn't I have a drink, just one – everyone else is having one.'

In order to guard against this 'addict head', I suggest Paul builds into his structure one or two meetings a week, a counselling session, regular nutritious meals and a meeting with a nutritionist to get expert advice. There are also many other things that can be built into his routine to strengthen his mind, that build up that good feeling and resistance. In order to overcome that 'addict thinking', when it comes, we need to have built up a store of good beliefs about ourselves, and a strong sense of identity that's separate from the addict side of our natures. If Paul doesn't feel good about himself, he's more likely to work extra hard physically and push himself so that he gets out of balance, and possibly even gets injured.

I want to get over to Paul the concept of detaching from the thoughts and feelings that are not going to benefit him. He can have the thought but he doesn't have to act on it. It takes a lot of work, but it's possible to observe the thought, and feel the feeling and acknowledge it, but at the same time to have a strong self that doesn't attach to the thought and doesn't act on it. For example, you might feel terrible because someone has rejected you, and it sends you back into a kind of depressed thinking. You might then get some other bad news, and just feel you can't take any more and your life's unbearable. You feel lonely, rejected, angry and you can't see a way out. At that moment you might feel like the pressure in your head is too much, and you want some relief. You want to act on this feeling by going to the gym/pub/cake shop/bookies so that you're feeling something completely different. You might be thinking of sabotaging everything – resigning from your job, walking out on your partner, getting the next bus home and never speaking to your friend again.

Alternatively, you might take a deep breath, phone someone or arrange to meet someone, and talk it all through. You might have a walk or run in the fresh air, do a yoga class, even some meditation – all of these things will put the actual problems you have into perspective. Getting someone else's take on a situation can be of invaluable help. If you have these good habits already in place, they come naturally at a time of crisis, and you have that store to draw on.

At the moment Paul runs with the feeling that he's not going to be satisfied until he gets to a certain weight, and that he won't be satisfied until he's achieved various external goals. I wonder if he could now prioritise his mind health over what he believes his body ought to be.

Paul

I've proved that saying, that an addict alone is in bad company, because that's when I relapse. I'm definitely an alcoholic, no doubt there.

An addict always wants something right now. What I'm worried about is putting on weight. I put on weight in Dubai, and at the clinic before then. And now I want to lose it all. I've done nine sessions in four days and I'm still worried about my weight. It's got me down again. I looked at myself this morning and I thought I'd lost a little bit more weight. I did two sessions yesterday, I ate last night, I drank two bottles of water, some Diet Coke and ate some popcorn. I think to myself, 'Good, I've lost weight.' I went to the gym, then I looked in the mirror again. It's an absolutely stupid thing I'm doing. I think to myself, 'What am I doing this for?' If I gave it time the weight would drop off me. I am getting into good condition, but it's really stability I need.

Once I get into the routine of going to meetings I'll be fine. I won't go to meetings until I've got the weight down. Another two weeks and I'll have done it. I've been on a crash diet and I want it straight away – that's me.

I feel like if I come to London I'm keeping other people happy, but what about me? If I knew there was work in London I'd move down here straight away. I don't fancy sitting on the train all the time commuting back and forth. People might think that I'm mad to put anything else before my health and my life. If London's going to help me get well, then why don't I move here now? Once I get my weight back to the way I want it, I'll speak to Chris, and maybe stay with him for a month in London and go to meetings.

I should have carried on with my coaching badges. Some people say the badges are so hard, but I didn't find it that hard, so maybe I should go back to that. I want to go back to football when I come out of the health farm. I'm really looking forward to the games in May.

It's true that the training is partly me trying to alter my mood. Training changes the way I feel, it lifts my mood. But I've got to the stage where I've gone past that, and now if I don't train, my mood that day will be shit. Look what happened last time I pushed myself after I'd damaged my neck skating. Once I'd been given the okay to train I went at it too hard. And I ended up in hospital. I'm a little bit worried about that, but it's still not stopping me.

It's true about starving yourself being like a withdrawal. I went from eating everything in the clinic and on holiday to now eating almost nothing, so it's like a withdrawal.

John

We need to keep finding ways for Paul to approach his obsession with weight, food and training. We talk a lot about structure, meaning the structure of how we use our time, both daily and weekly. I ask Paul about structure, how it's worked for him, and to take us back over some of the progress he's made with alcohol, OCD, bipolar and panic attacks, and to look at how it could help with food and exercise.

Paul

I know that a daily structure will help. A meal plan for each day, how many meals I'll have, roughly what time, when I'm going to train and for how long, and when I'm going to do a meeting. That's what's suggested. A food disorder needs structure to overcome it.

I've proved that structure works because I've done a plan with my OCD. You practise shutting doors and just walking away, and I have managed it. It's funny, as soon as I mention 'OCD' I look at the door. I just did it then. I can actually shut the door and walk away now. I don't touch light switches five times, I just turn the light off. I also used to have to switch off sockets in the wall. Say in a hotel corridor. I'd walk all the way up and down the corridors, checking to see if the socket was switched to 'on' but with no plug in. I had to have them all switched off. At Champneys I practised walking up and down the corridor there. Not switching off the sockets.

What's helped with the OCD is being distracted by other things, the medication a bit, and just practising good habits and structure. The thing with OCD is you think if you don't touch something three times or whatever, or if you don't do something or other, something bad will happen. I used to think it would mean I'd get run over.

I now think, 'Fuck it, if it happens, it happens.' I tried it – not switching lights off, or whatever. After a few days of nothing bad happening, I learned. I used to have to sleep with the light on. Now I sleep with it off. Being at Cottonwood helped with that. Having to share a room. So I've trained myself. It's like smoking. You can ask for help, and take stuff for it, but only you can conquer it. I've taught myself with the OCD.

When I hurt my neck I asked, 'Will I be paralysed?' The doctor said, 'Today you could walk across the road and get run over or you could have an operation and get better, you just don't know what's going to happen' – and that's true. I don't know what's going to happen and I can't control what happens, so I try to deal with things in that way now.

One thing, though. I'm okay on the arranging things in the right order, or light switches, opening and closing doors or switching off wall sockets – all that stuff. It doesn't get to me any more. Well, not much anyway. Not as much as it used to. But I don't know if I'll ever conquer OCD as regards numbers. Bad numbers and numbers that can protect me. It started when I was young. It was number five. Everything had to have five in it. I'd look at things five times. I'd touch things five times. I tried to get off five, and then it was thirteen. That was the bad number. And now it's number nine. And if I have loads of caffeine it really starts to get on top of us. If I let it. It doesn't take much caffeine – coffee, Coke, Red Bull – to trigger my anxiety. And that's when the superstitions about bad things happening if I don't do the numbers thing gets worse. I am trying to cut the coffee and other stuff down.

Doing all the right things and following the right habits does work to keep the OCD at bay. It's my own fault when I do the wrong things.

And compared to two years ago, I've managed to sort out the panic attacks as well. The more I talked about them the more I got conscious of them and I knew what was going on. When I came out of the clinic two years ago and got one of my first panic attacks I didn't know what was going on, so I spoke to someone else who suffered from them, and asked them how their panic attacks came on. And I realised that this was what it was, and I dealt with it. The very first time I had one was when I was in hospital, back when I had that injury at Lazio, and I didn't have a clue what it was. But now I take a few deep breaths, switch myself off, calm myself down. At first they lasted fifteen minutes but now they would only last about two minutes because I know how to deal with them.

Now, about the mood swings. Bipolar was diagnosed officially by the psychiatrist in Arizona. It's another condition that co-exists with my alcoholism. I say in the groups, 'I'm Paul, I'm an alcoholic.' When people ask how I am, I try not to say the word 'fine' – Fucked-up Insecure Neurotic and Emotional. In the clinic someone would be fine one minute and then saying nothing the next minute. One night there, I was lying in bed reading the *Big Book* (the main AA book, written by its founders Bill W and Dr Bob), and I got scared, thinking if Bill hadn't met Bob and set up AA, I think I'd be dead.

The programme's simple. Very simple. Being an alcoholic messes with my brain chemistry and sets up mood swings. I'm not the only one with bipolar and I'm not the only one who's an alcoholic. Thing is, I've got the bottle to tell everyone. Maybe I think my life would be a lot better if I could tell people when I'm sad. Best thing is to get on the phone to someone who cares for you.

I used to walk to the streets and stop and say hello to people, even when I was down, and stop for a photo, when I wasn't in the mood. I need to control the mood swings and learn to say 'No' in a nice way instead of saying, 'Yeah I'll do it,' and then getting fucked up. I need to say, 'No, sorry I can't do it – can I do it next week?' But I don't want people to not ask us to do things – I'll always do something that I'm asked to do, always. I've always done that. I can control mood swings if I use the right methods but, if I don't, my mood's shit and the only thing that'll cheer us up – instead of speaking to someone and telling them how I feel – is if I just go and have a few drinks, and then the next day I'm in a worse mood.

With bipolar, when I get a high or manic mood, I just want to spend money. I don't spend that much now, but I've got that beautiful Harley Davidson stuck in a garage in Jesmond. I can only use it in this country two months of the year because of the weather, and I'm sitting here with a spanking new Hot Rod.

I was on Red Bull once and I'd started to go into a high. It wasn't funny at the time because it was like being on cocaine. I ran outside – I was meeting a girl – but someone must have polished up the glass door, and I smashed straight into it. I was going so fast I just didn't see it. I went out to meet this girl with a tissue on my bleeding nose, and an ice pack on my eye, and said, 'Hello, nice to meet you.' The date didn't go that well.

It sounds daft now, but at the time it felt horrible.

It's hard not to have regrets. I regret so much what happened to young Steven, I regret that I didn't see as much of my son, Regan, as I'd like to, as I'd love to. Sometimes I think about the transfers I made. Also, if only I'd invested some money.

I have loads of regrets. The only great times I've had have been playing football. Or times with my mates. And now I don't have the football. All these thoughts are going through my head all the time.

John

I believe it's important for Paul to be occupied, when he's up to it and when he's ready to do something, because the nature of the addictive personality is that, when left idle or turned inward, it goes into self-destruct. Only the alcoholic can take responsibility for his condition. No one else can do it for us, for when we close that door at night, we have to be able to be the one who says, 'I'm all right, and I'm going to be all right.' We have to be the one who can deal with the negative thoughts.

Paul

I try my best to deal with those negative thoughts. I do need to start doing something soon, some kind of work or training. This Chelsea thing: I told Archie about the offer, and he said, 'You can't turn that down.' I'll get back in touch with José Mourinho when I come out of the health farm. I've had a fantastic offer from Alex Ferguson as well. I'm lucky. But the way I feel at the moment, I can't do anything until I get fit. I've just got to keep searching. I've searched before and found what I wanted. It's a case of digging deep. Maybe I have to get through the next couple of months to find what I want.

I couldn't have been more honest than I was in my last book, but this new book is more detailed and more me. This is what's really going on in

my life. In me heed. The first one was more football and career. I've come
to terms with everything I've got, I'm facing things and I'm a hell of a lot
better person than I was ten years ago and a hell of a lot better person than
I was three years ago. I've been told I've got this problem and that problem,
and I've had to deal with all of that.

The only problem I haven't really conquered to the best of my ability
is the drink, and that's me being honest. It's hard when you get invited to
parties and premieres. How am I going to sit there for three hours? I'm not
always the best at making conversation, unless I talk about football.

I'm always caring about somebody else – that's one of my problems.
I don't really care about myself as much as I really should do.

I mustn't cut myself off from people. I can't wait for this book to come
out. I might be a bit embarrassed, I don't want people thinking I'm a fruit
cake – because I'm not – but I have to deal with all these things I talked
about in our last session, and the life I've had. And I want people to know
the truth, not just rubbish they read in the papers.

It is stressful being followed everywhere, dealing with my ex-family,
the press, photographers, just totally watched 24/7. That's the type of world
I live in. I have to be careful about everything I say and everything I do.
Even now, three years after packing in football.

I went to watch a movie – this happened twice – and, when I came out
of the cinema to get some popcorn, my sister called us up saying it said in
the press I was staggering all over the place, in and out of the cinema. All I
was doing was getting popcorn, and it said in the press I was getting drunk.
I sometimes think I just can't live in this country. Maybe I could go off to
Australia for a year or something. I don't like living like this.

John

As we go on with the sessions in this book, we see it is like a jigsaw, and we're
putting together all the pieces, and seeing how they fit. There are different
aspects of Paul's illness, and they're connected with each other, and we're
gradually piecing together what those connections are.

One of the things that's so difficult for Paul at the moment is beginning this new chapter in his life, and not knowing where it'll take him. Everything he's known since being a very young adult has changed. He's got to get used to still having the pressure from the media, but without drinking, and without the fans singing his name every week. He is missing aspects of his old life, the 'good times' in the Premiership, but those have come to an end. Paul needs to grieve for this and then move on. Of course this is easier said than done. He is letting go of so much at the moment, and sometimes when I sit in a session with him, my feelings, or what we call in the field my counter-transference, swing from frustration to admiration. But I'm very aware that he's clearly doing the best he can with what he has at the moment, and one of the main ingredients of success is patience, on the part of the counsellor as well as the client.

We've gone back over where he's up to with various aspects of his illnesses: he's made good progress with managing his anxiety in terms of the OCD and the panic attacks. He even used his own version of cognitive therapy on himself to deal with claustrophobia, and realised that he could get himself through the experience of being locked up alone in a tiny space.

Paul knows what to do about alcohol, but he's struggling with accepting that meetings or some kind of regular support group needs to be part of his life. He's also grappling with the exercise and food. His self-esteem is dependent on his fitness and weight, and he doesn't want to lose control of that. That's good, but it's important for anyone that they lose weight slowly and with the advice of a qualified nutritionist. Dieting can deplete vital nutrients from the body, for example zinc. Deficiencies in these nutrients can in turn affect appetite and help contribute to food disorders. Balance is what we're aiming for, and that is achieved through hard work and discipline. There's still plenty of work for us to do.

———————

Dear Pauly

As you have been told many times, you are the most humorous son of a bitch I have ever met – not to mention rude, crude, obnoxious and insane individual I have ever met. Yet your honest, humble way of dealing with the issues of not only yourself but of others makes you one of the most sincere kind-hearted blokes I have known. You befriended me as I did you, knowing not a thing about each other or our pasts - that to me was the foundation of one hell of a good time during a very difficult time (at least for me).

Julie

Chapter Seventeen

Paul's seventh session: Letter to Paul

John

It's now the beginning of March. What I'd like to do in the session today is summarise the issues Paul and I have covered over the past few months, and look at a range of solutions. I'm going to read Paul a letter that I've put together, outlining some of the events of the past, linking them up with behaviour patterns, and looking at some steps he can take to keep well. This is loosely based on the Cognitive Analytical Therapy (CAT) tool called a 'reformulation letter'. Although we haven't had the opportunity to do a full sixteen-week CAT course, I use CAT in my approach with Paul, and this letter should help us concentrate on behaviour patterns, or what CAT calls 'procedures'.

> Dear Paul
> I'm writing this letter to acknowledge the main issues we have covered in our sessions together. This is in order to help you recognise your

problematic areas and to help you take more control of your life.

It has now been several months since you came back to see me for help. This time there was an added aspect to our relationship – 'to write a book'. It was clear that in order for us to do that, you needed to get back to basics again if you were to give yourself any chance of tackling the many issues that have been getting in the way of your happiness. These things have been affecting you for most of your life. These are the issues I have outlined below, and over the next few weeks we will be working on them specifically.

Ever since you were a young child there has been pressure on you to perform. You were a sensitive boy and seemed to 'tune in' to what others were feeling. You are the second eldest of four children. You grew up in a stressful home environment where money was hard to come by, and this meant that your parents were under great pressure to work, in order to feed and clothe you. Your father would have to travel abroad to find work and this meant that your mother was left to look after the four of you and go out to work. You shared with me that she had three jobs at one stage. She, like you, is sensitive and, I feel, has an anxious nature. You related well to your brother and sisters but, because of the many pressures, your brother Carl was put in a care home because he misbehaved. That was difficult for you to cope with.

You liked school and always wanted to be first in everything you did, especially sport. Outside of school you were always on the move and would attend a boys' club most days of the week. The joining age for that club was nine, but your father pretended you were older than you were and got you in from the age of seven. Despite the age difference you were able to compete with and often beat the other children at most sports. It was as if the club was a safe place for you and gave you an outlet – a channel for your stress and anxieties. It soon became clear that you had a natural talent for football.

Aged ten, you and the younger brother of a friend were out at the shops when he ran on to a road and was killed by a car. You held him as he died. That trauma heightened the already sensitive side of your character and you began to stammer and have physical tics. It was at this stage you began to be superstitious about certain numbers.

Your mother did what she could to help with these problems and your father took you to see a psychiatrist but you report this did not work, because he just made you play with sand. After one visit your father felt that it was a waste of time, so you never returned to those sessions. Clearly, there was not enough support to help you through that difficult period and you were left to deal with it as best you could – even today you feel responsible for that accident.

When you were about fourteen, your father was very unwell, and had a series of operations to deal with a brain tumour. One time he had an attack and you thought he was going to die right in front of you – another trauma, another time alone. His operations also meant that he could no longer go out to work, and this meant more stress at home. Sometimes this stress would boil over and your parents would argue and occasionally have physical fights, especially when alcohol was consumed. They would frequently separate.

It is no wonder that as you got older you took on the role of provider. This combined with the existing role of the 'funny guy': the one that made everyone else happy and okay. Aged fourteen, you knew you would become a successful footballer, and started practising your autograph. The praise and attention that you had always received from football increased, you were now achieving great things in your home town, and became a 'local hero'. What a relief – a way out of that old lifestyle – freedom! But not for you. You have shared with me over the past few months that instead of feeling better you felt worse. You loved playing football, but the rest of it got to you. There were lots of conditions attached. As well as the pressure to perform you had to lose weight. You had always been a little overweight but this was no longer acceptable. You were threatened with the sack if you did not lose weight. This was the start of another dysfunctional pattern, bingeing, purging and not eating. A pattern that would last till today.

It seemed that the external expectations of others, i.e. your family, friends, supporters and the media, were affecting you internally and you were struggling to cope. You did not have the right type of psychology to keep up with the changes. Football, the very thing that had supported and helped you, now seemed to be adding more problems. It's likely this is when your depression started.

Over the next few years, these pressures were magnified as you became more successful. You met your wife and had your son Regan. You were happy for a time but, due to arguments and pressure on you to perform, you would regularly separate. Yet more disruption.

Over a four-year period you progressed from local to national hero. The whole football world now knew of you. Your obsessive compulsive disorder went up and down depending on your anxiety level. So too did the food disorder. And there was now another problematic pattern emerging: your drinking pattern. Alcohol helped you relax and, to a degree, cope with the many stresses. But you could not drink like others did. You would lose control and this eventually brought you to your knees and you ended up in a clinic. You were told that you had the physiology (brain chemistry) of an alcoholic and that you had to abstain from alcohol.

Despite not liking that advice, you stayed sober for six months, but then started drinking again. On the football pitch you would still perform well but you were getting frustrated. You had been dropped from the England squad, your marriage was over and you were now in the newspapers for more negative things than positive. It was as if the adoration you had received for years was now turning into criticism: you were being portrayed as a failure. You felt betrayed, angry and misunderstood.

From that time to now you have been determined to carry on, to go forward and show that you are still that winner, that hero. You have been back into treatment for your alcoholism and bipolar disorder, but you still won't give up. It is no surprise that you now struggle to look after yourself – you were never shown how to.

I feel that in order for you to move forward in your life we should concentrate on the following areas:

1. To stay focused on your sobriety by attending AA meetings and following the programme as suggested. Never mind what you read in the papers – AA is a safe place. There are many people in your position who attend. This consistency will give you more control over your life and help you stay in touch with your sober friends.

2. Pay daily attention to your eating habits and stick to a food plan. We can do this plan together, but I suggest you sit down with a nutritionist and get that expert advice. Your food disorder needs special attention at the moment, and by not addressing it you are abusing your body. It may help to re-read some of the books that you have found helpful in the past.

3. Exercise is good for you – in moderation. I am going to suggest that you swap one gym session every other day for a meditation session. Being still and learning to relax will help you concentrate and feel better, and help you detach from your thoughts.

4. Write a daily journal at the end of the day, focusing on your moods. How you have felt that day, what things have affected your moods and what you might be worried about. This will help you focus on any signs of depression, or spot early signs of becoming manic. You should also note if there have been any panic attacks or signs of OCD.

5. Remember to say 'No'. It is your life, and people will only listen when you are clear with them. Don't blame anyone else and don't become a victim. You are a powerful man who is kind and considerate but who has needs, gets tired and needs rest – so stand up for yourself. Stop looking for other people to tell you that you are okay. You have proved that you are a success. You are good enough as you are. Learn to be yourself, Paul John Gascoigne.

You are already achieving some of the above but I believe you need to do it all. Over our next sessions we will be looking at how well you were able to achieve these goals. It is important that you ask your friends or me for help in achieving these aims. You are not responsible for your illness but you are responsible for your recovery.

Johnny

Paul

I think that letter gives a quick overview of my life, from being born to now. It sums it up quite well really. How it all actually did creep up on us.

In my village there were a lot of homes like mine. It wasn't unusual. It was quite normal, my home. But, like it said in the letter, the other boys were left alone to get on with it at the age of seventeen. I wasn't, I went to play for Newcastle. So I had to deal with the press and I wasn't ready for it. They really hammer you and put you down. I'd had quite a tough upbringing, and I just really couldn't understand why they wanted to put me down.

Unless you've got these problems, you're not going to understand what I'm going through. When people ask questions, as an outsider looking in, it's complicated for them because they don't get it. People think, 'He's been into treatment a few times now, what's up?' But it's not resetting a broken leg. People think, 'Why isn't he fixed now – he's been to hospital, what's the matter?'

No, there's people who've been to rehab nine times – more. I don't want to be in and out of clinics, but I'm not going to promise I'll never go back again, because I said that last time. I promised Bryan Robson. I said, 'I promise, I promise, I'll never touch drink again.' But I did. At the clinic they showed the damage drugs do to your brain, and that put the shits up me, it really did.

People say, 'How are you Paul?' 'Yeah, I'm all right at the moment,' I say, 'I'm writing a new book.' And I tell them the truth about my problems, and that it's not a problem if I stay on top of everything. Of course I'm always going to have the pressure on us, things are going to come down hard on us, my ex-wife and the kids, all of it. I'll have the worries I've always had. I'd like to see my son. That's sad. That is sad.

But I think, 'I'm lucky.' Gary McAllister's wife's just passed away with cancer and I just think, 'How lucky am I?' I've been thinking about him, and wanting to text him. They were a lovely couple, and she passed away at such a young age. I really want to go to the funeral. For me going to a funeral – it brings back a lot of sad, bad memories.

A letter like this makes you look back a bit at your life. I've been asked this question since I was nineteen: 'If you weren't a footballer, what would you be?' Thing is, I was a footballer, and that's it. I don't think, 'I could have been this or done that.' People say, 'Do you have any regrets?' Yeah, course I have fucking regrets. Why I make the most of the good times is because I know there are always going to be bad times round the corner. Whenever I had a good time I probably went over the top. But I wouldn't change me life. Yeah, I'd love to change all the fucking things I've got – these problems – but the fact is I have them and that's it. I've got to get over them. And challenge them on a daily basis, a day at a time.

Last week I was really down and I didn't want to do the counselling session. Unfortunately I have got these problems, and sometimes it's embarrassing for us talking about them. Last week I was really fed up, but this week's better. And I'm not far off the weight I want to be.

I've had a decent week. I hope it continues. These sessions are hard. It takes some time to recover from one. Sometimes I go to the gym and run it off. If there's traffic, it takes almost two hours to get back, and my thoughts are going round me head while I sit in the traffic. I don't want to talk to anyone or see anyone. I just have to be alone with it. I won't make arrangements to meet anyone for two days afterwards. In some ways I was looking for a fix, doing this book, but there isn't a quick fix. I thought, 'I'm going to come out of this really, really well, and I won't have any more panic attacks, no more alcohol, no more this or that.' But I'm taking it seriously. If I fuck about with these illnesses then they'll come back.

I remember getting a cry for help when I was doing me last book signing. I hardly put any of this stuff about my problems in me last book, but I still got people coming up to us and asking us stuff. I remember even ringing you, Johnny, about someone who asked me to call his house that night, who was depressed.

I had a phone call today from someone who started laughing, and he said, 'I've just been diagnosed with bipolar,' and he was on lithium. We both just laughed, because we knew. And that's a way forward for me a bit, being able to laugh about it.

My emotions are up and down. I'll tell you something, and this is absolutely ridiculous. I was watching football on TV, this guy scored a goal, and he was totally over the moon. The light on his face, his whole expression and everything, was just amazing, he was that happy. And I had a lump in me throat seeing it. I couldn't believe it, it wasn't even a team I particularly like. Any happiness I see at the moment, I get a lump in me throat. And I think, 'Where's that coming from? What the fuck's all that about?' I think it's getting in touch with my emotions again, that's the way I look at it.

I think a lot about what I'm going to do. There's loads of stuff I can do for charity. Stuff all over the world. But I have to wait till I've put me own house in order, then I can get into doing stuff like that again.

I loved being a manager and I loved working with Paul Davis. I thoroughly enjoyed it. The week before it was all over we won 4–1 in the Cup. Then, at the end, I had the most disastrous three days. We talk in the sessions about saying 'No'. And I said 'No' to that chairman. He wanted to do things at the club I didn't agree with. I said 'No', and it didn't work, he didn't like it. So for me, saying 'No' backfired on us. But I don't regret holding my own, because he doesn't know football like I do. I wouldn't say anything more about him, because I wouldn't do that. But I'm still glad I said 'No'.

What I've been thinking is, if I want to be a manager I can't just keep talking about it, I've got to do something about it. I've got to finish me badges, and get me next manager's job and take it by the scruff of the neck. I really think football's the only thing for me. I've got to start ringing people and listening to their advice. All these managers, they worked their nuts off to get where they are. They watch eight matches every weekend, searching

for players. They work really hard, never stop. I really want to give management a go, grab it by the horns.

I think, 'Fucking hell, why did I pack in football?' When I was at Rangers
I used to stay behind and train on me own, so I wouldn't go out drinking with
me mates, and Walter Smith spotted it and he knew why I stayed in the gym
till 4 p.m. And Walter helped us, as lots of other managers would or the
PFA. If a player asks for the help.

There isn't enough knowledge about drink for kids. I don't like the taste
of alcohol, but I drank it for the feeling. Now what chance have our kids got
if we're bringing out alco-pops, which taste sweet, so you haven't got even
the taste to put you off when you're a kid?

I saw a friend who goes to meetings this week, and she was really nice
and invited me for a coffee, and I appreciated that. She's absolutely living
evidence and proof that the programme of meetings can work. And she's got
lots of work, she's extremely successful. She's famous, and she tells people
she's an alcoholic. I can see that can happen for me, it's a possibility, if I can
put the amount of effort into it that I put into the gym.

I have got to stay on top of things. I try and look at the things I can
do. I do keep a journal and write things down. Well, I try to. I've been a bit
slack recently. These things will come when I'm ready. Diving into stuff's
not good. I dived into the training when I got back from holiday in Dubai.
And the Boston thing, China, Kettering, I dived into them. It wasn't to be.
It's a learning process for me.

I'd like to go to a men's group, where you see it's okay to vent your
feelings in front of other blokes. They told me there's a good AA and a good
NA (Narcotics Anonymous) men's meeting near where I live. A lot of people
go to both fellowships because NA covers all drugs – and alcohol counts as
a drug. And so do painkillers. I know if I take any type of painkillers, sleepers,
or drink, it does not help. I know that for a fact now, it makes it worse and
worse and worse.

I'll take it easier with the gym, go in at 9.30 and again at 5.30, and have
a steam and try and relax. Not getting up so early. I need to give meself time
out, and relax. I was going to come to London earlier, have a nice cup of

coffee and just relax. But what stopped us was the gym. It's a shame because I'm in a beautiful health farm, but I can't relax because of doing the gym. Steve and his girlfriend invited us for dinner, and I said, 'Oh, I'll be all right, thanks,' because I can't relax. Steve's a good guy and he loves his football. Arsenal fan. Really nice guy to be with. If you can't relax in a health farm, where the fuck can you relax?

Last week I was in therapy on Wednesday and Thursday, and after it took two days to chill out. And then here I am back in the session again. It's hard, but now that I'm coming here I'm glad I'm coming. I look forward to the sessions now.

That was a good letter for me to look at, and for other people to see what happened to me. From where I was very early on in my life, to where I am now. What I've had to try and cope with, to the best of me knowledge. But the skills I had weren't fantastic apart from football. I'll never play in the Premiership again, the FA Cup again, the World Cup again, but I will be able to play football. I know, I've had my time in the spotlight, but you can still play football. I can get over these illnesses if I stay doing the right thing and stay on top of it, and I can have a good life. There's proof out there, there are people who've done it and gone on to achieve things. I've met them, I've mixed with them, I've drunk with them – tea and coffee of course. I have seen living proof that it does work, and that's not just with the alcohol, it's everything that I've got. You can get out of it. I want to put that letter in the book.

The thing that matters more than everything is self-belief, confidence. Getting that back. I've got to remember about codependency. And letting go. Letting go's a big one. What helps me with letting go is Step One – like, I'm powerless over saying 'Yes'. I'm not going to be like Alan Sugar, saying 'NO!' But I need to be able to be who I am. And accept who I am. This is my personality. This is my personality sober. This is me having the balls to come out and say this stuff; if I can do it then I hope that it'll help others.

I've had a decent week, I don't know what it's going to be like next week, I really don't, but I'm staying in the moment. I looked forward to coming to this session. I'm happier with everything that's going on. I'm enjoying the day, I'm enjoying the session. I hope, now I'm nearing forty, I can have some time to enjoy some of my life.

John

Paul's speaking with so much clarity. It sounds like he knows what he wants, and he knows he can achieve it. He also knows it's going to be tough and there'll be days when he wants to throw in the towel.

He's taking responsibility for his part in things, which is all any of us can do. He's learning from the past, but trying not to regret it. He's been doing a lot of intense therapy, and a lot of thinking in between, and facing things.

We've talked about separating ourselves from the punishing thoughts. Paul mentioned applying the principles of the AA Step One – powerlessness – to his codependency, and we can do the same with the 'addict' when we say, 'I'm powerless over these thoughts.' So we stop trying to argue with them and engage with them – what we do is detach from them. We can learn to ignore thoughts that aren't real; for example, we might think that before we can relax we've got to do something by a certain time. These thoughts happen so often that we believe them, and the only thing we can do is to give into them. Like the alcohol craving that goes on so long that in the end we think, 'Fuck it, I'll just have a drink to get it out of the way.' Our own thinking tells us to do something that's actually bad for us. What on earth is that about? Put like that, doesn't it sound incredible? Why would my own head tell me I've got to do something that's bad for me, and dress it up in such a way that I think it'll be good for me? That's addiction.

A film that brilliantly portrays the concept of separating from a part of one's mind is Ron Howard's *A Beautiful Mind*, based on the book by Sylvia Nasar. The problem's obviously different, in that John Nash hallucinates, but the principle's the same. He learns that his mind sometimes tells him things and shows him things that aren't real. He teaches himself how to separate from that part of his mind, to recognise it, acknowledge it – even make friends with it – but not to believe it.

Dear Paul

You've been a true fuckin' mate. Stay true and stay honest to yourself. Keep letting the gas out. Farting keeps you sober. Thanks for all the laughs and wisdom. Keep in touch and stay sober.

Tony

Chapter Eighteen

Paul looks back on pigeon shooting and Jimmy shaving

Paul

Johnny's letter was good, full of stuff going over my life. I know it all, of course, as I've lived it, but it was interesting to read. In fact it was quite powerful. It was as if I'd written the letter myself, to myself. It reminds me where I've come from, what I've been through.

Then there's the five areas I have to concentrate on. That first one, about going to AA meetings, I know all that, been told it all before. I have gone to them over many years, but now and again, when I relapse, I don't go to them for a long time, when I know I should.

When I wake up in the morning, I hate the idea of my first thought being, 'Now, should I go to an AA meeting today?' What sort of fucking life is that? When I'm lying in bed, thinking about that, wondering how can I fit it in, I'll then think, 'What the fuck, I might as well buy a bottle of whisky today and get drunk.'

His remark about it being a 'safe' place. Yeah, it is. It's rare for people to stitch you up at AA meetings and sell a story to the papers. So that doesn't worry me – it's just waking up and realising I should go to AA. That's what I hate. Wake up, go to an AA meeting – if I'm doing that every fucking day I'll be like a robot.

His second point, about sticking to a food plan, I know all that as well. The trouble is I feel bloated all the time, when I know I'm not. It's just how I feel, in my head as well as my body. I often feel like eating a bar of chocolate, then I think, 'If I do that, I'll have to eat nothing for two days.'

I've seen a nutritionist before. I know what's what, what I should eat and not eat, but I think I've got a different metabolism to other people. I do watch what I eat, keep fatty stuff under control, but I hate doing it. It makes me depressed, the fact that I have to think about what I eat.

I know I should eat little and often, that makes sense. Johnny has given me a diet programme I should follow. I know it's all down to me. I've been given all the help and advice, but what happens is that I don't feel right with my body. I can feel this stomach now, and it feels bloated. I've got too much flesh round there. I want to get it off, because I want to be fit and thin for these games coming up.

It's another obsession I've got myself into. Most of the old ones are gone, but I seem stuck with this eating disorder. I just hope after this summer it will be all gone.

In his third point, he suggests I exercise in moderation – but I never do anything in moderation. When I was playing, I was the hardest and longest trainer – because I took it to extremes.

In theory, this should be a perfect place for relaxing, where I still am now, at Champneys, in a health farm. Steve, the owner, said to me the other day that I should really be relaxed, living here, but I'm not. It's not the environment, the place, because that's brilliant. It's me. Living with me, that's what makes me not relaxed. I still have all these demons running around in my head, battering at my brain to get out.

For twenty years, since I first became a footballer, people have been telling me to relax. It hasn't worked yet.

Point four is about keeping a journal. I did do one in Cottonwood, but

I haven't written anything for over a month. I'm in this cycle of training all day. I don't have time or the energy to write things down. When I'm not in the gym, I'm resting, waiting to go for the next session.

He's been on at me for some time about saying 'No' to people, which is his fifth point. I do try to say 'No', quickly, in a nice way, which I know is the best thing to do. But I find it so hard.

It's just happened again. Someone has asked me to play in a charity five-a-side. I know I can't play on the date they want, as my neck won't be ready in time, according to my surgeon. But instead of saying that, I didn't want to let them down. So I said, 'Yeah I'd love to, but we'll have to wait and see how my neck goes.' Yet I know it won't be right in time. Now they'll come back. It's all going round in my head now, festering away, wondering why I didn't say 'No' straight out. Stupid, or what?

So, all Johnny's suggestions are good. Can't argue with any of them. The hard bit is doing them. I'm so impatient, that's another of my problems. I can't wait. I'm rushing things now, to get fit, overdoing it, instead of slowly, patiently building myself up.

If I did do all these suggested things, it would be like starting a new life. I'd have to break the pattern of this life, the one I'm now in.

I think I'd find that just too hard. I certainly couldn't do it in a month.

Anyway, I will try. At least I'll bear them in mind and try eventually to work my way through them . . .

One of the things Johnny agrees with in that letter is that I haven't had an easy life. What has always pissed me off is people, even good friends of mine, who will say, 'Gazza you're looking well,' when I know I'm not. Then, if they realise I'm down, they say, 'You'll get over it,' which pisses me off even more.

They don't seem to understand or appreciate my situation. They just try to cheer me up, as if that will help, as if that will solve things. So it's nice when a therapist who is properly trained, and has had some of the personal problems I have had, tells you, 'Yeah, it hasn't been easy for you.' He's been there. And come through it. Those are the sorts of people I can relate to.

It's funny how I have the willpower to go to the gym twice a day but I don't seem to have it for other things. I don't understand it myself. I feel mentally drained at the moment. It's been a hard two weeks. I've done twenty gym sessions in twelve days. Yeah, I'm counting. I've been doing my first one at seven in the morning, instead of nearer ten, which means I'm hanging around, waiting for my next one, so I then I think I'll just fit another in.

I'm still speaking to nobody who calls me, except Jimmy or me dad.

Today I'm feeling a bit better. No I haven't started on any of Johnny's suggestions, but I feel quite cheerful, well almost cheerful. I've been concentrating my mind on this summer, when this cycle of fixation on training will be over, wondering what I should do next. It will be a chance to start a new life, so that could be exciting, well, at least interesting, if only I can think what this new life will be. The trouble is, I left school with no qualifications. I wasn't stupid, and could easily have passed more exams. I just couldn't be bothered. Once football seemed a possibility, I couldn't be arsed with anything else.

Now, twenty years later, it's as if I'm leaving school today, this moment, and I have to decide what I'm going to do, not just for a few weeks or years, but the rest of my life.

I've got to find something I enjoy, then I can put everything into it. So I sit and think of the things I enjoy, and football always comes out top.

But I do honestly think I'm getting better, so that makes me feel a bit cheerful. I can cope with my depressions more than I could.

One of the things they teach you in the clinics is what they call the tools – and I do believe I have enough tools now. Whether I use them or not, that's up to me.

I haven't had a panic attack for a while. I see them coming on, recognise the signs, mainly thanks to Johnny, and I can deflect them. You just have to do the obvious things, going for a walk, reading my *Day to Day* book for a few pages, or I put a film on the telly and watch it.

It was wonderful when I first spoke to Johnny about the attacks – he knew exactly what I meant. When I'd told other people, like Jimmy or my dad, they didn't understand. When I said to Johnny that I had a pain here, or I feel dizzy, that I was worried a panic attack was coming on, Johnny knew at once what I was going through. Jimmy or my dad would say, 'Don't worry, you'll be all right,' and that just made me more anxious, speeded up the panic attack.

It was such a relief to know it wasn't just me, that I wasn't imagining, that it wasn't unique to me. He let me see I wasn't alone. These things happen to people. That was so comforting.

So I am trying to relax and clear my head of negative thoughts, which is what I'm always being told is best.

When all this training is over, I will take up some of the hobbies I used to have, like fishing. I love fishing. I used to do it a lot. It was perfect for taking my mind off football. At most clubs I've been at, I've always managed to find a place to go fishing – even if it was catching the goldfish in the hotel's ornamental pond! Yeah, done that. At the moment, though, it's too cold, and I haven't got the time, with the training.

I also like shooting and hope to take that up again. When I first came to London and moved out into the country (firstly in a hotel and then in my own house for a while, in Essex), I always had a gun, just a 2.2 rifle which I kept in the boot of the car and shot at things, even if it was just Jimmy's fat arse.

One day the groundsman at Spurs was moaning on because of the pigeons on the pitch, eating all the seeds. I said I'd sort them. I got out my gun and fired a few shots so that frightened them. But there was one big fat pigeon I just couldn't scare away. Every time I got within shooting range, it flew off. It was taking the piss, this pigeon, so I thought I've just got to have it.

It seemed to disappear for a while then I noticed it had got up on top of the East Stand, where they have the golden cockerel on top. This was the old East Stand, before they rebuilt it. At the very top there was a TV platform with an open window. The pigeon was sitting on the open window, looking down and laughing at me, the bastard.

I climbed all the way up the stairs in the East Stand and eventually reached the entrance to the TV gantry. It was boarded up, as it was derelict and no one was supposed to enter.

The pigeon was still there, looking down on the pitch, wondering where I was. I was just fifteen feet away. I thought I'll just move one pace nearer, then I won't miss it. I took one more step – and I went right through the floor. I hadn't realised the floorboards were rotted.

I must have fallen about fifteen feet, bruising all my side and my legs. It was a Tuesday and I wondered if I'd be fit for Saturday. Venables did see the bruises next day at training. He asked what happened. 'A fucking pigeon did it,' I told him. But I was okay in time. Never did get that bastard pigeon though.

I was very close to Terry Venables's dad, Fred, a great character, who lived near the hotel I was living in, in Essex. There was a pub right next to his house that I used to go to, then pop round to see Fred.

I was with him one day, in his back garden, and I heard a noise which I thought was a pheasant in the field behind his house. He said, 'Yeah, it is a pheasant, but don't bloody touch it.' He looked upon it as his pet pheasant, which he'd been watching for about ten years. I said, 'Don't worry, I won't.'

I love pheasants, shooting them and eating them, and this looked a really juicy one. I thought if I get it, then in three days' time, when it's been hung, I'll get the hotel chef to cook it for me.

Next day, I checked Fred was not at home and got into the field. I chased this pheasant for about an hour – and eventually I shot it. I shoved it in my game bag and was just jumping back into Fred's garden – when he reappeared.

'What's in that bag?' he says.

'Nothing,' I said.

Now Fred was as crafty as his son Terry.

'I can see a feather sticking out.'

I don't think he had seen a feather, but he had guessed what I'd done and caught me out, so I admitted it.

'I'm telling Terry,' he said. I took him to the pub and we had a few pints and some games of darts. The pheasant tasted brilliant, but I wish I hadn't done it. Fred had liked his pet so much. Don't know why I did it. Selfish. Fred was a great bloke. I did miss him when he passed away.

I don't do such daft things any more, which makes me worry if perhaps I'll become boring, that people will find me boring, no longer the entertainer, the daft lad, daft as a brush.

One thing about my drinking days was that I did have some laughs. And not always when I was drunk. I generally did have some funny times. These days I don't do stupid, silly things. Haven't done so for at least three years. The laughs seems to have disappeared from my life.

I remember once with Jimmy, when we were up in Scotland, staying in this hotel, and a friend gave me some morphine tablets. They were in sachets, sort of like sherbet dabs.

Me and Jimmy went to the bar and I said, 'Let's have a drink and we'll each put a sherbet in our drinks, see what happens.' We ordered a couple of Bacardi Breezers and put a sherbet in each. After fifteen minutes, we both felt so nice, so relaxed.

I said to Jimmy, 'Do you think it's working?' and, as I said it, he suddenly slumps over the bar. But he comes to, looks around, and I say let's have an Aftershock. That's another drink. When he's not looking, I put another sherbet in his, but not mine. We ended up having about five Bacardi Breezers each. By this time, he's out of it, but feeling great. The morphine had made him feel happy, numbed his senses.

I managed to get him up to his room – which wasn't easy, he's a big lad you know – and he just collapsed on a couch. He's not much fun, so I was thinking, 'What am I gonna do now? I know, I'll do some shaving.'

I got out a razor and shaved half his hair off. Then I shaved off his eyebrows. I did his chest hairs as well. I found a black pen, the sort you use for signing photographs for fans. It's like a marker pen. Very hard to wipe off. On his forehead I wrote NUFC and then on his naked, hairless chest I wrote FAT BASTARD. Just for good measure, I found a coloured pen and coloured in his ears and nose.

I was pissing myself laughing, he looked so fucking funny. He was dead to the world of course, with no idea what I'd been doing to him.

I went to my room and fell asleep. First thing in the morning, I rang Jimmy. He was still asleep, so I woke him up. I could imagine him grunting and swearing, trying to find the phone. I'd stationed a mirror near the phone, so I knew when he answered he'd see himself.

I asked him how he was and he started to say, 'Eee that was a good night . . .' and then he goes 'NOOOOOOOO! You Bastard! . . .'

I could hear him screaming and swearing from further down the corridor.

When he got back to Newcastle, he sat for three days in a bath before the writing on his chest began to fade. But of course his head and eyebrows were still bare.

A delivery man arrived at his door with a parcel. He took one look at Jimmy and burst out laughing. 'Can I go and get my mate in the van and let him see you . . .?'

'Go on then,' says Jimmy. In the end, half the street was coming knocking at Jimmy's door, asking to see him. They all stood there, pissing themselves.

The first time I did that trick was to a hotel manager, very responsible man, always wore a suit. He was manager of a Swallow Hotel I stayed at when I first moved to Spurs and we became good friends.

When I moved to Rome, with Lazio, I had this big villa, so I invited him to come and stay with me. He was a great guy, good fun. I took him out on the town and got him well pissed.

When we got back to my place, he slumped on a couch and began singing some soppy song about 'I'm in love.' Then he fell asleep. While he slept, I shaved his head, leaving just a little bit at the back.

Next morning when he woke up, he went mad and I could hear him shouting as he ran round the house. 'Gascoigne, I'm going to kill you. How can I go back to work now?' I was hiding in his bedroom wardrobe at the time, waiting for him to wake up and see himself.

He stayed on another three days, but his hair hadn't grown at all. So

I said, 'Tell you what, I'll shave all your head this time, leave nothing at the back. It'll then just look as if you'd had a skinhead.' So I shaved it all off – but unbeknown to him, with the razor, I made a little cross on the top of his head. When he left to go home, he looked from the back like a hot cross bun . . .

Those tricks still make me smile, but I never do anything like that now.

Johnny's diet sheet that he gave me, strangely enough, does not contain pheasant. Here's what Johnny suggests, which of course I will try to follow, eventually . . .

John's food guide for Paul

Seeing a qualified nutritionist, and having a hair analysis done, is the best approach to getting the right nutritional advice. They'll recommend what you eat, and prescribe supplements based on what you're lacking.

Until then, here's a guide loosely based on the very healthy eating programme they follow at Champneys, Paul's regular haunt. There, the correct types of food – wholefoods, slow-burn carbohydrates, pulses and seeds, fresh fish and plenty of fruit and vegetables – are readily available with fantastic choices.

For food disorders, it is recommended to avoid sugar, processed foods, white flour, and fast-burn carbohydrates. So that means no white bread or pasta, potatoes or white rice – choose brown bread, wholewheat pasta and brown rice instead. Here's a list of the 'good' foods versus the 'trigger' foods that are more likely to make you want to binge.

Breakfast
Fresh fruit, natural yoghurt
Gluten-free muesli with unsweetened soya milk and pumpkin, sunflower and sesame seeds
Lightly boiled egg or a kipper

Avoid:
• White bread/toast, pastries
• Jam
• Fried foods

Lunch/Dinner

The lentil dishes, the short-grain brown rice, tofu, fish dishes, salads and stews are all excellent.

Fruit – give yourself a good selection, and natural live yoghurt (live yoghurt contains the 'good' bacteria which will need replacing after illness or dieting).

Avoid:
• Fried products (except fried fish)
• Vinegar/salt/sugar/ketchup added to food
• White pasta or other refined wheat products such as pizza
• Crisps/sweets/cakes/biscuits

Drinks: Stick to water. If you want tea or coffee, limit it to one or two cups a day, without sugar, and replace the others with herb tea such as peppermint. Avoid at all costs fizzy and diet drinks containing added colour, sugar, caffeine, aspartame or saccharine.

Sugar and processed starch are 'trigger' foods, which set off a craving for more. These foods are empty calories, not satisfactory to the body, so we eat and eat them trying to fill up that need for goodness which our body is telling us about.

However, if you eat enough fish and secondary proteins (beans/pulses/nuts/seeds/tofu), you will not feel hungry – you will feel satisfied but your stomach will not feel full or bloated. You will feel *good* – full of energy but still light and not full up.

Dear Paul

You're so real, so kind, so full of energy – a real pleasure.

You've added real joy to my stay here, laughs by the sack full (no, not your sacks . . .).

May your journey continue to be as successful and safe as it's been so far. Loads of love.

Col

XXXX

Chapter Nineteen

Paul's eighth session: The punishing voice

John

We all have internal voices, which we don't always notice. Individuals with addiction problems, depression and low self-esteem often have a louder than usual critical voice. This is programmed in at an early age and can often lead to approval-seeking and negative thinking. By the time we reach adulthood, we don't really know whose approval we're striving for, since the original task masters (parents or guardians) are long forgotten, left behind in childhood. We might look for someone to please – our boss, our partner, the public – but the real critic is inside ourselves. Although this punishing voice may now only be inside the mind, it's incredibly powerful, and has huge expectations of the addicted person. Even perfection isn't good enough, so that we push and push ourselves to succeed at work, or at sport, in the gym, with a diet, or whatever else it might be, striving for that approval we never got.

Today I aim to encourage Paul to recognise this voice, where it comes from, what it's saying to him at the moment – and that he doesn't have to listen to it. Paul starts the session by telling me what his state of mind is at this time.

Paul

I'm nearly at the end of my three weeks here at Champneys and I've been averaging two training sessions a day. That's what I'm aiming at. For my time here. Forty-two sessions in total. And I've nearly lost the stone I was hoping to when I arrived. I feel a bit better that way. My fitness is coming back.

John

We now track back to when Paul was a child at home. I ask what he remembers about his anxiety in those days, and what was driving it.

Paul

I was anxious as a kid, but only anxious about wanting to win everything. I wasn't worried about money or anything like that. The anxiety was about winning. When I played with me brother and sisters, we'd argue and fight over a game of monopoly – over everything we played.

Part of it was my embarrassment at losing. I always wanted to be the winner. Everyone knows I cried at the World Cup when I got booked and couldn't play in the final. But I also cried at the end when we got beat. When we weren't winners. We were out and I felt my life was over. It was also because of the fans. They had been so great and deserved the final. So did the players.

When I was younger, it was fear of losing that drove me. At school I wanted to be the best player in the park all the time.

Even when I won I sometimes cried tears of joy, and that was stupid really. I never really enjoyed my sport because I put myself under that much fear to win. I enjoyed playing it, but I couldn't wait to see the end result.

It was while signing copies of my first book that I got the idea to write this one. So many people came up to me and said it had helped. And I hadn't even scratched the surface of my problems.

Leaving the Princess Grace Hospital – with Jimmy's help – in January 2005 after recovering from pneumonia.

October 2005. A dream come true. Announcing my appointment as manager of Kettering Town. L-r: Kevin Wilson, Imraan Ladak, me, Paul Davis.

In the dugout with high hopes of being the gaffer for a long time.

There's a lot of pressure, but I loved being a manager.

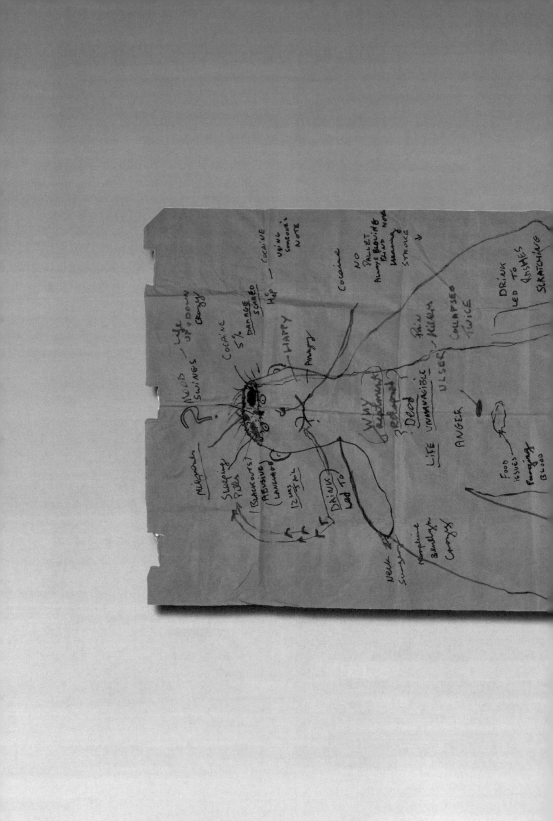

My Body Map. Cottonwood 2006.

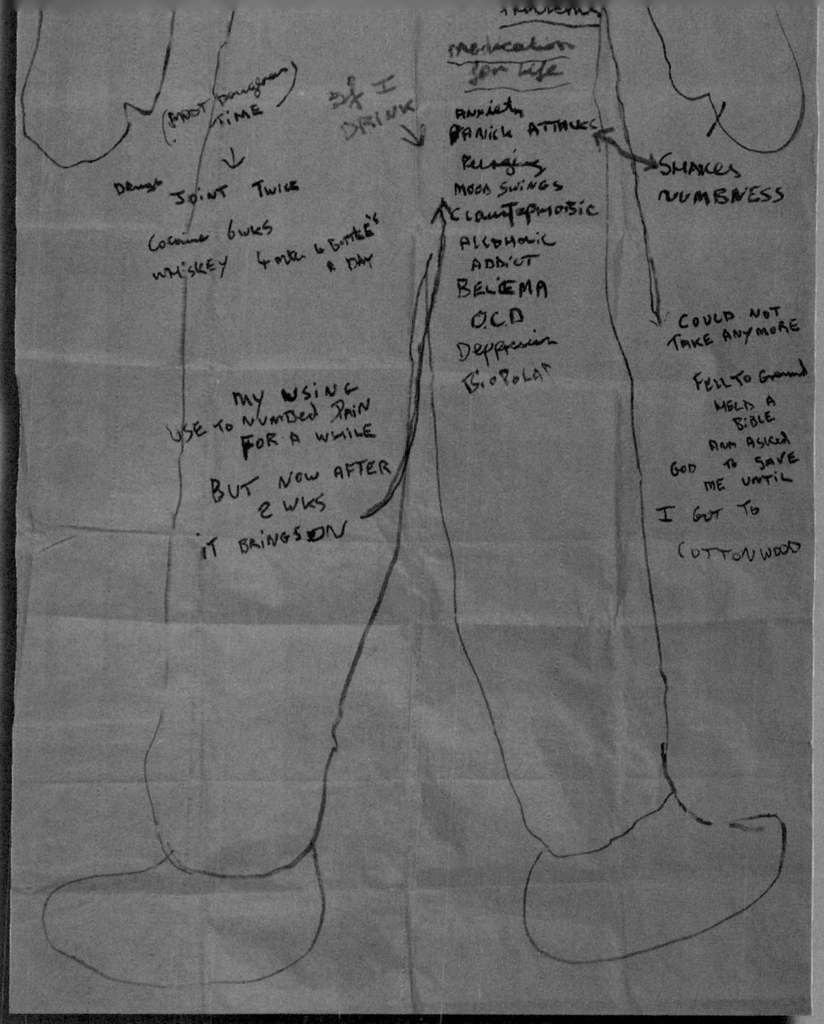
Medication for life
(MOST Dangerous) TIME
Drugs JOINT TWICE
Cocaine 6WKS
WHISKEY 4 or 6 Bottle's A DAY
If I DRINK
Anxiety
PANICK ATTACKS
Paranoia
MOOD SWINGS
Claustrophobic
ALCOHOLIC
ADDICT
BELIEMA
O.C.D
Depression
BIOPOLAR
SHAKES
NUMBNESS
COULD NOT TAKE ANYMORE
FELL TO Ground
HELD A BIBLE
And Asked GOD TO SAVE ME UNTIL
I GOT TO
COTTONWOOD
MY USING
USE TO NUMBED PAIN
FOR A WHILE
BUT NOW AFTER 2 WKS
IT BRINGS ON

At the charity do in Liverpool. December 2005. Relaxed and not drunk. I couldn't have imagined at this stage in the evening where I was going to spend the night.

Sir Bobby Robson has always been there for me with guidance and has supported my ambition to be a manager. He said, 'I know he has it in him.' Thanks Bobby.

Jimmy. My best friend. He always makes me laugh and helps me feel better.

The Dubai Masters. April 2006. Back playing for Newcastle with a ball at my feet after all my injuries. It felt great to reconnect with football again.

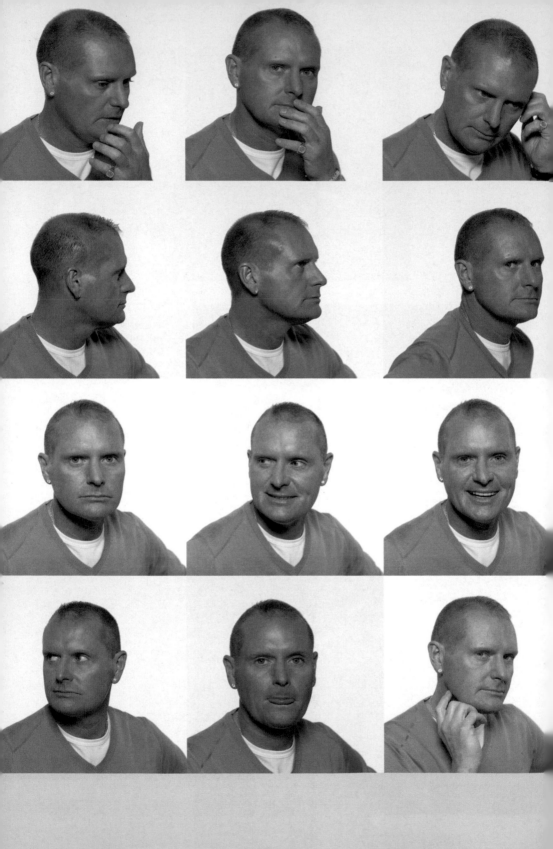

Would we win? And that was every sport, not just football: I was in the rounders team, I even played for the girls' netball team – goal shooter – also basketball, tennis, ping-pong, badminton, everything. I played in all the teams at school. I just never stopped playing. I played pool at the boys' club twice a week when I was seven. I went as often as possible, competing against older boys.

I was younger than the rest of the boys at the club – and I was little as well – but the other kids were brilliant. All the other boys had football strips on, and I had this yellow vest, because I couldn't afford a football strip. But it never bothered us, so long as I was playing football I didn't care. We often didn't have money for the kit and stuff but I still played football.

Me mam would buy new shoes and a new outfit for the school term, and we had to make them last the whole year. I remember once, on the first day of the new term, virtually taking the sole off my new shoe playing football. I couldn't wait for PE so I played in the school yard before lessons started. Me mam went mad. She couldn't afford to buy me new shoes so I went to school with a hole in me sole every day. It was embarrassing sometimes, so I tried to glue it. And it was like that in PE once as well. I'd done the same with my trainers – ruined them scraping along the ground and playing football. So I had no trainers for PE. I remember one PE session when my sister was doing PE before us, and I had to wait for her to finish and then go in the girls' dressing room and borrow her shoes so I could play football. It used to drive me mam crazy with me playing football. Ruining all the shoes. From then on, and even to now, I just thought, 'Me mam and dad must never want for nothing.'

I've carried them thoughts with me all this time, for years. I never forget my roots. I never forget where I come from: I'll always stay the same guy I was when I was seven.

Newcastle's my home. I've been away eighteen years. But I've always been in and out of the city, I'm always going back there.

I hate being on my own though. Even in Newcastle. When I'm on my own I start thinking about the career I've had, the great times, all that. I never watch myself playing football or anything because them times have gone, I'm never going to have them times again. But I remember all that. Then I think, 'What can I do next that's going to make me happy for the next twenty years?' That's why I go to the gym twice a day, because it takes my mind off things.

John

There's an anxiety, a drive, a restlessness, a need to get up, play something, join in with something, avoid our feelings. It's unease. Some people simply label it part of the addictive personality. That unease makes us act on how we feel, whether it's food disorders, drinking, or other habits. And Paul describes not just feeling lonely, but this energy inside him that stops him being able to relax, or just be.

It's hard for him to accept this stage of life that he's at. He's not alone with it, though people don't usually talk about this stuff. It's hard just to look back over your life and say, 'Yes, that was fantastic, but it's different now.' I ask Paul about whether there's a part of him that isn't yet ready to feel that, and to move on.

Paul

There's this arrogant side of us that says, 'Why should I have to move on? Why don't I get fit, have a good pre-season and play for a football club, even at the age of thirty-nine?' Okay, so some days doing this training, my knee's sore, and some days my hip's sore. But I still have the desire, even now. I look at Teddy Sheringham, he's forty and apparently they're offering him another year at West Ham. And Paul Merson and Dennis Wise, I see they're still playing football. And I think, 'Why don't I have another year just to see what it's like?' I've had a good career at the top level, and you might wonder why I'd go and play in front of a couple of thousand people. But I'm not bothered about that, just having that thrill again would be it.

But at the moment I'm putting myself under extreme pressure all the time. I'm always anxious to get back to that gym. I'll always try to squeeze in another session. What drives it? Thirty years of it, that's what drives it.

Since I was seven I've been pushing myself with the training.

I'm not eating right at the moment, as I've said. When I played, the managers were okay with me. They liked us a bit overweight, and I think I've played some of my best football when I've been, say, four or five pounds over. But I wouldn't feel good within myself. I felt I wasn't quick, sharp. Then I'd lose weight and I'd feel great and feel sharp. But then when I was lighter I didn't have the strength. So I'd put some weight back on – but then I wouldn't feel good within myself, I'd feel sluggish and all that, and I'd be back down to not eating and go through it all again.

There might be two spells of about a month in a season where I'd go to the gym at 8 o'clock in the morning, train at lunch time, train with the guys in the afternoon, and then train by myself later on. Sometimes I'd train five times a day and have one meal. No wonder I got injured. I just didn't know any different. I trained myself to do that. It's the obsessive side of it.

John

An important thing to recognise is that, in spite of being harmful, those eating and exercising patterns that Paul had did use to work for him at one time. Paul achieved an incredible amount. But now he's got to a different stage of life, and it's much harder to get away with such extreme regimes.

We look more at how this pattern with the food has affected Paul, and how it affects him now.

Paul

Since I was twenty-one, I've had injuries and operations. Some of that's because of not having the right stuff inside my belly when I trained, and tearing muscles, and not being strong enough.

I'm still in that pattern now. I'm not yet forty and I'm already thinking, 'I don't want to be buying bigger clothes when I'm fifty!'

As soon as I wake up, I start obsessing about food. I think, 'I can't have breakfast, because if I do I'll think, "Well, I may as well have lunch" – and so on.' The other pattern is that I'll have breakfast and then I'll be so pissed off

I'll have loads of lunch, etc. Food's going through my mind all day. But if I train, I can enjoy my food and just have salad with a bit of chicken or fish perhaps.

So how does that affect my mood? When I don't eat I feel down. Like today. I didn't train this morning and because of that I think I can't really eat anything at breakfast. And I'll miss lunch as well.

John

With this type of food disorder, we swing from saying, 'I'm fat or I'm overweight and I don't like myself' to 'I'm wafer-thin which I like.' Either way, we're abusing our bodies which has consequences. There's a constant inner dialogue.

Again we need to bring Paul's focus back to looking at where that punishing voice comes from, why it's not accurate, and what strategies work for Paul in contradicting it and not listening to it. That's where counselling comes in, and people and meetings and structure. And learning to let go of the control and get help from a nutritionist to work out your own diet plan that you stick to for a number of weeks. Then, when you wake up in the morning, you already know what you're going to eat so there are no decisions to obsess about. You're free from having to think about food. And, meanwhile, you get support from other people who understand the problem. Paul thinks it's stupid that he can't just sit and have an ordinary meal in a restaurant at the moment. But that's the food disorder, and thousands of people will identify with it – there's nothing stupid about it.

That's the voice that I want to challenge, the one that says, 'I can't eat now.'

Paul

The voice says I can't eat because I'll put on weight. Then if I do eat I'll think, 'It's not worth training today because I've eaten,' which is ridiculous.

It started when I've had coaches saying I'm fat. In Italy I got weighed four times every week. I remember being told off for being half an ounce overweight. That's not even a spoon of sugar. And I had to do thirty-five kilometres on a bike and an eight-mile run afterwards when I wasn't even half a pound over. You have to be an athlete, when you're a footballer.

I loved it at Glasgow, I could eat normally and enjoy my football. And I loved my football at Lazio, but that coach he was a tough coach, with regards to the weight anyway. He wouldn't let us join in training. He'd make us go with another coach – the fitness coach. All the lads were laughing, looking at us. I was overweight. He said Casiraghi had a bad game just because he was one pound overweight, but I was six pounds overweight sometimes. If you want to keep up with their standards you have to match them and stick to that lifestyle. If you haven't got as much skill you have to be even more physically strong and very fit.

John

If the power of the punishing external opinion is more powerful than your internal opinion of yourself, this form of criticism is a big problem. If in a newspaper someone says you're an idiot, somewhere in your head you think, 'No I'm not, he doesn't know what he's talking about.' But that comment has the power to make you behave in a way you don't want to behave, and to feel hurt or angry in a way you don't want to feel.

To shelter ourselves from the external critical voice and from the internalised critical voice we need to learn to 'parent' ourselves – to look after and encourage ourselves, to forgive ourselves and teach ourselves good habits.

Paul

With the food, I could parent my own son, I would never force my kid to eat, but I'd ask him if he was hungry, and I'd get him something good and healthy to eat. I'd make sure he eats properly and regular. Of course.

But with the press, it's hard. In some ways I wish I was like Chris Evans. He just doesn't let anything bother him. I wish I could be like that with the press. How does he do it? Well, one, he doesn't get the newspapers. And two, he just does whatever he likes. It's his life. And when he had a rough time in the press he didn't really let it get on top of him. He's got a place abroad where he could shoot off to, and he had good support round him. It's good to see Chris back and doing well again. He's got a job for life, and he's very talented. With football, it's a short life-span.

Not listening to that punishing voice is hard. I think, 'I've got to do two sessions, I've got to get back to the gym.' I just don't want to do anything but training at the moment.

John

There's a point I want to raise about Paul working hard all his life to train his body, learning different techniques to achieve different types of fitness. In a similar way, he's already learned mind techniques through counselling and other methods. But it's an ongoing process. Perhaps Paul needs media-skills training, for example. And to learn how to switch off, how to relax. A lot of people who are successful get help and training of all kinds. Paul's taught himself how not to listen to the anxious voice of the OCD. I ask if he can use that technique with the food – not to listen to his 'addict voice'.

Paul

It's like with the alcohol, the addict voice won't go away. The food is like alcohol, which is like OCD.

People reading this are probably thinking, 'How fucking daft is he?' I know it's daft, but by talking about it and letting people know, and letting myself know how stupid it is – like how stupid it was to turn light switches off all the time – I hope it helps. The food one *is* stupid, really, because in the health farm everything that's served is healthy, there's no fat in it whatsoever, it's all healthy stuff. Steve's been good and keeping an eye on us, and he's been telling us: 'Make sure you eat properly,' and 'This is good for you.' When I've been going down the gym he's been coming down and saying, 'Get this down you, eat this.' He's been a different class.

It's probably a good thing I'm in the health farm and training the way I am – I think if I was back home and training like this I'd be injured by now, because I wouldn't have eaten anything at all. At least there's food there. Talking about this is quite embarrassing really, because someone reading this is going to think, 'Imagine having that for the rest of your life. But I'm not going to have it for the rest of my life, because I've got most of it under control, and this is just the battle I'm going through at the moment. I can't all of a sudden turn it around in one session of talking about it. I have to get it under control and enjoy food again.

There was a programme on TV about these fat kids and some of them won't live longer than their parents because they're so overweight, and I felt so sorry for them. I went to the shops last night, and there were two tramps sitting outside on the step. I gave them a tenner because I knew they wanted some beer – they just had one can between them. I knew what it felt like because I've been in that position myself. I know what those fat kids feel like as well.

Seeing other people's pain gets me. I sometimes think about going to another part of the world. This last year, I've been thinking our country is mad, as regards everything that's been happening. You hear about kids overweight, kids getting abused, deaths, robberies – all that's been affecting me. I don't think I've listened to the news so much in my life. One of my favourite programmes – you won't believe it – is watching the debates in the House of Commons, seeing what Tony Blair's got to say about our country – never mind what's happening in Iraq. Everything in our country's bothering us.

I feel selfish at the moment, because I'm doing a book and I get to talk about my problems, and there are so many people in this country who've got problems and really have to struggle through life. They can't afford to talk to anybody, or they're too embarrassed to talk to anybody, and they think people are going to think they're screwed up. They've got their backs to the wall, they feel there's no hope for them. So I feel guilty in a way. I can honestly tell them not to be afraid to talk to someone about things. You're clearing your head, and especially if it's someone with experience they can talk to you back and help you deal with it. Not a lot of people in this country do that, not enough.

I know there are some people out there who can't leave the house, or it takes them two or three hours to leave the house because they can't shut the fucking door behind them. I had that real bad in China. I know I'm better now – but I only know that because a lot of people say it to me. I wish I could see it, I wish I could relax.

When I have addict thoughts, the normal way I manage them is I just go against them. If my addict says, 'You can't eat,' I just say, 'Fuck, I'm going to eat.' By challenging the thoughts and not believing them, I've conquered some of the problems I've had to go through.

I think, when I go to Newcastle, just at the train station there's a bagel shop, and I can see myself getting two big bagels.

John

Sometimes we need to try saying, 'Hang on, I'm not going to beat myself up. Instead of worrying about food, I'm going to ring up a friend, and meet up.' It's about taking a small risk, trying something different in a small way.

When we've got more time on our hands, that's when we have to watch that addict. The addict puts on a different costume: one minute he's an alcoholic pestering you to have a drink, and you say, 'No'. The next minute he pops up in the kitchen as a chef, asking you to overeat. The addict pops up in different disguises. And that's what we call cross-addiction. When one addiction gets arrested, another one appears.

It's good for Paul to remind himself that he's not at all stupid, that he's suffering an illness which isn't his fault. So he needs to let himself off, but at the same time accept it, and take responsibility for what he can do about it.

Paul

One of the big things is acceptance. The more I accept it the easier it is. If I write down everything – the panic attacks, the mood swings, everything

– it's easier. A girl saw us once writing everything down, and she said, 'Oh my God!' I wanted to laugh. And I said, 'Yeah, I've got all of them.'

I think if I accept it, it really works. Like with OCD: I've accepted I have OCD and now I can walk away from the light switches. Same with the food, if I accept I have the weight and food problems, I can just eat sensible. You can eat stuff that doesn't put weight on you and still enjoy it. If I'm honest though, I don't think I've quite accepted all that with the food yet. I haven't quite conquered that.

Trying to lose this stone in three weeks instead of in three or four months is exhausting me. I think, 'Why have I punished myself like that? Training and not eating. Do I need to do that?' And then when I've done it I'll think, 'Well, what can I do next?' I don't seem to live a day at a time, I don't relax.

I'm still obsessed with football, I absolutely love football, and I get invitations to matches and I don't take them up. Whether that was a good thing, taking the manager's job, I don't know. Because having a taste of it for just such a short time – it's still in me mind now. I'd love to be a manager again. And I've learned from it the last time, from my mistakes. With anything anybody wants to do, they have to learn it.

John

Not eating properly affects our brain chemistry, which in turn affects our mood. Then, feeling low, we won't do the things that could help us, like ringing a friend or taking some first steps to change things. I've suggested to Paul to try having two balanced meals: a healthy breakfast, and lunch. If we don't eat, our bodies start to get eaten into, and vital nutrients are missing.

Not every thought we have is an accurate thought. If we think, 'I mustn't have breakfast today,' that doesn't mean that's healthy for us just because we think it. Learning not to engage with the addict voice can take years of practice.

Paul's in a very difficult stage at the moment. He's dealing successfully with his OCD, his panic attacks, his alcoholism, and tackling the food and exercise. And he's uncovering what lies beneath. What we've done previously together has been mostly counselling rather than psychotherapy. But now we've started doing some therapy – looking at where some of the thought and behaviour patterns originate. People-pleasing, having to rescue people, keeping the peace, having to fix everything, having to be the perfect weight, not being good enough just as he is – the punishing voice. We look at where some of these ingrained beliefs have come from. And of course he's going to feel up and down while we're digging things up.

Paul's body is still recovering, and that's part of why he's been depressed. Also he's not stimulated enough, and hasn't got the job he wants yet. But he talked about acceptance, and he's struggling to accept the way things are at the moment. Some things have gone, and it's no use worrying about them, but there are some things which hopefully he can change. To quote philosopher Reinhold Niebuhr, we need 'The serenity to accept the things we cannot change; courage to change the things we can; and wisdom to know the difference.'

Dear Paul

You're a top man. People love you just as you are. You don't need alcohol. Please stay sober.

Lots of love mate

Jack

Chapter Twenty

Paul looks forward – to life and the World Cup

Paul

I'm about to have my final session with Johnny. I was scared yesterday morning, though not about the session itself. I woke worried about what I'm going to do next. It's at the back of my mind all the time. I could go round the country giving talks, 'An Evening with Gazza', but I'm too young to do that. I've got bits and pieces of TV and DVD work, but I just have the one goal – to be a manager. Will I achieve that or not? That's what worries me. I do feel I have conquered most of my problems. Well, I've minimised them. They'll always be there, but with a bit of luck and willpower, I'll stay on top of them from now on.

After I've seen Johnny tomorrow I hope I'll have no appointments again, none of that once-a-week, or twice-a-month appointments written in my diary which I've been doing for almost a year. No more will be pencilled in. It'll be the end, for now. I'm hoping to manage without him, now

I have the tools. I have my own GP in Newcastle, and when I need any new medication, he'll prescribe it.

I'm checking out of Champneys tomorrow. I've been in this one, at Tring, for three weeks, then before that I was six weeks at Henlow Grange. Jimmy is coming down to drive me home to Newcastle. I'm moving back into my apartment in Jesmond.

It felt a bit lonely living there earlier on, when I got it two years ago, so I haven't really unpacked. But now I'm looking forward to it. I think I'll cope okay now, as I'm in a much better state. It'll be nice to have a proper place of my own for a change, till I decide whether to buy a house or not.

On Saturday, there's a party for my dad's sixtieth birthday, a big family gathering, so that'll be good. I'm sure I won't get tempted by the drink. Then on Sunday I'm going with Kenneth Shepherd, son of Freddy Shepherd, to watch Newcastle United.

I don't see going back to Newcastle as a danger. Not the game, obviously. I mean moving back there. I survived two years last time, living up there without drinking. I want to be back with my old mates. The press are always describing them as hangers-on, but to me, they're true mates.

I'll keep on training, up in Newcastle. Now the weather has at last got better, I'll do some road running, just around Gateshead. And gym work in a hotel.

A six-a-side tournament in Dubai is coming up, which Sky will televise. I'm playing for a Newcastle veterans team, along with Chris Waddle. I'll be seeing more of him now, when I get back. He is my oldest friend in football. And I still haven't forgotten that Santa Claus text. Careful, Waddler – I might not be as daft as I used to be, but I've still got a few tricks up my sleeve.

I used to say he was in my genes, because I seemed to follow him around. He started at Newcastle, like me. I first met him when I had to clean his boots. One day he said I hadn't cleaned them well enough. 'Boots are the tools of your trade and you have to keep them in top condition,' so he said. 'Fuck off,' I replied.

I was only sixteen and pretty lippy. So he gave me a kick. A dead leg.

I managed not to cry in front of everyone in the dressing room, but after that I didn't give him any more cheek.

Chris moved on to Spurs, and so did I. He went abroad, and so did I. He played for England, and so did I. At the end of his career, he played for a lower league club, as I did. He had a spell at managing, like me. I said to him the other day, 'I hope you win the fucking lottery, cos that means I will as well . . .'

I'm looking forward to being back in the North East, going to watch Newcastle play. And of course I can't wait for the World Cup.

What pissed me off, during the weeks leading up to it, was everyone saying, 'This is the best England team since 1966.' It's bollocks. What has this team won? Nothing so far. A team can only be the best team, or better than another team, if they win something.

They come out with this sort of shite before every World Cup and European Championships. They said it in 1994, 1998, 2002, 2006 and I bet you any money they'll be saying it again in 2010.

When I was in the 1990 World Cup, and Euro '96, we got to the semi-finals each time. This present team has yet to get anywhere near that, so how can they be better? On each occasion, we got knocked out in the semis by Germany on penalties. And you know what Mourinho says – being beaten on penalties doesn't count as losing. So, yeah, it did annoy me, all the talk about this lot being the best England team ever.

There are some good individual players, but it's playing as a team that will matter, how they all perform, on the day.

Obviously I hope England win, or at least do well, and I'm sure they will, but I'm not looking further forward than the semi-finals. I see the four semi-finalists as being England, Brazil, France and Italy. Out of those four, if it happens, I hope England draw Italy. Our football is so different from theirs, with all the pressing we do, working them hard. Italians don't like that, they don't like our style, so we could have a chance against them. If we face Brazil or even France, it will be harder and I wouldn't reckon our chances of making the final itself.

Even as individuals, I don't think they are better than in the past. There is one truly outstanding player, Rooney, but that's about it. Of course Beckham, Lampard and Gerrard are world class as well, and very experienced.

But are they better than individual players in the past? In my day, we had Bryan Robson and Paul Ince in the middle. They were world class, but also grafters. They did all the work, then gave the ball to me. So no, I don't actually think today's individuals can be said to be much better. Joe Cole, he's good. I forgot him. I like him.

I don't worry about the so-called problem of having no one on the left. Good players – which Beckham, Lampard and Gerrard all are – can work anywhere. When I was in the England team, Chris Waddle was officially a winger, but he would be tucked into the midfield when there was a need, and he did a good job. That's what all good players have to do.

Most fans and players in England today have no problem with England's first eleven, and the five subs. There's a solid sixteen players there we all agree on. They pick themselves, when fit and in form.

Some people have gone on in the past about having to choose two from Sol Campbell, John Terry and Rio Ferdinand. I don't see it as a problem. They are all good. I think if I was manager, and they were all fit and in form, I'd think about trying to play all three together. Up front, well, there's no argument, it's Rooney and Owen.

As for the rest of the squad, well, everyone has had their say on that. I probably would have chosen Crouch and also perhaps that boy at Wigan, Jason Roberts. He's done well this season when I've been watching him. In fact I sent a text to Paul Jewell, saying he should be pushing Roberts for the England squad, but I didn't hear anything back.

I wonder at the last moment if anyone will come through, have a late spurt, or take the place of someone who gets injured or loses form? It's still two months to go, so we don't know yet.

For the 1990 World Cup, I was keeping my fingers crossed to be in the squad, but I wasn't sure. My best hope was to get in the squad and sit on the bench, then poor Neil Webb got injured. I took his place, got in the team, and never looked back. That might happen again to someone. You just have to stay on your toes, then jump at any chance that comes up.

I have no problems with Sven. He was ridiculed and criticised by the press, especially when he got stitched up by the fake sheik, but I feel sorry for him. He took the bait, so he made a mistake, but it was all the work of the media.

It's as if the English media don't want England to win. They hounded Sven and tried to get him sacked. They stalk all the England players, or their wives and girlfriends, making their lives hell, putting them under such pressure. They never help England's cause, do they? You would think they would. It's in their interest, if they really are genuine England supporters, as they say they are.

Sven's record is good. All the players I've spoken to privately have no problem with him. They all like him. And so do most managers I've met. It's just the press that's been against him.

I think being the England manager is a harder job than being the Prime Minister. You need the hide of a rhino to survive, or you stay at home and never go out. It will be interesting if England do win. The press will suddenly start shouting 'Don't Go Sven'. That could be funny.

It doesn't bother me that Sven never appears emotional on the bench. Mourinho gets criticised for being too emotional. You can't win.

All the England manager has to do, basically, is keep his nose clean and pick the best twenty-two. Then when he's got his best twenty-two, if each is performing well, he stays in, if not, he's out.

What is a good manager anyway? What is a good player?

I think Wigan's Paul Jewell and Blackburn's Mark Hughes are good managers because they have had little money. Their teams are not flash, they don't have stars, they play simple 4–4–2, and yet they work so hard and get their rewards. To me, that's a mark of a good manager.

A manager who can spot a kid at fourteen and see him through into the first team and then the England squad, that's also a good manager. Fergie and Wenger, they both have good eyes for young players.

A manager with more resources, and a large squad of world-class players, and yet one who can manage a rotation system and keep everyone happy, that to me is also a good manager. Mourinho has that ability. And he also has this quality of being able to change players just at the right time in a match. He reads a game to perfection.

A manager who has a team of stars, who win most games, and yet manages to keep everyone motivated, that's a good manager too. I'm thinking of Walter Smith when I was at Rangers. He had twenty players who were internationals, in a team where we were 3–0 up in many games by half time – but he then had to keep us working and focused to the final whistle. That's good going.

There are lots of ways of defining a good manager, just as with players. A player playing well in a shit team is a good player.

All the millions of pounds swilling about in football today doesn't worry me. I was very well paid, compared with the generation before me, if not quite as well as today. But I'm not bothered they can now get £100,000 a week. I'm not resentful. A star player gets followed all the time, and his family. He gets slaughtered each week in the press by someone. I think they deserve all the money they can get. The clubs are raking it in. So is the television. The press is living on the back of football, selling millions of copies, doing extra supplements for things like the World Cup, without paying. So good luck to the players if they can screw as much as they can for themselves.

All the diving, that does worry me though. I don't blame the players, or the managers. Diving has always gone on. Players will always try to steal an advantage and con the ref – and if it works managers don't care. But now it's got out of hand. And I blame the refs. They should be able to spot it and clamp down on it.

I think what would help would be if refs went and watched some Premiership training sessions. When teams play practice games, they play to win, and play hard – but they don't dive. You wouldn't dare, not against your own players. They'd either just laugh at you, or thump you. In training games, when someone falls down, it's for real. In real games, they do it because they think they can get away with it, that refs won't know the difference. If the refs were to watch training sessions, they'd be able to differentiate between a real fall and a pretend one.

I am sorry that kids don't play football in the streets or the parks any more, as I did, not so long ago. Jumpers for goal posts and all that. You hardly see it now, even up in Newcastle and Gateshead. The streets are full of cars, that's one reason. I think it's also because parents are scared, worried about any weirdos wandering about, or bigger kids. You hear about these fourteen-year-olds beating up eleven-year-olds, stealing their mobiles or trainers, or just knifing them for fun. No wonder responsible parents don't let their young kids out in the street to play.

I often wonder what our football would be like today, without all the foreign players and managers. We seem to be obsessed at the moment by Mourinho, he's in the papers all the time, as if we didn't have any English-born managers. But I think we would be a lot poorer without the foreign guys.

My real worry is the level of coaching being done in our football academies. I don't think they are all as good as they could be. In Europe, they do seem to teach them better, which is why Arsenal is always buying all these good European kids. If the British ones were as good, they'd buy them. I worry more about a talented English kid not getting a decent enough training over here, rather than his way being blocked by some imported foreign player. If you're a shit player, no one will pick you. If you're good enough, someone will pick you.

But if a kid starts thinking he's going to have no chance, because of all the foreigners ahead, then he will have no chance – because his mentality will be wrong. You have to believe you will make it.

There is such pressure on all managers today, so you can understand what happens. If the choice is between a seventeen-year-old English kid, who has come up through the academy but is still learning, and an experienced foreign player of twenty-seven, you can see the manager's dilemma. He tends to think in the short term. He doesn't want the sack if his team gets stuffed. So he has to play safe, unfortunately.

Rooney has come all the way through the English system, and his natural talent has flourished, but he was carefully looked after by David Moyes at Everton. I was there at the time and I remember Colin Harvey, the academy director, telling me to look at this lad. Rooney was a little freckled kid, only fourteen. He came on as sub for the academy Under-17 team and scored two goals. I never talked to him, but I could see he was brilliant for his age.

I do think he's already almost on a par with Ronaldinho, who is of course today's best player in the world. Rooney is usually bracketed with Messi, when people speak of world-class young players. Messi is really a new Chris Waddle. But with a better hairdo. Not hard. Rooney is a different player entirely. He can't be compared with Messi. I think Rooney is better. He can attack, create, defend.

I never get fussed about who should be the next England manager. I'd like, in theory, the England manager always to be English, but it doesn't bother me if he was foreign.

Personally, I would go for any older manager, such as Terry Venables. He's had so much experience and is a brilliant coach and manager. If it has to be someone a bit younger, I'd have Bryan Robson. He's done an amazing job at West Brom, with little money. But I don't expect either of them to get the job. Loads of yous will know, by the time you read this, what happened. I wonder if I am right.

People in the press often say, when writing about Rooney, that me and George Best should be a warning to him. But when I broke into the England team, a few years older than Rooney, mind you, people said the same to me – that I should take heed, and not turn into another George Best.

Okay, we have alcohol in common. Which has been bad. Obviously. And people are right to draw attention to the dangers of alcoholism. But they forget how much I achieved. I didn't throw it all away. But for injuries, I'm sure I would have got near 100 caps, not just 57. And George achieved a lot. He didn't play in World Cups because Northern Ireland didn't qualify. But look what he did achieve at Manchester United. He won the European Cup for fuck's sake.

Anyway, alcoholism is a disease. There's no point in warning people against it. It happens. You get it or not. I don't think Rooney will have that problem. He seems fairly stable. I like the fact that he's still with his childhood sweetheart. That must be a help. I wish it had happened to me.

I often wonder how my son Regan will turn out, if I'll be used as a warning to him. At the moment, he's more interested in being a ballet dancer than a footballer. That's fine by me. I hope he does well. It's what his mother wanted to be when she was young, so perhaps he's inherited her genes. I hope he doesn't inherit OCD from me, but I don't think he will. I just hope he has an enjoyable life, and gets left alone by the media. Perhaps when he's grown up, we might get close again. He might understand more what I have been through, and that I'm not all bad.

There's lots to look forward to football-wise at the moment for me, which is good. And you know what, when I'm doing all this mad training to get ready for these charity games and testimonials, I often have lurking at the back of my mind the thought that, hmm, could it just happen? Could I possibly get one last crack at it?

Ah well, just a thought. I'm sure it is too late now. Or is it . . . ?

———————

Dear Paul

You made me laugh when I thought I could not and seemed always to put me in a better shape. This disease is your worst enemy, don't let it beat you. I will always remember being in my room on my first morning shaking like a leaf and you were the first person in the community I ran into. I saw the fire in your eyes and your disdain for this disease ('fuckin' relapse'). How friendly and at home I immediately felt. Thanks for all your help.

Phil

Paul's ninth session: The final countdown

John

In this final session I'd like to talk about what helps Paul more than anything with his state of mind, his health and his happiness. Whether it's friends, his parents, meetings, counselling, working – whatever the ingredients are that he needs to feel well.

Paul

The last couple of weeks have been mixed really. I wanted to get fit, to get myself back in trim, look after myself, and I think I've done all that. I'm quite excited because I'm leaving the health farm. I've got the memorial dinner to go to with Calum Best for George. I'll be sad, but being there for Calum's a good thing.

I've been isolating myself from everybody. But now I've got a few matches coming up, so May's going to be a good month. I'm making sure

I'm going to be busy. It's been frustrating not doing stuff, but the fact is I've had to come through a hell of a lot during the last year and a bit, and I had to work on that. I've still got these problems for the rest of me life.

It's time to get myself back into real life, out of the health farm. I've been a bit worried this week about money, how some of the investments I've made in the past have backfired on us. It wasn't a brilliant weekend.

There's lots of things I've got planned that I'd like to do, but the last few days I've been doing some negative thinking. I've lost confidence. I need to get a feel for football again. I haven't done any interviews on the football side of it, just worked on this book.

I feel quite nervous going back home, seeing the family. When I go to Newcastle I'll see homeless kids, and there's nothing worse than seeing a homeless kid. At the traffic lights they're washing cars in the freezing cold and I really feel for them.

My head's gone again on what I'm going to do with the rest of my life. I want a steady job and a decent income. I want to get something that'll really make us happy. I'm not depressed, I've just got mixed feelings at the moment with regards to everything. Why am I thinking this way again, when last week I was really on top of everything?

The big question for me is, what do I want to do after the World Cup? As you know, I'd like to be a good manager, to really work hard on that. It's great saying I want to be a manager, but I'm going to have to put in the work. Bryan Robson came straight into it at a young age, and he's worked himself real hard for it. Obviously I'd love to get another manager job. But I'm not going to set meself big targets yet, only small achievements to aim for, otherwise it'll be too much while I'm still sorting myself out.

John

I'm not surprised he's feeling like this because he's been in the clinic, then came the holiday when he didn't relax at all, then came this intense period of therapy and training. I've said to him before, and I say it now: this is like a growing-up period, going from one phase of his life to another, a transition.

It's quite normal to feel scared, to feel nervous, to worry about financial responsibilities, what you're going to do, where you're going to end up living. I think the most important thing is for him to be really kind to himself at the moment – to look after himself. To allow himself to say, 'I am worried about not drinking, I am worried about situations, I am watching my food, my exercise.' To try to nurture himself over the next few weeks. He's got a very busy couple of months ahead.

I tell Paul I was talking to my supervisor, and he said this is like sitting in the cockpit of our plane. Sometimes what we want to do is get the parachute and bail out. We don't want to take the controls – the responsibilities. Ultimately, Paul's now in control of his plane. No one else is doing the piloting. Previously he's been in the back of the plane, so being the pilot is new, and it feels scary.

Paul

Last night I had cravings for everything. I was worried and scared. And this morning I feel like I'm going mad again. I can't put me finger on it. I'm thinking negative thoughts all the time. I'm thinking, 'What am I going to do in Newcastle? What am I going to do about training?' I can't think of anything positive.

John

I ask Paul whether he's had any breakfast this morning, and how many cups of coffee he's had. We work out he's had about six cups of coffee, and no breakfast. Caffeine is a powerful drug, and it makes us anxious. On an empty stomach, the effect is magnified. The Chinese see caffeine almost like a Class C drug. To them it's a mood-altering stimulant. You go to an acupuncturist, and the first thing they do is tell you to stop drinking caffeine.

Paul's drinking lots of water, and I also suggest that after this we get some lunch. You can't drink six coffees and get away with it. We've all done it – or something just as extreme that we know at the time we're going to pay a price for – but we go ahead and do it anyway. I can only have one, or maybe two, coffees a day. Any more than that and I get anxious. Paul's got worries, fear is still an issue, but put caffeine into that equation and he's going to feel extremely anxious.

Paul

I've had that much more coffee than usual this morning. I feel tired as well, from all the training. I'm glad I'm talking about it, to be fair. It just hit us last night: I haven't been communicating with anybody. Loads of things have been racing round me head. There are loads of things coming up that I can do. I suddenly felt, like, from doing nothing I have to keep myself busy now. My confidence went out the door.

But I'm looking forward to Newcastle, seeing Jimmy, and my family at home. It will be nice to chill out as well. I'll find a happy medium I think. I'm so pleased I'm talking about this now, because it must have been the coffee – I haven't felt like this for a long time – it's mad having that much coffee.

John

I'd like Paul to try and get to an AA meeting, just to go and listen, to realise he's not alone – because he's alone with this stuff at the moment. It's simple, but if you don't talk about it, and you keep going round and round the same worries, with caffeine on top of it, it feels like the world's going to end.

What I've done is draw three columns on this bit of paper, headed: Morning, Afternoon, Evening. We're going to write down the daily basics of Paul's day. Paul's got some big projects coming up, but I think before he writes lists for those, we should do this simple schedule.

Paul

Let's get started then. Basics. Wake up, take meds. I must admit I will have a coffee. Okay, let's put down ONE cup. And breakfast if you say so. If I'm really starving I'll have half a slice of toast or cereal without much milk.

And I will try soya milk. That nutrition sheet you gave us the other day, tailored to the menu at Champneys, it had soya milk on there. I like soya milk. Then after breakfast I have to have a good workout, so let's put that down there in the morning.

Next thing I need to do in a day is check the diary, or check with Jane, my agent, what's on that day. There might be something on in the afternoon, but if there isn't that's my main worry – the afternoons. I have to try to keep myself busy. At the health farm I was just steaming. Stuff like that. The whole of April I'll probably train in Newcastle, in the mornings. Training and gym work. I'm going to have to start looking at some stuff, like, if it warms up a bit, do some fishing. I love fishing. I've got to get myself into the habit of going to the AA meetings. I know. I enjoy meetings but it's just getting into the habit of going. I don't want it to be so that I've got to go to a meeting every day, but I like being around people who've got the same problems. When I was down, going to meetings cheered us up a little bit.

Anyway, I'll put down doing two or three meetings a week, which I can do. I can go in the evenings as well.

John

We've put down meals as basics. I know I've mentioned it a lot, but Paul's got to put food in the tank at the moment. It's not massive meals we have to have, but what we do eat has to be the right stuff. Fish salad is great.

Paul

I love me fish. I'll always have that. I will eat healthy stuff.

John

I've put here – morning, afternoon and evening – 'Watch thoughts'. That's the cockpit stuff again – you're in charge of your thoughts, they're not in charge of you.

Paul

Over the last couple of days I've been thinking again about what I had and what I fucked up. I've never really had any regrets before, about my career or things I did in my personal life, only they've started to creep in a little bit recently.

Some days I feel depressed and I don't want to go anywhere, don't want to see anyone, don't want to do anything. Then there's some days I feel on top of the world.

John

Paul hasn't any validation from a job at the moment, and that's a key thing he needs to do next – get involved somehow with a club. In the short term, he's going to be in Newcastle for a few weeks, so it would be good to clear it with the staff at Newcastle that he's going in to train, and work out which days and times that's going to be so the lads know what days he's going in. Meanwhile, other longer-term offers will come in.

Paul's doing really well. If I was in his position, would I follow all these suggestions I'm giving him? I'd like to think I would, but I don't know, and I understand why it's hard. It sounds easy and looks easy on paper but, when you're caught up in your own battle, it's a different story.

I ask Paul if he thinks he'll be able to check each day with this basic list we've done, and look after himself, keep to the basics, keep it positive. If he'll be able to say, 'I feel shit, I feel uncomfortable, but I know if I look after myself it will pass.'

Paul

Hopefully I will be able to do that, because I know it's worked in the past. I went into the clinic, had thirty days or so in the clinic, then I came back from the holiday, then the health farm, and I look at myself and I think, 'Am I further down the line, have I took a little step backwards, or have I moved forwards?'

John

When I go to a football match, or when I listen to other people's problems, it can distract me from my own problems. For Paul at the moment, because of the intensity of the book – we're going through every issue he's ever suffered with in one big hit – and because he hasn't got a job or anything big on at the moment, it's full-on. It's eat therapy, sleep therapy, everything therapy. So, although in the previous session he mentioned getting invited to matches, but not being bothered about going, I think going to the games will be a positive distraction.

JM: You are a thinker, you think a lot, don't you? And I wonder sometimes, do you think too much?

PG: Yeah, it never stops.

JM: So at this stage could going out and doing something different help, to give you a rest from the thinking?

PG: Yeah. A friend phoned me a couple of times and said, 'Why don't you come to California for a month? We'd be doing some meetings and some surfing and relax with a load of people.' It sounded quite good. But then I thought, 'No, I'll be the same as I was in Cottonwood, feeling I want to get back home.'

JM: Remember this, you're dealing with a lot. Okay, let's try this, it might sound silly, but what if you're in your room and God suddenly turns up. What do you think He'd say to you at the moment?

PG: I think He'd say, 'Just hang in there. There's things in life you can look forward to, and things will start happening.' You're right, sometimes doing this talking does bring up stuff. It brings back old memories. Like memories of the OCD. That feeling that if you don't touch something, something bad is going to happen that day.

JM: It's a control thing, but we don't have that control. OCD relies on an illusion of control, stemming sometimes from a trauma – you felt unsafe, out of control, so you're then trying to re-establish control. When I had that it was really bad. I'd think I was safe walking down this street, but not down that one – all sorts of things about staying safe. I've still got the odd little routines I do now and then, to ward off bad things.

So, what about taking up some offers while you're in Newcastle, going to some games?

PG: I love being up there in Newcastle, I must admit. I will treat myself to a few games. I went through this feeling, where I got myself really excited and I went to watch football one night, thinking about managing. It's hard work. Some of these managers really struggle if they haven't got money to spend on players, and they face relegation, and it's a lot of pressure. But I suppose if someone can do it, then I could do it as well.

JM: Maybe, in the short term, you could do your badges and your coaching, like Stuart Pearce did, learning the skills. The invitations are there, and you can learn from the best people, without having to carry the can. I want to pick up on this issue of looking after yourself. It's an inside job. I think what God would say to you is, 'Look after yourself.' So you could start planning your next move a bit more – okay, you might not even get paid to start with, but you'll be learning, managing. Clubs will see you're serious. And if you're also serious about training they'll see you're having a good pre-season. And say to yourself, 'If I can prepare a plan for where I want to be next year, move slowly towards it, do my badges, be a coach – it's a guide, a direction to move in.' Does that make sense?

Paul

Yeah. I do want to put the effort in first, for free, and then in the future things will start to pick up again.

I'm obsessed with football, because I've been doing it all my life. With the managing side of it, where do I start? I need to be positive about myself.

John

I'd like Paul to try and remind himself each morning about the structure, and remind himself, 'Today I'm going to be okay, I might have a shit day, but I'll be okay.'

I'd like to suggest that he sits down over the next couple of weeks, and lists the top five or six clubs he'd like to go to in order to learn from the manager, or maybe as a coach. Then, perhaps in July, with someone he feels comfortable with, go round each of the clubs and see what they've got to say. Just to get five or six options.

Paul

That's what I've been thinking about doing meself anyway. The other thing is, there are players around getting on a bit like us, with good fitness. I want to see how I am, see if I am fit, what I'm capable of. See if I could have another year or two of playing. It would be brilliant if I still felt fit enough to play. Then, I don't know why I keep thinking of Australia, but I keep thinking of fucking off to Australia for three months. There's loads of things going through my mind. But the most important thing is that I want to get back to football training. To see how I feel with a ball at my feet – and to get my confidence back with football in general.

John

I hand Paul the beginning of the list of clubs. Where would he like to be? What work would he need to do to get there? I know he can work hard and train hard. My only worry is him pushing himself *too* hard.

Paul

I heard Andy Gray said, 'Has anyone seen Gazza? We don't know where he is.' I've been away doing the clinic and the training and therapy for that long. But you're right, Johnny, football's where I belong. I know it's gonna be hard work, and I'm working on the hard work. I'm going to get back out there and see what happens.

John

I hope Paul can be himself. He's been going through a transitional stage of his life and he's trying to turn it round. He's done a lot of intense sessions in a short period of time, and he needs a break. He's leaving for Newcastle. But I hope he'll still come and see me whenever he can, get to some meetings and, most of all, look after himself.

Dear Paul

I'll stop using your words like clems and fuck and wanker and I'll just leave a few of my own. You've been an amazingly kind, caring, generous, loving friend to so many people here Paul. I hope you don't forget to leave some for yourself. But if you do man, I'll give you whatever I got. It's like that. Bros for life.

Jed

Paul sums up Paul

Paul

I don't know what will happen to me. People ask me that all the time. They also keep asking my friends what they think I'll end up doing. Fuck knows. The press, they know of course, being fucking experts. They're convinced I'll end up in the gutter, wasted, a dead loss and skint. That's what it feels like they wish for me, sometimes.

But the country as a whole is on my side I reckon. The sales and the reaction to my book showed that. They sympathise and understand that I have problems I'm trying to deal with. And I still am, if not very well. But I did manage two years without a drink. For ten years I have not hurt anyone, not since that awful moment with Sheryl. Even that photographer, I didn't really hurt him. I think he sympathised with me in the end.

I've given the press acres and acres of free stories over the last twenty years. They've fed on me. Okay, they often paid me for stuff as well. That's because I often felt I had to defend myself against what other papers have said. They make up all these lies about me. Then others repeat the lies. I'd much prefer never to appear in the papers at all.

The press can ruin your life. They can make a sick person much sicker. I really believe they helped to kill off George Best. I really do. They're certainly making me sicker than I am already . . .

My number one ambition, in my fantasy world, is still to be a manager in the Football League. It doesn't have to be the Premiership, not at first. Any club out of the ninety-two in the Football League, that would do me. I'd be happy then. And just to finish off that particular fantasy, I'd like a three-year contract, so it becomes a steady job where I can work away slowly and quietly. I know that doesn't happen in football. That's why it's fantasy.

My second desire in life is to settle down with someone. I'd like to be with a woman I love and have kids together. It would need to be a woman I can trust. She would be my best friend and partner. I have quite a few married mates who often tell me about their wives and they say, 'She's my best pal.' I'm dead jealous when they say it. I wish it could happen to me. Must be wonderful.

It wouldn't matter where we lived. And I wouldn't worry where she was from, English or Russian, Asian or American or whatever. I just want a woman I can trust.

Funnily enough, I've just heard from that American girl I met at Cottonwood. She rang me up to ask me why I haven't been in touch. We had a good laugh on the phone, talking about when she was singing the ABC song in a funny childish voice. We were in hysterics. I teased her about being educated and all that, yet she sang the ABC song in that silly girlish voice.

She asked me how my book was getting on and I told her she gets a mention, in one of the messages to me at Cottonwood. She laughed, but doesn't object. She's a nice lass.

At the end of our conversation, when she was laughing at things I was telling her, she said we should meet up again. I should come out to California and see her. Perhaps we could arrange to be locked up inside again, on a bipolar session.

She's just a friend, that's all. I've yet to meet my soul mate. It might be in the chip shop, or at a bar, or a coffee shop. It can happen anywhere, but let's hope it does, some time soon.

If I had to choose between these two fantasies, getting my ideal job, or meeting my ideal woman, and I could only have one, well, thinking about it seriously, I'd have to say the job. That would have to come first. That's how I feel.

If neither of those things happen, I won't go around regretting things. I think I've had a brilliant career and a brilliant life. I got to a World Cup semi-final, and a European Championship semi-final, played 57 times for England, won cups in England and Scotland. I've travelled the world, done loads of TV shows, all the things I would never have done if I hadn't been a footballer. I have been married, have a lovely son, so I've had that experience, even if it didn't work out, the marriage part. I've done everything, really, I ever wanted to do. So far. Managing a Football League club, that's my remaining ambition.

When I look back, even though I don't regret things, I often find myself thinking, 'Why did I do that, why did I go there?'

I loved Spurs. I went as England's most expensive ever transfer. I loved it there, did well for them, and they all loved me – and yet I willingly left them and went to Lazio. Why? That's what I often ask myself.

I know there were specific reasons, things happening at the time. I got into a sequence of events that landed me there, but now I can't quite remember or understand what happened. Why was I so keen to go? I had a world-class manager in Terry Venables. Why didn't I stay another two years at least?

I'm not saying I didn't like it at Lazio. I did, apart from all the injuries. I'm not knocking Lazio. Something that must have been clear in my mind at the time has gone hazy. It seems a bit of a mystery now, what my motivation was for leaving. I suppose that happens to lots of people, looking back at their life.

Then at Rangers. I just seemed to find myself there, wake up one day and there I was. But I settled in and loved it. Next thing, I'm at Boro. Nothing wrong with Boro, but why did I leave Rangers? I can't quite remember now. Then at Everton, I was playing well in the Premiership. I was fit and well, got myself a nice apartment – but I then left for Burnley. Sometimes I'm a mystery to myself.

Yes, it's true that Everton ended after I had made my first visit to Cottonwood, but the year before that, I was sober and doing well.

I think I must get bored, that could be it. Or, as Johnny suggests, I self-sabotage. It's a pattern I must get out of.

I said earlier I was worried about becoming boring as a person. Now that I think about it, what I worry about is being bored. Being sober is pretty boring. Doing all this training is pretty boring. Going back to therapy sessions or AA meetings, that won't exactly be exciting or good fun.

Often when I was in a minicab, coming to London to see Johnny, I looked out at people bustling along the pavements. I looked into their faces and wondered what they were thinking, where they were going. Were they excited because they knew they were going to do something good? Or worried about something bad. Or were they just generally depressed and stressed out . . .?

One way I try to cheer myself, when I get into this cycle of feeling depressed, is to think about how I succeeded in the past. In my career, I had thirty-one operations – yet I recovered from each of them, and was able to to play again, even though some experts said I never would. I got over them all and returned to the first team, playing at the top till I was thirty-five. I did it then. I can do it again. I can recover.

Okay, I also keep relapsing. I've been four times to Cottonwood, which isn't good, but I did manage to take myself there each time, to face up to what I was doing and get help.

Of all those things – all the operations, going to the clinics – doing this book has been the hardest thing in my life. Honestly. I've found it so tough, going to all these therapy sessions, and then trying to describe how I feel.

All week I worried about the session, and then I worried about what I'm revealing. I worry that people will think I'm mad, that no one will ever employ me again, or go out with me.

Then I think, 'It takes balls to do what I'm doing. I'm proud to have done it openly, and to have done it properly, putting all my effort into it.' Because that's what I do if I decide to do something. And I do hope it will help other people, who might have some similar problems. Let them see what it's been like for me. When I meet people in future, after they've read the book, I'll willingly talk to them, listen to their problems.

I'm not looking for sympathy. I hate sympathy anyway, friends trying to cheer you up, feeling sorry for you. I'm just describing what happened to me. How I tried to cope – or not, as the case may be.

It's been harder than being in a clinic because in a clinic you can say, 'Sod it,' then walk out, sit in the sun, watch the birds, and never go back. With all these sessions, and then talking about them, I've been stuck inside four walls, trapped with myself. I could of course have packed it in, early doors, which I did at one time want to do. But I decided to carry on – and that's when I felt trapped, that's why it's been so hard.

Has it all helped? That's the Big Question.

Well, I regret I've done it so intensely, packing so many sessions into such a short time. That's me, that's how I do it, taking things to extremes. At times I've felt I'm going to explode.

But, given all that, it's still helped me. No question. I wouldn't have continued with all this, if I didn't think it was helping me, or would help me.

First of all, through therapy and stuff, you get given the tools. That's the phrase they always use in clinics. Things to do, how to distract yourself, re-focus your mind when you have a problem.

Then it gives you understanding. I mentioned those panic attacks. Talking to Johnny about them, and him explaining them to me, I could see he understood what I was going through. That was a huge help. You feel you are not alone, you are not some sort of one-off nutter experiencing something no one else has ever experienced.

You also learn, from understanding something about your problem, when an attack is coming on. You can recognise the signs and symptoms better. You can get ready, or try to. That all helps.

I'm also grateful for the medications that clinics and doctors have prescribed for me. They have helped calm me down, reduced the chance of panic attacks or my OCD coming back. With OCD, I'm definitely improved, compared with how I was, thanks partly to the various pills I still take.

Medication can also help with depression – but the trouble is, your GP might just be ramming you full of tablets without really knowing the root of the problem. He probably hasn't got time to talk it through with you.

And finally, just talking to someone, letting all the shit come out of your head, that's definitely helpful. You might not at the time feel you've come away with anything positive, with a plan of attack, far less a cure, but talking is like a safety valve that gets released.

I know a lot of people will think, 'That Gazza, he's not a good example of therapy working, hasn't done him much fucking good, has it? He's confessed he's had a few drinks over the past few months when he's meant to be on the wagon, and he's still putting his stupid finger down his stupid throat.' Perhaps I shouldn't have admitted that. On the other hand, it's only happened once in the last year. Okay, three times then. But it was far worse in the past. I am getting better, all the time. Honestly. I do believe it.

And things will continue to get better, as long as I don't try to rush things. I have to be patient.

Already, I find people asking me for advice. Me of all people, as if I know fuck all.

Friends who have been worried about their drinking, thinking they're becoming an alcoholic, have often spoken to me, asked for any help. I usually do the obvious and easy thing – give them Johnny's number. I ring him first like, to see if he minds.

I did recommend one friend who has OCD, who was checking doors all the time, going mental because he couldn't stop. He had one session with Johnny and, bingo, his OCD was finished.

It does happen, that in one session you can be sorted, first time out. But other people need lots of sessions. You just don't know when you start how long it might take.

If a therapist doesn't help you with OCD, there is one specialist OCD clinic in Philadelphia. I haven't been there, but I'm told it's good.

With some friends who are alcoholics or addicts and are trying to cure themselves, I always tell them – don't do cold turkey, not on your own. Say you've been drinking solid for four months, then suddenly you force yourself to stop and have four days without drinking – the withdrawal symptoms will be far worse than the addiction. In fact, it's pure hell. That's when you could top yourself, or do something really stupid. If you are trying to withdraw, you must do it with a friend, in company, or with your doctor's help. Doctors can also give you special tablets to cope with withdrawal.

The other advice I would give to anyone is – don't be afraid to talk, to admit your problems. It has to be someone you can trust, of course, and who will understand. You don't want someone who'll just dismiss it, or just tell you to get a grip – that you'll soon get over it.

One thing I will say to other footballers with problems is, 'Don't keep it to yourself.' I wish I had revealed more to my various managers about what was really happening to me. I didn't tell them early enough, when I knew what was happening, what I was doing.

I know there are footballers who take cocaine. It gets out of your system after three days, and if they're given from Saturday to Tuesday off they can go and drink water and sweat it out of their system before they next play. If there are any players reading this book who are taking it, it will affect your football. You can tell your manager and the manager will keep everything discreet.

Things eventually will get into the papers, about bad habits and behaviour, but the papers will get it wrong, so that won't help. It's best to confess as soon as you can to your manager. They'll then keep it quiet, help keep it out of the papers. I wish I'd done that.

If you feel you can't approach your manager, for any reason, ring the Professional Footballers Association, speak to Gordon Taylor. I've found him helpful. He was always there for us. If you say, 'I'm struggling with this, I don't want anyone to know,' I know Gordon and the PFA will help. And keep it very discreet. After all, as a pro footballer, you pay them a fortune in subs, so they are there to help you. I wish I'd done that more often. But I didn't have the knowledge.

These days, the PFA is better equipped and more understanding when dealing with personal problems than in the old days. And these days, the personal problems are more personal, brought on by all the stress, all the temptations and distractions. There's always been stress, but not to the same extent as today. Not many people, even in football – except a few of the old style, old sweat coaches – honestly think that the solution is a cold shower, and that you'll snap out of it.

My therapy sessions have now come to an end. That's what I hope. For now, anyway. I expect to need Johnny less and less in the future. He has given me the areas I have to work on, which I will, once this summer is over.

But he'll still be a friend. I will still ring him up, perhaps go and watch Everton with him. I'll contact him again, professionally, if I get into a panic or fear I'm relapsing.

What you have to realise, when you have problems like mine, is that there's not likely to be a miracle, sudden cure. I have to live with me. But there are ways of coping. And I think I have coped pretty well, during my career, all things considered. I *will* do even better in the future. I know it won't affect any management job I get next, because I know what to do now. And I'm sure it won't affect any relationship I might get into. I am improving, all the time.

I know much better than I ever did how to cope. And I suppose, when you think about it, that's what life is all about, for everyone. How to cope.

And just before I go, I want to tell you all something amazing. Something that has made me cry. Not surprising you might say. When you are talking about Gazza. But these were tears of happiness.

It happened just last night. I was in Dunston, where I used to live. In the Dun Cow pub to be exact, with my brother. I was watching him play darts and playing some pool with other mates. I was having a good time, drinking Diet Coke, enjoying everyone's company. That made me feel good. But that's not the amazing thing.

My phone went off. I didn't recognise the number, but I answered it anyway. Don't know what made me. I don't usually if I don't know who it is. But I did this time – and it was the most important call I've ever had in my life.

I heard a small voice. It was Regan, saying how much he missed his dad. It was the best news I'd had in years. I hadn't seen him in months. I could tell he was emotional and I spoke to him for ages. I was crying my eyes out. Half the pub came out to see if I was okay. Bringing me my Coke and ciggies. They were brilliant. They could see I was overcome with it all, but happy.

I am going to see him tomorrow. When he's out of school. I'll drive down. I spoke to Sheryl and she was fine about it. Saying I could come down any time I was ready. I'm ready now. I can't wait to see him. This is the start of the next stage of my life. I know it. I'm feeling really positive for the first time in a long, long time.

That's it from me. Now fuck off. I'm going training. And tomorrow I'm going to see my boy . . .

Hey Paul

My stomach still hurts from laughing with you. I know your life is busy as is mine, but let's keep in touch. My experience here was made easier because of you. If there is something in the future you think I have to offer, it's yours.

Fond memories to you mate – stay fucking clean!

Yours

Christie

PS Send me a copy of your new book you door knob . . .

John's summing up

John

Over the past few months Paul's had a lot to deal with. We've seen through the session notes that he has shown courage and commitment, and despite the recent relapses and being rejected from his first job as manager he was determined to bounce back. He has put a lot into our sessions and I hope has gained a lot too. Paul is more aware of his addictions and aware of the reasons why he behaves as he does in certain situations.

He has wanted the world to know what it's really like being Paul Gascoigne, and as you can see it's not easy. I hope as he moves into this next stage of his life he has the courage to be himself. For now we've finished our sessions together, but his work is by no means complete. As we've seen, Paul has substituted one addiction for another and at the moment his obsession with his weight has triggered his food and exercise disorders. This is still a tricky time for him since full recovery cannot be properly established until all addictive behaviours are arrested. Paul will always need to keep an eye on his addictions and his bipolar disorder, like many millions of sufferers around the world. He has learned some more techniques, ways he can help himself, but he needs to put them into practice on a daily basis to get the benefit and be truly free.

He has lived life in a fish bowl for us all to see and I think he always will. I hope as he develops ways of being comfortable in his own skin, he will stop looking for attention from harmful things and people (including the press) to tell him that he is okay. He's been honest in this book but has fears that people may misinterpret why he is doing so. That is a risk, but he has been determined to go ahead. He genuinely feels for others who have similar stories and by sharing about his treatment he hopes to share a message of hope – that help is available.

I too have struggled at times writing this with Paul. It has thrown up all sorts of dilemmas, which I've spent many hours discussing with my partner, therapist and clinical supervisors. Paul and I have discussed time and again how it should be written and what we want to achieve. But I know that the process we've been through in charting Paul's progress (writing his own personal case study) has helped him to recognise and revise his old patterns of behaviour as he interacted with people around him. These insights gained through counselling are very valuable. For example, when Paul has to assert himself and say 'No' to people he risks hurting their feelings, which he finds difficult even if they have been behaving badly. This pattern goes back to that anxious child who had experienced so much trauma at an early age and who just wanted everybody to be happy. Those unmanageable feelings have contributed to Paul drinking alcohol to change his mood, which eventually triggered his alcoholism.

I hope that he re-reads this book once a year for the rest of his life. I also sincerely hope that there are some readers who, after reading about Paul's journey, will take the brave step to ask for help. I have attended too many funerals due to the illnesses described in this book, and I guess that's where we should end: in the reality of what being ill is really like, the loneliness, the self-hatred and the desperation of addiction and mental illness.

Paul inspires me to continue in this field of work. He won't give up despite the many setbacks he's experienced. Whatever he goes through in his life I'll be there for him no matter what.

Introduction to the appendices

This section provides further information on the various conditions mentioned in Paul's story. Each appendix concentrates on one 'illness', and is a brief outline of what the illness is, what the symptoms are, and what treatments are available. I have also provided some basic advice and a questionnaire to be filled out by anyone who thinks they may need to look into one of these issues. These are not psychometric tests; in other words, they will not replace a professional diagnosis, but should help to indicate whether there is a need to seek help. Should you have any doubts at all about any of these conditions, in relation to yourself, a family member or friend, it's always advisable for the person concerned to have a consultation with their GP and talk the matter through. It may be that you have another, related, condition, or that you need a full health check-up. If, in fact, there's nothing wrong, having that confirmed will put your mind at rest. However, if you do need treatment, it's always better to arrest the illness at as early a stage as possible.

The final appendix, 'Where to get help', gives a list of organisations that can provide information, support and treatment for various conditions, including some of the self-help groups that meet both in the UK and in many other countries of the world.

Alcohol

Alcohol has a massive impact on our society. There are nine million problem drinkers in the UK, and 7% of our adult population have alcohol dependence[1]. Around 33,000[2] die each year because of alcoholism, and many more suffer health problems such as liver disease, pancreatitis, diabetes and heart problems.

The families of problem drinkers also suffer. Most domestic violence and death at home is caused through drinking too much. Of men who hit their partners 60% to 70% do so under the influence of alcohol. 800,000 children are living with parents experiencing serious drink problems.

Alcohol is a factor in 60% to 70% of homicides in the UK[3], and almost half of all violent crime is committed while the offender is under the influence of alcohol[4].

What's an alcoholic?

Alcoholism is the excessive and repeated use of alcohol in a compulsive and addictive way. According to some experts, the electrical brain-waves in people suffering from alcoholism are different from those who are non-alcoholics, meaning that alcoholism is a physical as well as a psychological disease.

So how do you know if you're one of these 'problem drinkers'? Try this basic questionnaire as a first step to finding out.

1. Do you ever drink to relieve emotional stress?
No ❏   Occasionally ❏   Always ❏

2. Do you ever drink alone?
No ❏   Rarely ❏   Once a week or more ❏

3. During the past year, have you ever felt remorse after drinking?
No ❏   Once or twice ❏   More than twice ❏

4. How many times in the past year have you tried to cut down or stop drinking?
Never ❏   Once or twice ❏   More than twice ❏

5. How many times in the past year have you missed work because of a hangover or drinking?
Never ❏   Once or twice ❏   More than twice ❏

6. On a typical drinking day, how many drinks do you have?
1 or 2 ❏   3 to 5 ❏   6 to 8 ❏   9 or more ❏

7. In an average week, how many days do you drink?
None ❏   1 to 2 ❏   3 or 4 ❏   Every day ❏

8. How often do you have more than six drinks in one go?
Never ❏   Less than monthly ❏   Weekly ❏   More or less daily ❏

Scoring

In each question, give yourself a score of 0 for the first answer; 1 for the second answer; 2 for the third answer, and so on. For example, in question 1, if you ticked 'occasionally', that's answer number 2, so you get 1 point.

If you scored –

- 0 to 3: It's unlikely that your drinking is harmful to you.
- 4 to 7: It's unlikely that your drinking is hazardous, but you should check and remain within the recommended safe limits of alcohol, to be sure your drinking does not cause you health problems.
- 8 to 10: It's possible that your drinking is becoming harmful to your health, and you should ensure that your alcohol intake is within the recommended safe limits, and seek further professional evaluation.
- 10 to 14: It's likely that your drinking is harmful to your health, and you should seek further professional evaluation.
- 15 to 19: Your score is believed to indicate a problem with drinking, it's likely to be harming your health and well-being, and you should seek further professional evaluation.

This questionnaire is only a basic first guide, and cannot replace a professional consultation; if you are in any doubt about your drinking you should always contact your GP.

Recommended safe limits of alcohol

- Men should drink no more than **21** units per week, and **4** units in any one day
- Women should drink no more than **14** units per week, and **3** units in any one day

What's a unit?

- Half a pint of ordinary beer, lager or cider
- A small pub measure of spirits
- ²⁄₃ of a small glass of wine

How do you work out your units?

- 2 small glasses of wine = 3 units, the daily limit for women
- 2 pints of beer = 4 units, the daily limit for men
- 1 bottle of wine = 9 units, so a maximum of 1½ bottles per week for women and 2⅓ bottles per week for men
- 1 litre of strong beer = 6 units, so the maximum for women is 2 litres per week, for men 3½ litres per week

If you think you have a problem with your drinking, talk to your GP or use the information at the back of the book and contact someone who could give you confidential and accurate information. The longer you put it off the worse it will get.

Food disorders

The Eating Disorders Association estimates that about 165,000 people in the UK have eating disorders with 10% dying as a result, but experts believe it could be higher. Most sufferers are women, but one in ten are now men.

If you have an eating (or food) disorder, you use food to alter your mood – rather than for nutrition. You might do this by:

- starving
- overeating
- bingeing
- purging

– or a mixture of all of these. The behaviour brings short-term relief from depression, stress or intense anxiety, until it builds up again and the action is repeated. The desire for control is a big factor. People with eating disorders often have a distorted view of the size of their bodies (body dysmorphia); they often have an exercise addiction as well; and use nicotine and caffeine to help stop hunger pangs. Two types of common food disorder have been given their own names:

Anorexia nervosa – this is a self-starvation syndrome involving body dysmorphia and intense fear of weight gain, in which the sufferer typically loses 20% or more of their original body weight, leading to muscle wasting. Sufferers usually have low self-esteem and intense feelings of shame and guilt, but are in strong denial about having a problem.

Bulimia nervosa – this is characterised by secret 'binge' episodes involving eating large amounts of very high-calorie foods, often followed by 'purging' either by vomiting, swallowing of laxatives and diuretics, or obsessive exercise to rid the body of the calories consumed. Sufferers have the same low self-esteem as anorexics, but are usually more aware that they have a problem.

This pattern of seeking relief from negative feelings is typical of any addiction – e.g. to drugs or alcohol. People often don't know or deny to themselves that they have a problem. Sufferers can recover using the same model of addiction as any other type of addict – although, instead of abstaining completely from food, they abstain from the addictive foods (foods like refined flour and sugar are known to alter mood), and eat three nutritious meals a day and nothing else. Thus, this model of treatment involves:

- admitting the problem
- medical assessment – some sufferers may be dangerously ill
- supported abstinence from the addictive procedure
- getting ongoing support with the feelings that prompted the behaviour in the first place – possibly including medication for depression

If you know someone with a food disorder, it's pointless getting bossy or frustrated with them and trying to get them to eat more, or less. They're in an addictive process and they're powerless over the behaviour. If you try to stop that behaviour, the person's underlying negative feelings will escalate until they're unbearable, and they'll be forced to react. So the sufferer has to be shown that there's another way to deal with those terrifying feelings, at the same time as quitting the addictive cycle.

However, if you do know someone with food problems, do ring the Eating Disorders helpline and ask how to best get them help. It's important to say that food disorders are potentially very damaging to physical and mental health, and can be fatal. Anorexia nervosa can result in sudden death, believed to be due to heart failure, and other organs are adversely affected by the malnutrition accompanying this disease. Anorexia also causes amenorrhoea, low blood pressure, decreased heart size, dry skin, hair loss and cold intolerance (leading to increase in body hair). The self-induced vomiting of bulimics can lead to swelling of salivary glands, erosion of tooth enamel, electrolyte and mineral deficiencies, oesophagus tearing and irregular heart rhythm, while laxative abuse can cause long-lasting damage to bowel function.

Most food disorder sufferers begin with strict dieting, exercising, or overeating, and the condition escalates from there. Spotting the potential problem in the early stages can prevent years of misery and ill health.

How's my relationship with food?

Try this simple quiz as a first step to finding out:

1. I worry about being overweight.
Yes ❑   No ❑

2. I'm usually on a diet of some sort.
Yes ❑   No ❑

3. Every day I spend a lot of time thinking about what to eat and what not to eat.
Yes ❑   No ❑

4. I quite often feel guilty after eating.
Yes ❏   No ❏

5. If my favourite food's not in the house, I'll hunt around the shops at night to buy some.
Yes ❏   No ❏

6. When I exercise I'm thinking about how many calories I'm burning up.
Yes ❏   No ❏

7. I often eat until I feel bloated.
Yes ❏   No ❏

8. I sometimes use laxatives to help me lose weight.
Yes ❏   No ❏

9. I don't like going out to dinner or eating in company.
Yes ❏   No ❏

10. I feel more in control when I don't eat.
Yes ❏   No ❏

11. The thought of just having normal meals makes me miserable.
Yes ❏   No ❏

12. I'll only be happy when I'm the right size and shape.
True ❏   False ❏

If you've answered 'Yes' to six or more of these questions, it's suggested you seriously think about getting some help:

- talk to your GP and ask for a blood test to make sure you're not anaemic or deficient in any other vital nutrients (such as vitamin B12)

- if your GP agrees you have a food problem, ask their advice; you can ask to be referred for counselling
- if you have dangerously low body weight, you may be admitted to hospital for treatment
- contact the Eating Disorders Association – details in 'Where to get help' in the back of this book
- ring the Overeaters Anonymous helpline and ask for advice
- you can be referred into residential or day treatment programmes, either subsidised or paid privately – some are listed at the back of this book

If you're a yo-yo dieter, a mild overeater, or someone who worries about weight and food but hasn't yet got a serious problem, make an appointment with a qualified nutritionist (try the Institute of Optimum Nutrition at the back of this book for a nutritionist near you) and learn how to feed your body regular nutritious meals in a balanced way that can be maintained for life – no more diets, no more starving yourself, just simple self-care and an end to guilt and worry. Meanwhile, do something about your emotional pain – counselling, self-help, or even a life coach or good friend who can help you put together a plan to get your needs met.

This questionnaire cannot replace an evaluation by a professional, and is only a first guide in the assessment process. If you are at all worried about your relationship to food, please seek a professional diagnosis.

Obsessive compulsive disorder (OCD)

Some 2–3% of people in the UK are thought to suffer with some form of OCD. Some manage it on their own and find ways of coping and negotiating their peculiar habits without drawing too much attention to themselves. Others suffer badly with the condition, and it affects their lives both personally and socially. At its worst the individual can become completely debilitated by it, even housebound, and this could lead to suicide or self-harm. OCD is one type of anxiety disorder, of which there are several different kinds.

What is OCD?

We've all driven up the motorway worrying that we've left the oven on or the front door open, or we avoid a certain unlucky number. It's normal sometimes to have doubts, worries or superstitious beliefs. But with OCD they become so excessive that they control your daily behaviour. OCD involves behaviour, or compulsions, in reaction to a set of obsessive thoughts that are continuous, repetitive, anxious, time-consuming and often out of proportion to reality. In other words, you keep thinking you've got to do something according to a certain rule, or else something bad will happen. The compulsions are ritualistic and repetitive actions – far worse than everyday rituals or habits – that temporarily relieve the obsessive thought. For example, checking door handles several times in order to prevent an accident from happening to a loved one. Or counting an exact number of steps before getting in the car. A common form is anxiety about illness and germs, and the sufferer will repeatedly wash hands and clean themselves and their surroundings.

This need to 'act' on the thought and obey certain rules is powerful and convincing. It usually alleviates the anxiety for a short time, but the obsessive thought will return and gradually get worse. The condition often develops in childhood and gets progressively worse in teenagers.

There are many types of OCD: obsessively checking things, washing and cleaning, orderers (constantly placing objects in a certain order) and repeaters (repeating the same action), hoarders and people with scrupulosity – in other words, having to be thorough.

How to get a diagnosis

If you or someone you know is suffering with any of the symptoms described, there is help available. The first thing to do is visit your GP and ask to be referred to a trained clinician for a diagnosis, which is made on the basis of the symptoms you describe.

Related conditions

Common conditions that closely resemble OCD are tic disorders – for example a vocal tic disorder such as snorting. Tic disorders are involuntary behaviours in response to a feeling of discomfort. It's much more common for OCD and tic disorders to occur together when the conditions began in childhood. Many OCD sufferers also have depression, and some have accompanying food disorders.

Treatment

You might be recommended a course of therapy – usually Cognitive Behavioural Therapy (CBT). If you don't have a CBT practitioner in your area, you could try Cognitive Analytic Therapy (CAT).

You might be prescribed medication for the condition. It's believed that decreased serotonin levels in the brain are linked to OCD, and certain antidepressants that increase serotonin levels have been shown to be effective in treating the condition.

Treatment of other anxiety disorders

Most anxiety disorders are treatable through a combination of medication and counselling or psychotherapy. Whether the patient is treated with medication alone, therapy alone or both, and exactly which type of medication and which type of therapy, will depend on the anxiety disorder and the preference of the prescribing doctor and the patient. It's important to be honest and thorough when telling your doctor about your symptoms, because the only information they have to make the diagnosis is what you give them, and it's vital to get the correct diagnosis so that the right treatment can be given. Try not to be embarrassed – your doctor will have heard these symptoms many times before and regard them as part of a medical condition which is not your fault, and nothing to be ashamed of.

Do I have OCD?

A simple questionnaire cannot diagnose you, but you could try answering these questions before you visit your doctor, to get an idea of the kind of information the doctor will need.

1. I have to repeatedly check doors and windows every time I leave the house.

Yes ❑   No ❑

2. I feel anxious if lights are left on, because I'm worried they won't get turned off.
Yes ❑   No ❑

3.There's a special number of times I have to do certain tasks.
Yes ❑   No ❑

4. My hands are sore and dry from constant washing.
Yes ❑   No ❑

5. I have to cancel out every 'bad' thought with a 'good' thought.
Yes ❑   No ❑

6. I keep a lot of items at home that other people would throw away.
Yes ❑   No ❑

7. I always put things like towels, clothes, books or other objects into a special order or pattern that has to be just right.
Yes ❑   No ❑

8. I go over and over in my head events, things I've said, or things I've put in an email or text message.
Yes ❑   No ❑

9. I spend a lot of time each day cleaning objects or the house.
Yes ❑   No ❑

10. I hate using public lavatories and don't touch door handles with my bare skin.
Yes ❑   No ❑

11. I have to repeat tasks until it feels to me that they've been done just right.
Yes ❑   No ❑

12. I feel anxious about certain words and phrases being spoken.
Yes ❑   No ❑

13. I feel worried every time other people leave the house.
Yes ❑   No ❑

14. I avoid driving in case I cause a road accident.
Yes ❑   No ❑

15. I get very worried about illness and don't like being near people who are ill.
Yes ❑   No ❑

16. Tasks have to be done in a strict order and in a certain way, and if it doesn't go perfectly I have to start from the beginning and do them all again.
Yes ❑   No ❑

17. The things I do help to stop disaster from happening.
Yes ❑   No ❑

If you've answered 'Yes' to four or more questions, it's suggested you speak to your GP. Tell your GP about your anxiety and rituals in detail so that they can decide whether you need help. Contact the organisations listed at the back of this book who will talk to you in confidence. If a full assessment concludes that you have OCD, remember, help is available – this condition is treatable.

This questionnaire is only a basic guide, and cannot replace a professional evaluation – if in any doubt always contact your doctor.

What are anxiety disorders?

The most common are:

Generalised anxiety disorder (GAD) involves chronic and constant excessive worry and anticipation of disaster in every area of life. Symptoms include insomnia, headaches, sweatiness, fatigue, trembling, hot flushes and difficulty swallowing.

Panic disorder involves repeated and sudden panic attacks characterised by pounding heart, weakness, dizziness, tingling, chest pain, nausea, choking, terror, fear of loss of control and impending doom.

Post-traumatic stress disorder (PTSD) can develop after a terrifying event such as violent attacks, natural disasters, accidents and experience of war. The symptoms include persistent frightening thoughts and memories of the ordeal, sleep problems and traumatic nightmares, emotional numbness, loss of interest and motivation, and even aggression and violence.

Social phobia involves overwhelming anxiety and self-consciousness about ordinary social situations. Sufferers are so nervous and fearful of being judged by others and are so embarrassed by themselves that the condition affects work, school, and friendships. Symptoms include trembling, nausea, blushing and sweating.

Specific phobias are irrational and extreme fears of a thing that is actually little or no danger, which lead the sufferer to go to extreme lengths to avoid the object of fear. Some examples are fear of flying, tunnels, water, dogs, spiders, heights, rodents, blood.

Obsessive compulsive disorder involves anxious thoughts and rituals that control the sufferer's life and compel them to stave off disaster through acting out certain behaviours according to specific rules. It takes many different forms, but the feelings of intense anxiety and the need to act out rituals to relieve the anxiety are common to each.

AppendixFour

Bipolar disorder (manic depression) and depression

Bipolar disorders and depressive disorders are classified as types of mood disorder. Major mood disorders are the leading cause of suicide in the UK. The mortality rate of bipolar disorder is two to three times higher than that of the general population. About 10-20% of individuals with bipolar disorder take their own life, and nearly a third of patients make at least one attempt at suicide.[5]

People with alcoholism are more than six times more likely to suffer from bipolar disorder than the general population, and almost four times more likely to have major depressive disorder[6]. When there is a dual diagnosis of alcoholism occurring together with another psychiatric condition, this is called comorbidity or dual disorder. The alcoholism (or other addictive illness) often makes diagnosis and treatment of the second psychiatric illness more difficult, because the behaviour and symptoms of alcoholism mask the symptoms of the other illness, and also prevent the patient seeking help.

Bipolar disorder, formerly manic depression, is described as a mood disorder, because it severely affects an individual's emotional responses. Moods swing from high to low, from one pole to another – sometimes in a very short period of time, sometimes over days or weeks – but when it does happen it's always severe.

There are two types of bipolar disorder: bipolar 1, the most severe type involving mania, and bipolar 2 disorder, still very serious, involving hypomania. Hypomania is a less severe form of mania not usually requiring hospitalisation. There is also substance-induced mood disorder, which is brought on by the physiological effects of a substance, e.g. cocaine, ecstasy or prescribed medication.

These disorders can be difficult to detect, especially in the early stages. The main points to look out for are:

The highs – mania[7]

Inflated self-esteem or grandiosity – feeling on top of the world, imagined special connections with people in high places or powerful positions, imagine others think very highly of you

Decreased need for sleep – going to bed late and rising very early, surviving on little sleep but still feeling refreshed

Pressure of speech – hurrying, inability to get the words out in time, difficult to interrupt, usually loud and emphatic, continuing to talk even when no one is listening

Flight of ideas – accelerated speech, thinking of one thing then another, speech becoming incoherent

Distractibility – moving from one project to the next, can't sustain attention, easily distracted

Psychotic episodes – paranoia, imaginary friends, delusions, hallucinations, impairment of ordinary everyday activities

Increased involvement in goal-directed activities – workaholism, obsessive behaviour

Psychomotor agitation – cannot sit still, fidgeting, pacing around, inner tension

Excessive involvement in pleasurable activities with a high potential for painful consequences – substance abuse, sexual acting out (several partners in a short period of time), excessive gambling and spending sprees

The lows – depression

What goes up must eventually come down, so on the other end of the bipolar scale the mania will usually at some stage switch into a major depressive episode. Your depression may last for months, weeks or only a few days before you return to mania or hypomania.

Major depressive disorder is major depression only, without the mania. If you feel you're suffering with depression only, then the symptoms listed below will also act as a guide. Dysthymia is a milder form of depression, more subtle than major depressive disorder, and therefore not always easy to recognise. Dysthymia doesn't attract as much sympathy from family and friends because it appears as if sufferers are just feeling sorry for themselves. But it's a diagnosable condition in itself, and needs treating.

Signs of a depressive disorder include:

- strong, consistent feelings of sadness
- change in normal appetite leading to weight loss or gain
- loss of interest in normal activities
- helplessness
- lack of energy
- negative thinking
- low sex drive
- loss of normal sleep pattern
- hopelessness
- crying
- insomnia or hypersomnia
- suicidal thoughts and planning

To meet the criteria for bipolar disorders, most of the high and low symptoms must be persistent and continuous over a sustained period of time (or less if you have needed to be hospitalised).

If you do identify with even a few of the above symptoms from either section and are worried, it's strongly recommended that you visit your GP and describe the problem. Your doctor should refer you to a psychiatrist for evaluation. The important thing to remember is: *if in doubt – check it out*.

If you do have any of the symptoms listed, or can relate to some of the issues Paul described – or if you think a family member or friend is suffering – it doesn't necessarily mean that you or they are suffering with bipolar disorder. There could be many reasons for some of those highs and lows. If you have recently been detoxed for alcohol or drug dependency, you may still be in the early stages of recovery, and mood swings are normal at this stage. If, however, you've been in recovery from addiction for several months, and recognise some of these symptoms described, you may have a dual disorder. Getting a diagnosis for a secondary condition will not interfere with your twelve-step recovery – in fact, you may be in danger of relapse if this goes untreated.

Another cause of highs and lows could be that you're suffering with another type of mood disorder. Or you may have been feeling on a natural high due to something going well at work or in your relationship, and then that has come to an end, and you now feel really low and down.

If you feel you have been suffering with any of the conditions described above, then give yourself a break and get the support you need. Paul did. We live in an age when the science of psychology and pharmacology is beginning to receive the recognition and support it deserves. There have been massive advances in psychotropic medication for mental illness. There are many types of medication that help with mood stabilisation that can make a huge difference to the way you live your life. These types of drugs are non-addictive. It might be that you need a course of counselling or psychotherapy to help you deal with and understand your illness. Most National Health medical centres now have a counsellor on site. If you want to find out more, there is a wealth of information on the internet and in the psychology sections in larger bookshops. For contacts, ring the Bipolar Organisation listed under 'Where to get help'.

Codependency

Codependency is a set of compulsive and maladaptive behaviours learned in order to survive in an emotionally painful and stressful environment, In a family or group set-up. It was at first defined as originating in families where addiction, mental illness or severe physical illness existed, but it's now understood that these behaviours can be passed on from generation to generation whether alcoholism is present or not. The dysfunctional pattern of relating to others is developed during childhood according to family 'rules'.

Those family rules might include:

- other people are more important than you
- it's not okay for someone to have a bad mood – it could lead to disaster
- you have to earn approval
- keep your problems to yourself
- keep your feelings to yourself

- if you're feeling bad, it's your own fault
- be strong
- do everything perfectly
- don't be selfish
- don't rock the boat
- don't speak about anything difficult or painful
- if you don't obey these rules, you won't be loved or liked
- if you don't obey these rules, everything could fall apart

Codependency is especially common when verbal, physical and sexual abuse or violence is present. When children grow up in an environment where there is drunken or abusive behaviour, or neglect, they have to learn to cope with the chaos and unpredictability. One way of coping is to be the family 'fixer' or 'rescuer'. This role usually consists of trying to look after one or both parents, often breaking up family disputes and acting as peace-keeper. The child quickly learns to put their needs second to others in the family, and subsequently when they grow up are attracted to partners who are either addictive in some way, or emotionally unavailable and need looking after.

Most of us have elements of codependency. In fact, it's very important that at times we consider others before ourselves. However, for some codependency sufferers it gets in the way of happiness and can lead to ill health or addiction.

Am I codependent?

Here are some of the main features and characteristics of codependency, presented as questions for you to answer:

1. Do you have an unhealthy dependency on your relationships?
Yes ❏   No ❏

2. Do you say 'Yes' when you should be saying 'No', at a cost to yourself?
Yes ❏   No ❏

3. Does your family have a history of addiction or psychiatric illness?
Yes ❑   No ❑

4. Have you been in previous harmful relationships, putting up with behaviour that you shouldn't?
Yes ❑   No ❑

5. Have there been signs of addiction in your past or present relationships?
Yes ❑   No ❑

6. Have you put up with physical, sexual or verbal violence or bullying?
Yes ❑   No ❑

7. Do you work long hours for no extra reward, or not take your allowed holiday?
Yes ❑   No ❑

8. Have you covered up for others' drunken or intoxicated incidents, lying on their behalf?
Yes ❑   No ❑

9. Have you bailed someone out financially, lending them money, paying gambling or drug debts, or turning a blind eye when they've stolen from you?
Yes ❑   No ❑

10. Do you feel guilty for standing up for yourself?
Yes ❑   No ❑

11. Do you feel anxious if things are not perfect?
Yes ❑   No ❑

12. Do you try to control others' behaviour?
Yes ❑   No ❑

13. Do you find it hard to trust others?
Yes ❑   No ❑

14. Do you take excessive precautions against real or imaginary disasters or accidents?
Yes ❑   No ❑

15. Do you need constant reassurance from your partner/spouse/child?
Yes ❑   No ❑

16. Are you prone to jealousy?
Yes ❑   No ❑

17. Do you feel that if you don't do what your loved one wants, they might leave you?
Yes ❑   No ❑

18. Do you often lie awake watching your loved one sleep?
Yes ❑   No ❑

19. Do you try to anticipate what mood your loved one is going to be in when you next meet?
Yes ❑   No ❑

20. Do you purposely start arguments to get your loved one's attention?
Yes ❑   No ❑

If you've answered 'Yes' to five or more of these questions, you may fit into this category. Don't put off seeking help. On the surface it might not appear as harmful as a chemical or alcohol addiction problem, but being dependent on someone who constantly lets you down is bad for self-esteem and can lead to depression. Ask yourself if you're happy with how you respond to your family, friends and colleagues.

If you're living with an addicted person and you're codependent, not only are you suffering but you might not be helping the person that is ill, if you keep tolerating their lies and excuses. Children copy our behaviour, so if you're a parent it's important to seek help, look after yourself and put appropriate boundaries in place.

How to get help

The understanding and treatment of codependency is still in its infancy in the UK, but there is help available and there are many excellent self-help books. In some parts of the UK the self-help group Codependents Anonymous (CoDA), is available. There is also a twelve-step programme called Adult Children of Alcoholics (ACoA), which addresses some of the issues discussed for those whose parents were addicts or alcoholics. Most major addiction treatment centres now treat codependency.

As the condition stems from childhood it will be important to look back over some of those painful issues with a counsellor, therapist or even a group in which you feel safe. You can find a counsellor or therapist through the UKCP or BACP, both of which are listed in 'Where to get help' at the back of this book.

Some clinics and treatment centres run 'family weekends' which involve the family of the ill person attending a weekend workshop. Additionally, there are weekend workshops held, for anyone who wishes to attend, which concentrate on various aspects of relationships, codependency and boundaries (contact details in 'Where to get help').

Gambling

It's estimated there are currently around 370,000 problem gamblers in the UK. This is an estimate because a lot of problem gamblers do not declare themselves or seek help, and gambling is often not recognised as an addictive illness. However, the behaviour of problem gamblers causes extreme disruption and hardship both in their own lives and in the lives of their families. Debts mount up, homes are lost, families split up and gamblers can acquire criminal convictions.

In just five years, the amount gambled on sports alone in the UK has risen from about £7bn per year to £40bn, according to Professor Leighton Vaughan Williams, a government adviser on gambling[8]. This year, £1bn will be staked on the World Cup. It's now easier than ever to place a bet — through the internet, mobile phones, and television. The 2005 gambling laws and proposed 'super casinos' offer yet more opportunities to gamble. Online gambling in particular has taken off in the last few years. Gamcare, an organisation offering support and information about gambling (listed in 'Where to get help'), says that the average debt reported by people looking for advice is £25,000, but this is likely to be under-reported. Young people are particularly vulnerable to slot machines, internet gambling and scratch cards. And the problem is growing: Gamcare receives 52,000 calls per month.

Because gambling can be seen as glamorous – attending exclusive casinos requiring vast minimum stakes – high-earning, highly pressurised professionals such as Premiership footballers are often attracted to it as a form of relief, relaxation and entertainment. It is, however, deceptively easy to fall prey to the 'habit', and even those with money to burn can literally lose everything.

Why do people gamble?

'At that point I ought to have gone away, but a strange sensation rose up in me, a sort of defiance of fate, a desire to challenge it, to put out my tongue at it. I laid down the largest stake allowed – four thousand guilden – and lost it. Then, getting hot, I pulled out all I had left, staked it on the same number, and lost again, after which I walked away from the table as though I were stunned. I could not even grasp what had happened to me.' – Fyodor Dostoevsky, *The Gambler*.

Gambling creates a high, a rush of adrenalin, which is exciting and, like other addictive behaviours, blocks out all other considerations, concerns and emotional pain. It's not winning that the gambler becomes addicted to – it's taking the risk. That's why the gambler goes back and loses all their winnings – they're not doing it for the money, they're doing it for the feeling.

What is problem gambling?

When your gambling disrupts either your work, family life, social life, psychological or physical well-being, then it's called 'problem gambling'. When problem gambling becomes pathological it qualifies as a progressive addiction. At this point the gambler needs to bet more and more often and larger and larger amounts, and becomes restless and irritable when they try to stop or when they can't gamble. They become preoccupied with gambling, they chase losses (trying to recover losses by gambling more and more) and continue gambling despite increasing negative consequences of their behaviour.

Addictive gambling involves denial about the problem, an inability to stop or control the gambling, mood swings and depression. Like any other addictive disease, pathological gambling has phases. These include chasing the first win (always trying to have again that first wonderful high when winning), experiencing blackouts (periods of gambling of which the gambler has no memory at all) and using gambling to escape emotional pain. Addicted gamblers experience low self-esteem, they use rituals, and are driven to seek immediate gratification. There's also a significantly high suicide rate amongst compulsive gamblers.

Questionnaire

If you think you may be gambling too much, try answering these questions as a first step towards working out if you need help.

1. Have you ever gambled to relieve stress or worry?
Yes ❑   No ❑

2. Have you ever borrowed money to gamble?
Yes ❑   No ❑

3. Have you ever lied to friends or family about your gambling – how often you gambled, or how much you lost?
Yes ❑   No ❑

4. Do you often go gambling to celebrate something – a birthday, or a new job?
Yes ❑   No ❑

5. Have you ever missed work because of your gambling?
Yes ❑   No ❑

6. Have you ever thought about stealing or getting money in other illegal ways to gamble?
Yes ❑   No ❑

7. Do you think about gambling quite often when you're doing other things, like working or socialising, or when lying in bed at night?
Yes ❑   No ❑

8. After you've lost money, do you feel an urge to keep going to try and win it back?
Yes ❑   No ❑

9. Do you feel regret or remorse about gambling?
Yes ❑   No ❑

10. Have you often gambled until every last penny was gone?
Yes ❑   No ❑

11. Have you ever gambled money you needed to pay bills?
Yes ❑   No ❑

12. Do you promise yourself you'll stop after a certain point or after spending a certain amount of money, and then find yourself carrying on, unable to stop?
Yes ❑   No ❑

If you have answered 'Yes' to four or more of these questions, it's possible you have a gambling problem, and it's recommended that you see a professional to get an assessment. (This questionnaire is only a basic guide, and cannot replace a professional evaluation. If in any doubt, always contact your doctor.)

How to get help

Here are a number of steps to take to get help:

- visit your GP
- contact a specialist addiction treatment centre for an assessment and diagnosis (some are listed at the back of this book in 'Where to get help')
- contact Gamblers Anonymous (listed at the back of this book in 'Where to get help') – self-help meetings for people who think they may have a gambling problem
- make an appointment with a counsellor or psychotherapist (via UKCP or BACP, listed at the back of this book)
- contact Gamcare – details in 'Where to get help'

The addictive personality

Addiction is responsible for many deaths, causes devastation to family units and wrecks communities around the world. Addiction often runs in families, and many experts believe that predisposition to addiction is a combination of biological, psychological and environmental factors. A common term for this predisposition to addiction and the progressive alteration of personality during addiction, is the 'addictive personality'.

Addiction is defined as a disease of the mind, body and spirit. When we take or do something that makes us feel good, it's normal to want to do it again. If you have an addictive personality, you will *definitely* do it again. Some describe addiction as having a 'hole in the soul', because of the constant search to find the missing piece – the thing that's going to make you feel complete. But that feeling of completion is elusive – it only ever comes in short bursts, after which its absence is felt all the more keenly.

Addictive behaviour is mood-altering, i.e. changes the way we feel. Messengers are sent to stimulate the pleasure centre in the brain, which then produces dopamine, a chemical that makes us feel good. So we go back for more and more, and this creates dependence – thus begins the addictive cycle.

Types of addiction

Here are some of the more common forms of addiction:

- prescription drugs, e.g. sleeping pills, painkillers
- alcohol
- food
- street drugs, e.g. cannabis, cocaine, ecstasy, amphetamine, heroin
- sex
- shopping
- gambling
- exercise (addiction and bulimia)
- relationships addiction (often called codependency)

Am I an addict?

Diagnosis of addiction requires a thorough examination by a professional. However, below is a short self-assessment questionnaire as a first step to finding out whether you have the disease of addiction. When answering the questions, apply them to your chosen substance or behaviour. For example, if you go shopping to make yourself feel better, apply each question to your shopping habits. If you have more than one habit, apply the questions to the one that affects you most frequently.

1. Do you continuously use the substance or act out the addictive behaviour, despite knowing there are harmful consequences?
Yes ❏   No ❏

2. Do you sneak or hide consumption or behaviour, for example, covering up how much money you have spent/gambled, or sneaking away to purge after a meal?
Yes ❏   No ❏

3. Do you lie to friends, colleagues, family or doctors to disguise the behaviour?

Yes ❑   No ❑

4. Have you had accidents, or been in dangerous situations due to consumption or addictive behaviour?

Yes ❑   No ❑

5. Have you lost a job due to the addictive behaviour/consumption?

Yes ❑   No ❑

6. Have any relationships with friends or loved ones been broken as a result of the behaviour/consumption?

Yes ❑   No ❑

7. Do you minimise your use of the substance or addictive behaviour (i.e. pretend you use/do less than you actually do)?

Yes ❑   No ❑

8. Have you tried to stop and failed?

Yes ❑   No ❑

9. Do you have continuous feelings of shame, guilt or remorse?

Yes ❑   No ❑

10. Are you always thinking about the next high, the next meal or bet?

Yes ❑   No ❑

If you have answered 'Yes' to more than two of these questions, it's likely you have an addictive personality, and it's recommended that you see a professional to get an assessment. (This questionnaire is only a basic guide, and cannot replace a professional evaluation. If in any doubt, always contact your doctor.)

How to get help

Here are a number of steps to take to get help:

- visit your GP
- contact a specialist treatment centre, most of which offer a thorough assessment and diagnosis (some are listed at the back of this book)
- contact a self-help group (listed at the back of this book)
- make an appointment with a counsellor or psychotherapist (via UKCP or BACP, listed at the back of this book)
- get informed – search for charities and organisations on the internet
- be honest with yourself and share it with someone you trust – addiction thrives on secrecy

You might be guilty and ashamed of your behaviour but it's important to be honest – do not minimise or maximise your problem. Addiction is easy to deny, and even the most experienced practitioners don't fully understand its nature.

What treatment?

Statistics show that the most effective treatment is abstinence, where applicable. Experiences in my own life and of working with many clients who suffer with addiction problems suggest that cutting down seldom works, and neither does substituting one addiction for another, e.g. swapping alcohol for cannabis.

Addiction is always progressive, and the consequences become more painful and more dangerous with time. If you have already crossed the line identified by the questionnaire, you'll need support to get you through the difficult process of withdrawal and into some kind of recovery programme. Addiction is a primary rather than a secondary illness, that often requires urgent assistance. There are normally deeper psychological reasons for the use of substances or behaviours to make oneself feel better, but until you address the addiction you won't be able to examine those underlying issues and get better.

Once an addict always an addict? Perhaps, but with the right support you can change – millions have.

Where to get help

Self-help groups

Alcoholics Anonymous – for anyone who thinks they may have a problem with alcohol
0845 769 7555
www.alcoholics-anonymous.org.uk

Narcotics Anonymous – for people with problems with any kind of drugs
0845 373 3366
www.ukna.org

Gamblers Anonymous – for anyone who thinks they may have a problem with gambling
08700 50 88 80
www.gamblersanonymous.org.uk

Debtors Anonymous – for people who have problems with spending, debts or finances
020 7644 5070
www.debtorsanonymous.org.uk

Overeaters Anonymous – for overeaters, anorexics, bulimics and people with other food disorders
07000 784985
www.oagb.org.uk

CoDA (Co-dependents Anonymous) – for people with codependency issues
07000 263645 (answer phone)
www.coda-uk.org

Al-Anon – for people whose lives are affected by a problem drinker or addict
Alateen – for children affected by alcoholism in someone they know
020 7403 0888
www.al-anonuk.org.uk

Families Anonymous – for people whose lives are affected by drug addiction in the family
0845 120 0660
www.famanon.org.uk

ACOA – Adult children of alcoholics
USA 310-534-1815
www.adultchildren.org

Organisations

UKCP – UK Council of Psychotherapists – professional body regulating
psychotherapists, which can help you to find a therapist in your area
020 7014 9955
www.psychotherapy.org.uk

BACP – British Association of Counsellors and Psychotherapists – to find a
counsellor or therapist in your area
0870 443 5252
www.bacp.co.uk

Action on Addiction – addiction research, advice and support
020 7793 1011
www.aona.co.uk

Chemical Dependency Centre – charity helping those with chemical
dependency
020 7351 0217
www.thecdc.org.uk
– SHARP London – a day programme for alcoholics and addicts in London
020 7349 5772
– SHARP Liverpool – a day programme for alcoholics and addicts in Liverpool
0151 703 0680

OCD Action – charity offering advice and support for people with OCD
0845 390 6232
www.ocdaction.org.uk

OCD-UK – charity for people with OCD, including list of support groups
www.ocduk.org

The Institute of Optimum Nutrition – nutritional advice and diagnoses
0870 979 1122
www.ion.ac.uk

Eating Disorders Association
01603 621414
www.edauk.com

Gamcare – gambling addiction and problem gambling help, advice and support
020 7378 5200
www.gamcare.org.uk

MDF The Bipolar Organisation – support and information for those with bipolar disorder
08456 340 540
www.mdf.org.uk

SANE – information and support for those with mental health problems
0845 767 8000
www.sane.org.uk

Association for Cognitive Analytic Therapy (ACAT)
020 7188 0692
www.acat.me.uk

John McKeown
www.johnmckeown.org

Treatment centres and hospitals

Cottonwood de Tucson – USA private residential treatment centre for addiction and other psychological disorders

020 7486 6222

1-800-877-4520 (USA)

www.cottonwooddetucson.com

The Priory Hospital – group of private residential psychiatric hospitals (most with addiction unit attached)

020 8882 8191

www.prioryhealthcare.co.uk

Priory Hospital North London – walk-in and residential psychiatric services including addiction unit

020 8882 8191

www.prioryhealthcare.co.uk/Find-a-centre/Facilities/Priory-Hospital-North-London

Priory Hospital Roehampton, South London – walk-in and residential psychiatric services including addiction unit and specialist eating disorders unit

020 8876 8261

www.priory-hospital.co.uk

Clouds House – residential treatment for all addictions – private and health authority funded

01747 830733

www.clouds.org.uk

Promis – treatment centre for all addictions, specialising in food disorders and gambling

020 7581 0222

www.promis.co.uk

Hazelden – USA private residential treatment for all addictions for adults
and adolescents
1-800-257-7810 (USA)
www.hazelden.org

Crossroads Centre – Eric Clapton's treatment centre for addiction in Antigua
0800 783 9631
1-888-452-0091 (USA and Canada)
www.crossroadsantigua.org

Broadway Lodge – treatment centre in west of England
01934 815515
www.broadwaylodge.org.uk

Notes to the appendices

[1] Department of Health Strategy Unit Alcohol Harm Reduction Project: Interim analytical report, 2003.

[2] Alcohol Concern (www.alcoholconcern.org.uk).

[3] 'Alcohol and Crime: Breaking the Link', All-party group on alcohol misuse, 1995.

[4] Home Office Statistical Bulletin, 'Violent crime overview, homicide and gun crime 2004/2005', ONS January 2006.

[5] Muller-Oerlinghausen B, Berghofer A, Bauer M., 'Bipolar Disorder', *Lancet* 2002 May 11;359(9318):1702

[6] *Comorbidity of Alcoholism and Psychiatric Disorders – an Overview*, Ismene L. Petrakis, M.D., Gerardo Gonzalez, M.D., Robert Rosenheck, M.D., and John H. Krystal, M.D., National Institute of Alcohol Abuse and Alcoholism, November 2002.

[7] *Diagnostic and Statistical Manual of Mental Disorders – Fourth Edition (DSM-IV-TR)*, American Psychiatric Association, Washington D.C., 2000.

[8] Sean Coughlan, 'Billion pound game', *BBC News Magazine*

Picture credits

Section 1
Page 1: Steve Double; **page 2:** Action Images; **page 3**: Getty Images (top), Empics (bottom); **page 4:** popperfoto.com (top), Dennis Stone/Rex Features (bottom); **page 5:** John Frost Newspapers; **page 6:** Action Images (top), Getty Images (centre and bottom); **page 7:** Action Images; **page 8:** Getty Images (top), Empics (bottom)

Section 2
Page 1: bigpicturesphoto.com (top), Rex Features (bottom left and right); **page 2:** Empics (top), Getty Images (bottom); **page 3**: Action Images; **pages 4 and 5:** courtesy of Paul Gascoigne; **page 6:** Liverpool Daily Post & Echo (top), Will Walker (bottom); **page 7:** Empics (top), bigpicturesphoto.com (bottom); **page 8:** Steve Double